er
rg

Available in the same series

Amsterdam
Athens
Berlin
Brussels
Copenhagen
Florence
Frankfurt
Hamburg
Hong Kong
Jerusalem
London
Madrid
Munich
New York
Paris
Rome
San Francisco
Singapore
Tokyo
Venice
Vienna

Baedeker's

AA

Hamburg

THE AUTOMOBILE ASSOCIATION

Imprint

Cover picture: The Port of Hamburg with the "Michel" and "Tele-Michel"

80 colour photographs
16 perspective drawings, 14 ground plans, 5 special plans, 1 transport plan, 1 city plan

Conception: Redaktionsbüro Harenberg, Schwerte
Text: (part): Dr Gerhard Eckert
Completion, editorial work and updating: Baedeker-Redaktion
General direction: Dr Peter Baumgarten, Baedeker Stuttgart

Cartography:
Ingenieurbüro für Kartographie Huber & Oberländer, Munich
Falk-Verlag GmbH, Hamburg (city plan)

English translation: Alec Court

Source of illustrations:
Baubehörde Hamburg (1), Baumgarten (1), Hagenbeck (2), Hamburg-Information (3), Historia-Photo (6), Museum für Hamburgische Geschichte (1), Sperber (68), ZEFA (1)

Following the tradition established by Karl Baedeker in 1844, sights of particular interest, hotels and shops of particular quality are distinguished by either one or two asterisks.

To make it easier to locate the various sights listed in the "A to Z" section of the Guide, their coordinates on the large city plan are shown in red at the head of each entry.

Only a selection of hotels and restaurants can be given: no reflection is implied, therefore, on establishments not included.

In a time of rapid change it is difficult to ensure that all the information given is entirely accurate and up to date, and the possibility of error can never be entirely eliminated. Although the publishers can accept no responsibility for inaccuracies and omissions, they are always grateful for corrections and suggestions for improvement.

1st edition

Licensed user:
Mairs Geographischer Verlag GmbH & Co., Ostfildern-Kemnat bei Stuttgart

Reproductions:
Gölz Repro-Service GmbH, Ludwigsburg

Printed in Great Britain by Jarrold and Sons Ltd, Norwich

ISBN 0 86145 325 5

Contents

Preface

This Pocket Guide to Hamburg is one of the new generation of AA Baedeker guides.

These pocket-sized guides, illustrated throughout in colour, are designed to meet the needs of the modern traveller. They are quick and easy to consult, with the principal sights described in alphabetical order and practical details about opening times, how to get there, etc., shown in the margin.

Each guide is divided into three parts. The first part gives a general account of the city, its history, prominent personalities and so on; in the second part the principal sights are described; and the third part contains a variety of practical information designed to help visitors to find their way and make the most of their stay.

The new guides are abundantly illustrated and contain many newly drawn plans. In a pocket at the back of the book is a large city map, and each entry in the main part of the guide gives the coordinates of the square on the map in which the particular monument, building, etc. is situated. Users of this guide, therefore, will have no difficulty in finding what they want to see.

Facts and Figures

Arms of Hamburg

General

City State

The "Free and Hansa City" of Hamburg is a city state, a *Land* (province) of the Federal Republic of Germany, surrounded by the *Länder* of Schleswig-Holstein (north of the Elbe) and Lower Saxony (Niedersachsen – south of the Elbe).

Geographical location

Hamburg lies in the North German Plain at 10° E longitude and between 53° and 54° N latitude. The city extends along both sides of the Elbe, into which the Alster and the Bille flow from the North, about 100 km (62 miles) above its outflow into the North Sea near Cuxhaven.

Climate

A characteristic of the weather of Hamburg is its variability. The proximity of the North Sea and the Baltic determines the climate in this area. It is milder than the climate in the hinterland to the east, since the water restricts extremes of temperature. The average annual temperature is about 8·9 °C (48 °F); the average temperature in spring is 7·9 °C (46 °F), in summer 16·9 °C (62 °F), in autumn 9·3 °C (49 °F) and in winter 1·2 °C (34 °F). On average the warmest month is July, 17·5 °C (63 °F) and the coldest January with 0·1 °C (32 °F).
Precipitation is spread throughout the year; on average some 747 mm (29 in) fall on 206 days. The driest month is March and the wettest are July and August. There is fog or mist on about 70 days in the year; in the winter the weather is predominantly windy and even stormy. "Schmuddelwetter" (dirty weather) occurs quite frequently and brings penetrating drizzle.

Ecology

As is only to be expected in a metropolis with a high concentration of population, the quality of the environment is in general not of the best. Although Hamburg has some 6300 ha (15,560 acres) of public open spaces as welll as 2650 ha (6550 acres) of nature reserves and, therefore, holds a leading place when compared with the other German *Länder*, nevertheless the problems of pollution (air, water and soil) and of noise are extremely serious.
Not until the end of the 1970s was an authority created which, with the Ministry of Regional Affairs, Conservancy and the Environment, concerned itself urgently with problems of the environment. In 1982 it published an informative document "Umweltfibel Hamburg" (environmental textbook).
The greatest difficulties for the people of Hamburg are caused by the Elbe, which has today practically degenerated into a navigable sewer. Even in Czechoslovakia, where it has its source in the Riesengebirge, the Elbe and the Moldau (Vltava) have to accept effluent from Prague and the river is then increasingly polluted by waste from the industrial areas around Dresden, Halle, Leipzig (via the Saale) and Magdeburg, all in East Germany, and from the metropolis of Berlin (via the Havel). Hamburg, however, gives the river its death blow by emptying insufficiently treated waste from houses and industrial plants.

◀ *Hamburg Congress Centre surrounded by parks*

In order to maintain the harbour basins and the channel at a navigable depth, large amounts of mud and rubbish are constantly being dredged up and discharged farther away; most of the land so won is contaminated with heavy metals. Few fishermen now operate in the Elbe and the fish which are caught, such as eels and bream, are in poor condition or contaminated so that only a very small part of the catch can be marketed. – Bathing in the Elbe and also in the Alster is extremely risky.
Farther down the course of the Elbe between Hamburg and its estuary near Cuxhaven more industrial effluent is fed into the river from various chemical and metal works. In addition the temperature of the river is raised when it receives the water which has ben used in cooling plants, in chemical complexes and nuclear power stations.
The amount of air pollution caused by industrial and vehicle emissions is also a matter of considerable concern, especially as a consequence of the increased amount of dust containing a threatening percentage of heavy metals. – Nearly 18 per cent of the total population is affected by aircraft noise in the area of the International Airport Fuhlsbüttel, situated not far from the city centre.

Telephone Dialling Codes

Within the Federal Republic: 040
From UK: 010 49 40
From US and Canada: 011 49 40

Area and Population

The entire area of the city state of Hamburg including the islands of Neuwerk and Scharhorn in the estuary of the Elbe, extends over 755 sq. km (291 sq. miles), of which 60 sq. km (23 sq. miles) are water. The greatest distance across the city area is a good 40 km (25 miles), the length of the state boundary is over 200 km (124 miles). In 1984 the population of Hamburg was about 1·6 million; this corresponds on average to a population density of about 2130 per sq. km (5570 per sq. mile) – in Eimsbüttel nearly 5000 per sq. km (12,950 per sq. mile). In Hamburg together with the six neighbouring districts in Schleswig-Holstein and Lower Saxony which make up the "Region Hamburg" live 2·8 million people in an area of 7300 sq. km (2818 sq. miles).

Administration

According to the constitution of 1952 the citizens of Hamburg elect the 120 members of the parliament of the *Land*, who serve for 4 years; the Senate consists of 10–15 Ministers who, in their turn, elect a president (First Bürgermeister) as "primus inter pares" – first among equals – and his deputy (Second Bürgermeister), each for one calendar year. The departmental ministries bear the designation *Behörde* (authority). A watch committee supervises the observance of constitutional agreements.

Districts (*Bezirke*)

For administrative purposes the city is divided into 7 districts; these are Hamburg-Mitte, Altona, Elmsbüttel, Hamburg-Nord, Wandsbek, Bergedorf and Harburg. At the head of each of these districts stands a district administrator (Bezirksamtsleiter = Bürgermeister), elected by the current district council. The districts are, in their turn, subdivided into so-called *Ortsämter* (localities).

DISTRICT/ Locality/Ward

- HAMBURG-MITTE:
  Hamburg-Mitte: Hamburg-Altstadt, Hamburg-Neustadt, Sankt Pauli, Sankt Georg, Klostertor, Hammerbrook, Borgfelde, Hamm-Nord, Hamm-Mitte, Hamm-Süd
  Billstedt: Billstedt, Billbrook, Horn
  Veddel-Rothenburgsort: Veddel, Rothenburgsort, Billwerder Ausschlag, Kleiner Grasbrook, Steinwerder
  Finkenwerder: Finkenwerder, Waltershof
- ALTONA
  Altona: Altona-Altstadt, Altona-Nord, Ottensen, Othmarschen, Groß-Flottbek, Bahrenfeld
  Blankenese: Blankenese, Nienstedten, Osdorf, Lurup, Iserbrook, Sülldorf, Rissen
- EIMSBÜTTEL
  Eimsbüttel: Eimsbüttel, Rotherbaum, Harvestehude
  Stellingen: Stellingen, Eidelstedt
  Lokstedt: Lokstedt, Niendorf, Schnelsen
- HAMBURG-NORD
  Hamburg-Nord: Winterhude, Hoheluft-Ost, Hoheluft-West, Eppendorf, Groß-Borstel, Alsterdorf
  Barmbek-Uhlenhorst: Barmbek-Nord, Barmbek-Süd, Uhlenhorst, Hohenfelde, Dulsberg
  Fuhlsbüttel: Fuhlsbüttel, Ohlsdorf, Langenhorn
- WANDSBEK
  Wandsbek: Wandsbek, Eilbek, Marienthal, Jenfeld, Tonndorf, Farmsen-Berne
  Bramfeld: Bramfeld, Steilshoop
  Rahlstedt: Rahlstedt
  Alstertal: Wellingsbüttel, Sasel, Hummelsbüttel, Poppenbüttel
  Walddörfer: Volksdorf, Bergstedt, Lehmsahl/Mellingstedt, Duvenstedt, Wohldorf/Ohlstedt
- BERGEDORF
  Bergedorf: Bergedorf, Lohbrügge
  Vier- und Marschlande: Curslack, Altengamme, Neuengamme, Kirchwerder, Ochsenwerder, Reitbrook, Allermöhe, Billwerder, Moorfleet, Tatenberg, Spadenland
- HARBURG
  Harburg: Harburg, Heimfeld, Eißendorf, Marmstorf, Wilstorf, Rönneburg, Langenbek, Sinstorf, Gut Moor, Neuland
  Wilhelmsburg: Wilhelmsburg
  Süderelbe: Moorburg, Altenwerder, Neuenfelde, Francop, Cranz, Neugraben, Fischbek, Hausbruch

Population and Religion

Population

The growth of Hamburg into an important metropolis is due in no small measure to the arrival of incomers, in the 16th c. from the Netherlands, Spain and Portugal (including numerous Jews), in the 19th c. from Holstein, Mecklenburg and Lower Saxony. In contrast to the peak of population about the middle of the sixties of this century, when it approached 2 million, the number of inhabitants has since declined. In 1984 it amounted to about 1,607,000 distributed among the seven Hamburg districts as follows.

Wandsbek	373,388
Hamburg-Nord	287,760
Eimsbüttel	232,537
Altona	255, 673
Hamburg-Mitte	217,395
Harburg	182,969
Bergedorf	87,969

The decline in population can be explained partly by the fact that many Hamburg citizens have moved to the outlying districts on the perimeter of the city in Schleswig-Holstein (Ahrensburg, Norderstedt, Pinneberg) or Lower Saxony (Lüneburger Heide). The proportion of females in the population is about 53 per cent, foreigners number approximately 10 per cent.

In his demeanour the Hamburger is somewhat reserved, at times obstinate. The upper classes conduct themselves in a generally conservative way and keep newcomers at a distance. Long residence in Hamburg is a necessary precondition for social acceptance. On the other hand business people in Hamburg have always shown a friendly approach, as they did in Hanseatic times.

Religion

Hamburg is predominantly a Protestant city. About three-quarters of the German population belong to the Evangelical Lutheran Church; only about 8 per cent are professed Roman Catholics, 0·1 per cent are of the Jewish faith.

Among foreigners living in Hamburg a considerable number are Muslims.

Transport

Suburban Transport

The city of Hamburg, its suburbs and its periphery have a well-developed transport system. Suburban transport is catered for by the S-Bahn, U-Bahn and buses and, on the Elbe and Alster, by boats. All suburban means of transport in Hamburg are incorporated in the Hamburger Verkehrsverband (HVV) and tickets, within the various tariff zones are valid on all forms of transport.

Trunk Roads, Motorways

The Europa Routes E3 and E4 meet in Hamburg. Not far south of the city the Federal Motorways A1 (Hansa Route: Cologne – Bremen – Hamburg – Lübeck – Oldenburg/Holstein; E3/E4) and A7 (Würzburg–Kassel–Hanover–Hamburg–Flensburg; E4/E3) converge. The A1 crosses the North Elbe and skirts the town centre in the south-east. The A7 utilises the new Elbe

Tunnel and traverses the north-west of Hamburg. The A24 (E15), completed in 1982, links Hamburg and Berlin (there is a transit stretch across the German Democratic Republic). The A23 to Itzehoe and the A25 to Bergedorf are of regional importance.

Federal Trunk Roads

The following important trunk roads lead through Hamburg or start from the city;
B3: Hamburg–Hanover–Kassel–Frankfurt/Main–Basle
B4: Kiel–Hamburg–Brunswick–Harz
B5: Lauenburg–Geesthacht–Hamburg–Elmshorn–Itzenhoe–Brunsbüttel–Heide–Husum–Danish border (Tønder)
B73: Hamburg–Buxtehude–(Altes Land)–Stade–Cuxhaven
B75: Travemünde–Lübeck–Hamburg–Bremen–Leer–(East Friesland)
B207: Hamburg–Mölln–Lübeck–Puttgarden (Fehmarn)
B431: Hamburg–Wedel–Elmshorn–Glückstadt–Meldorf (Holstein)
B432: Hamburg–Bad Segeberg–Scharbeutz (Baltic Spa)

Rail

In rail traffic Hamburg plays a very important role, especially for the European north–south traffic – the Vogelfluglinie ("as the crow flies" route) to and from Scandinavia. There are also important rail connections with Berlin and East Germany. Since the completion of the railway bridges over the Northern and Southern Elbe in 1872, all the long-distance rail traffic uses a single route between Hamburg Altona Station (via the Dammtor Station and the Main Station) and Hamburg-Harburg. Hamburg is the terminus of motorail traffic in the north of the Federal Republic of Germany (loading and unloading at Hamburg Altona Station).

Maschen marshalling yards

About 20 km (12 miles) south of Hamburg in the territory of Lower Saxony lie the German Railways' marshalling yards at Maschen, the largest of their kind in Europe. They were completed in 1980 and have an area of about 5 sq. km, 7 km long and 700 m wide (2·7 sq. miles; 4·3 miles long and 765 yards wide). There are about 300 km (186 miles) of track and more than 1000 sets of points. On average every day some 270 goods trains with a total of up to 11,000 wagons are marshalled with the help of a computer for nearly 100 destinations in Germany and abroad.

Airport

Hamburg's airport at Fuhlsbüttel in the north of the city, is one of the oldest in Europe; its origins go back to 1911. In contrast to other large cities, Hamburg's airport is relatively close to the city centre (only about 10 km (6 miles) from the middle of the town), which imposes a dangerous level of noise on the inhabitants living in the vicinity.
Measured by the number of passengers movements, Hamburg takes fourth place among the airports of the Federal Republic, coming after Frankfurt am Main, Düsseldorf and Munich. There are more than 130 towns throughout the world to which there are regular flights about half of them operated by established airlines. For air services to and from Scandinavia, Hamburg represents an important link. The plan to build a major new airport farther north in Schleswig-Holstein between Bramstedt and Kaltenkirchen has been abandoned for the time being.

Lufthansa workshops

Also on the airport site are the hangars and technical base of the Lufthansa airline. Here the aircraft of the Lufthansa airline, together with their engines, are serviced, repaired and overhauled.

Transport

Port

Whenever one speaks of Hamburg, one immediately thinks of the port, the largest German seaport. In the chain of European North Sea ports it is the most easterly. It has direct connection with the Baltic through the Kiel Canal (Nord-Ostsee-Kanal) between the Kieler Förde and the Lower Elbe.
Hamburg harbour is an open tidal harbour without obstructive locks between the river and the harbour basins. Modern terminals for the transhipment of goods, warehouses, stores, compounds and railway goods yards as well as a multiplicity of industrial concerns (wharves, refineries, metal works, etc.) to which ocean-going ships directly deliver raw materials, are concentrated around numerous docks in an area of about 100 sq. km (38 sq. miles).
Hamburg is known as the "rapid" all-purpose port providing transit or storage capacity for practically every kind of merchandise shipped throughout the world. Of particular significance are the extensive areas for the important container traffic, terminals for individual consignments, facilities for roll-on/roll-off traffic as well as special terminals for fish, semi-tropical fruit, timber, mixed and bulk freight and, last but not least, the many cold stores.

Free Port

The heart of the port of Hamburg is the fenced-off area of the Free Port, one of the oldest and largest installations of its kind in the world. Within this customs-free area goods of all kinds can remain stored, can be handled or even processed for any length of time.

Speicherstadt (Warehouse Town)

A curiosity is the huge Speicherstadt with its tall brick facades, gables, cornices and towers which was built at the end of the 19th c. On the "floors" of the warehouses valuable imports are stored.

Port Navigation

Within the port area goods are transported by the Port Navigation Company (Hafenschiffahrt) with a considerable fleet of launches, tugs and lighters.

Landungsbrücken

The Landungsbrücken (floating landing-stages) at St Pauli, near the Old Elbe Tunnel, are used for passenger traffic: harbour ferries, trips round the port and down the Elbe, ferry to England. Not far upstream, within the area of the lower harbour, is the Überseebrücke where cruising ships, visiting naval vessels, training ships and windjammers tie up.

Lower Elbe

A lifeline for the port trade is the 100 km (62 mile) long course of the Lower Elbe between Hamburg and the estuary near Cuxhaven. After much deepening and widening of the channel ships up to 100,000 tons laden weight are able to reach the port; a chain of radar stations controls navigation.

Upper Elbe

The Elbe has long been a waterway link between the central European hinterland and the North Sea. In inland shipping traffic with Czechoslovakia, East Germany and Berlin the Elbe still plays an important part.

Elbe Lateral Canal

The Elbe Lateral Canal, completed in 1976 between Artlenburg, north of Lüneburg near the modern ship-hoisting installation at Scharnebeck and the Mittelland Canal near Wolfsburg (115 km (71 miles)), provides a direct connection with the other German inland waterways.

The port of Hamburg, an important container transhipment point

Elbe tunnels

The Old Elbe Tunnel, built between 1907 and 1911, runs under the Elbe between St Pauli and Steinwerder; the New Elbe Tunnel for the federal motorway A7 (E3) was constructed between 1968 and 1975; a third tunnel is planned.

Bridges

With altogether 2200 bridges, of which about 1000 cross waterways, Hamburg has more than any other town in Europe. The largest and longest bridge is the Köhlbrandbrücke, completed in 1974, which links the eastern with the western parts of the port; the most recent bridges have been built over the North and South Elbe for the new S-Bahn route between the Main Station and Harburg, and over the South Elbe for the Harburg eastern ring road (B4/75).

Culture

General

Hamburg is the undisputed cultural centre of North Germany and plays a leading part in the whole of the Federal Republic. The broad cultural provision is based on two universities and several colleges of higher education, a number of research institutes, nearly 100 publishing houses, about 30 theatres, several museums as well as numerous libraries and archives. Of great importance are the news media.

Language

The speech of the native Hamburger is High German with distinctive characteristics; slightly nasalised pronunciation, often a quick delivery and the well-known "S-tolpern über'n s-pitzen S-tein" (literally "stumbling over a sharp stone", but actually indicating a tendency to pronounce the initial "s" before certain consonants as in English and not as "sh" as in normal German). Unmistakable – especially in the vocabulary – is the influence of Plattdeutsch (Low German dialect) which persists in popular speech in the port area and which is also enjoying a certain revival (popular plays in the Ohnsorg Theatre and television programmes). A particular linguistic creation is the "Missingsch", a mixture of High and Low German (for example the stories of "Klein Erna").

Hamburg University

The University of Hamburg, founded in 1919, was considerably enlarged after the Second World War. Meanwhile north-west of the Dammtor Station around Von-Melle Park an extensive university quarter has grown up.

Teaching (for about 42,000 students including some 2000 foreigners) is carried on within the framework of 19 faculties supplemented by particular fields of research (marine research, shipbuilding, international economics, environmental protection, phychosomatics, endocrinology, etc.) and various institutions directly under the Senate (Computer Centre, Interdisciplinary Centre of College Didactics, Institute of Shipbuilding, etc.), as well as some integrated courses, undertaken in conjunction with other colleges. A traditional feature of the University of Hamburg is the encouragement of the study of other countries (foreign languages, geography, ethnology, international law, marine law, world economy, etc.). Among the numerous medical establishments the University Hospital in Eppendorf and the Bernhard Nocht Institute of Marine and Tropical Diseases should be mentioned.

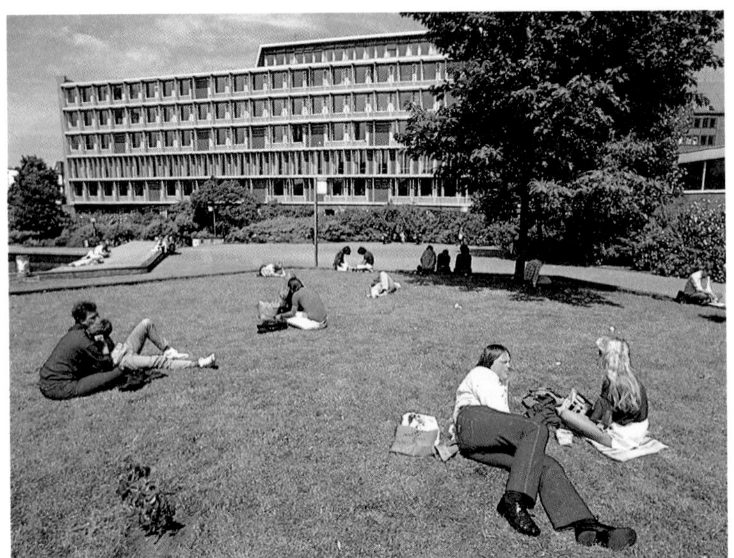

Hamburg University, one of the largest in Germany

Carl von Ossietzky State and University Library

Associated with the University is the Carl von Ossietzky State and University Library (over 2 million volumes) which developed from the City Library, founded in 1479, which was the oldest cultural institution of Hamburg, and which acquired its own purpose-built premises in 1982 with the most modern technical facilities.

Technical University of Hamburg-Harburg

Since the beginning of 1979 the Technical University of Hamburg-Harburg (TUHH), the most recent university in the Federal Republic, has been under construction. Students are admitted in 1982.

Colleges and Institutes

In addition to the universities there are in Hamburg a College of Fine Arts, an Institute of Music and Interpretative Art, an Institute of Economics and Politics, a Specialist Institute with 13 predominantly technical departments, a Special Institute of Public Administration, the Hamburg Military Institute, as well as the largest adult education institute in the Federal Republic.

Research Institutes

Of the great number of research institutes in Hamburg the following should be mentioned; the German Hydrographic Institute (DHI) and the German Oceanographic Data Centre and various research vessels; the Federal Institute of Hydrology (coastal division); the Federal Research Institute of Fisheries; the Federal Research of Forestry; the Hamburg Experimental Institute of Shipbuilding (HSVA); the Meteorological Observatory; the Max-Planck Institute of Meterology; the Hamburg Observatory (in Bergedorf); the Hamburg Seismatic Station (in the Haake near Harburg); the German Electronic Synchrotron (DESY); the GKSS Research Centre at Geesthacht (use of nuclear energy and marine resources) with the deep-sea-diving simulator GUSI; the Institute of Economic Research (Hamburg World Economic Archive, HWWA); the German Overseas Institute (DUI); the Hans Bredow Institute of Radio and Television and the Institute of Peace Studies and Political Security.

Theatre

The theatre in Hamburg has a long tradition. The Comödienhaus which was named the German National Theatre two years after its foundation in 1767, gave Lessing the impetus to write down his "Hamburgische Dramaturgie" which has remained topical until the present day. Lessing's "Minna von Barnhelm" received its first performance here.
As a cultural metropolis Hamburg has now some 30 theatres, among them such well-known ones as the Hamburg State Opera (with its leading international ballet under John Neumeier), the Deutsches Schauspielhaus, the Thalia Theatre, the Hamburg Kammerspiele (for many years directed by Ida Ehre) and the Ernst-Deutsch Theatre. The Ohnsorg Theatre and the St Pauli Theatre have a great public following with popular plays in Plattdeutsch or in Hamburg dialect ("Missingsch"). A number of small-scale and cellar theatres as well as cabarets and companies using platform stages (including the one on the only seaworthy theatre-ship in Europe) have devoted themselves to the cultivation of intimate theatre. The Hansa-Theater professes to be the last true variety theatre in German-speaking countries, the Piccolo-Theater is said to be the smallest theatre in the world. At the Alstervergnügen (pleasures of the Alster), performances which take place in the late summer, artists of many nations perform plays, music and dance.

Culture

Tradition of Music

Even Hamburg's musical life can look back on a past rich in tradition. Georg Philipp Telemann and Carl Philipp Emanuel Bach both worked in Hamburg as directors of church music; the composers Johannes Brahms and Felix Mendelssohn-Bartholdy were both born in Hamburg.

Classical Music

Hamburg's great home of music, the Hamburg State Opera, founded in 1678 as the first German Opera, is among the leading opera houses of the world; its ballet enjoys international fame. Three important orchestras are based in Hamburg; the Philharmonic State Orchestra, the Symphony Orchestra of the radio and television company, the Norddeutscher Rundfunk, and the Hamburg Symphony Orchestra. The centre of concert life is the Hamburg Musikhalle, built 1904–08, where the celebrated conductor Karl Muck organised his philharmonic concerts between 1922 and 1933.

Church Music

Mention must be made of the church concerts which are particularly fine in Hamburg, with first-class performances of choral and organ music.

Popular Music "Hamburg Scene"

The "Hamburg Scene" is a synonym for jazz, rock, folk and pop. Many individuals and groups, which have become internationally famous, began their careers in Hamburg, among them, of course, the legendary Beatles. The communication centres Fabrik and Markthalle or premises such as the Cotton Club, Hamburg's oldest jazz club, and Onkel Po's are known far beyond the borders of the city. Rendezvous of the "Hamburg Scene" are to be found in the Grossneumarkt, in the university quarter, in Pöseldorf and in Eppendorf. Here, and also in many other parts of the city, artists from Hamburg and from all over the world appear in clubs, cellars and bars. In summer there are often performances in parks and squares.

Music Publishers and Record Producers

Several music publishers, a number of music and recording studios, as well as many record producers employ over 1700 people in Hamburg. Producers of records and cassettes in the city, although concerned with serious music but mainly geared to popular music, account for more than 50 per cent of the total output in the Federal Republic.
The Federal Association of the Phonographic Industry and the German branch of the International Federation of Producers of Audio and Video Programmes have their headquarters in Hamburg. The German Phono Academy (Hamburg/Berlin) fosters young musicians and awards the German Record Prize.

Fine Art

A personality in the field of of Fine Art in Hamburg and one whose influence is still felt today, was Alfred Lichtwark (1852–1914) who contributed a great many works to the Kunsthalle and who founded a tradition of civic painting. For more than a century Hamburg has featured in art in works by Max Liebermann, Max Slevogt, Lovis Corinth, Pierre Bonnard and Oskar Kokoschke. Ernst Barlach worked in Hamburg between 1888 and 1899. Today modern figures such as Horst Janssen and Paul Wunderlich are leaving their mark on the artistic scene.
The Museumsinsel (museum island) with the Kunsthalle, Kunsthaus and Kunstverein, situated not far from the Main Station, is Hamburg's most important source of artistic knowledge. In addition about 100 art galleries exhibit works of various epochs and styles.

The Musikhalle, with bronze sculpture symbolising Brahms's music

Sculpture

A great number of sculptures can be found in squares, parks and gardens, public buildings and churches, including works by Joannis Avramidis, Gerhard Brandes, Thomas Darboven, Fritz Fleer, Barbara Haeger, Claus Hoffmann, Alfred Hrdlicka, Martin Irwahn, Max Klinger, Richard Kuöhl, Hugo Lederer, Bernhard Luginbühl, Waldemar Otto, Jörn Pfab, Maria Pirwitz, Ursula Querner, Werner Reichhold, Ulrich Rückriem, Hans Ruwoldt, Friedrich Schaper, Edwin Scharff, Johannes Schilling, Victor Oskar Tilgner, Annemarie Vogler, Hansjörg Wagner, Georg Wrba, as well as many other well-known artists.

Architecture

Most of the old architectural monuments of Hamburg were destroyed in the Great Fire of 1842 and by aerial bombardment in the Second World War. The three principal churches of St Petri (St Peter's), St Jacobi (St James's) and St Katherinen (St Catherine's), are a reminder of the Middle Ages; the Church of St Michael is an impressive achievement of Hamburg Baroque. In the course of time, however, all these churches have had to be restored after destruction or damage.

In its present form the inner city of Hamburg is fundamentally a creation of the 19th c. (the layout of the Inner Alstar, the Kleiner Alster and the most recent City Hall building). The newly redesigned Rathausmarkt (1977–82) approaches, in a later realisation, the proposals of the great architects Gottfried Semper and Alexis de Chateauneuf to create in Hamburg a Hanseatic Markusplatz (St Mark's Square). Largely spared from wartime devastation is the Speicherstadt (warehouse town) in the Free Port.

At the beginning of the 20th c. North German building in brick had a real renaissance in Hamburg under the Chief Director of

Bismarck Monument

Chilehaus

Building, Fritz Schumacher (from 1909). Fine examples are Schumacher's buildings in the Holstenwall (craftsmen's rooms, Museum of Hamburg History), Fritz Höger's Chilehaus (1922–24) and the office blocks of Messberghof (1923–25), Mohlenhof (1928) and Sprinkenhof (1927–31).

Following reconstruction after the Second World War a new university quarter arose in Rotherbaum, and to the north, on the far side of the Stadtpark, a complex of purpose-built multi-storey offices known as City Nord. The recent past has produced impressive additions to Hamburg's communications network, including the Kennedy Bridge (parallel to the Lombards Bridge over the Alster), the Heinrich-Hertz Telecommunications Tower ("Tele-Michel"), the long span of the Köhlbrand Bridge in the port, the New Elbe Tunnel for the A7 motorway and the extensive subterranean S- and U-Bahn junction Jungfernstieg. During the building of this railway junction part of the Inner Alster had to be temporarily drained. Noteworthy new buildings in the inner city are the Axel-Springer publishing house, the three-winged star-shaped high-rise administration building of the Unilever concern, the building of the Deutscher Ring Insurance Group, the Hamburg Congress Centre, the vertically stacked skyscraper of the Hamburg Plaza Hotel and the headquarters of the Landeszentralbank. Development and building of many shopping passages, galleries and arcades has given a new look to the inner city between the Gänsemarkt and the Rathausmarkt.

Old Hamburg

Many hundred historically valuable cultural features have been placed in protection. In addition, in recent years efforts have been made to restore squares and rows of streets to their original form. Mention should be made of the Krameramtswohnungen (merchants' dwellings) near St Michael's Church, the old patrician houses on Deichstrasse (backing on to the picturesque Nicholaifleet), the Beyling Institution with its characteristic inner courtyards in Peterstrasse and half-timbered houses in Bäckerbreitergang (near the Musikhalle), in Reimerstwiete and in Lämmertwiete in Harburg.

Literature

Leading figures in the literary life of Hamburg in the 17th and 18th c. are the poets Johann Rist, Paul Fleming, Friedrich von Hagedorn and Barthold Hinrich Brockes. Between 1770 and 1803 Friedrich Gottlieb Klopstock worked in Hamburg where he completed his "Messias" (Messiah); Heinrich Heine, Friedrich Hebbel, Detlev von Liliencron, Gustav Falke and Richard Dehmel all lived from time to time in Hamburg. The two writers in Low German, Gorch Fock (=Johann Kinau) and his brother, Rudolf Kinau, originated in Finkenwerder. Wolfgang Borchert, Hans Henny Jahnn, Siegfried Lenz and Peter Rühmkorf all achieved recognition both at home and abroad with their writings. Other names from the Hamburg scene of the present day are Hermann Peter Piwitt, Hubert Fichte and Margot Schröder.
Various literary events of popular character take place throughout the year.

Periodicals, Newspapers

In the Federal Republic Hamburg is considered the leading news media and communication centre. A large proportion of the popular periodicals and magazines on sale throughout Germany come from publishing houses in Hamburg. These include "HörZu", "Funkuhr", "Fernsehwoche", "TV Hören und Sehen", "Neue Post", 'Stern", "tina", "Bravo", "Das Neue Blatt", "Neue Revue", "Brigitte", "Petra", "Für Sie", and "Der Spiegel". Hamburg publishes about a quarter of all German daily newspapers ("Bild-Zeitung", "Hamburger Abendblatt", "Hamburger Morgenpost", etc.) and 85 per cent of weekly and Sunday papers are published here ("Bild am Sonntag", "Die Zeit", "Welt am Sonntag", "Deutsches Allgemeines Sonntagsblatt").

Publishing

The largest publishing houses in Hamburg are Axel Springer, Heinrich Bauer, Gruner+Jahr, the Jahreszeiten-Verlag and the Spiegel-Verlag. Among the many other establishments are the book-publishers Hoffmann und Campe ("Merian"), Paul Parey (agriculture), Felix Meiner (philosophy), Friedrich Oetinger (books for children and young people), Hans Christians (publications about Hamburg), the specialist publishers Falk (maps), Sikorski (music) and the publishers of the Hamburg Directory.

Radio, Television, Film

The Norddeutscher Rundfunk (NDR) is the second largest regional broadcasting undertaking in the Federal Republic and a member of the ARD. It provides three radio programmes and participates from Hamburg in the common programme of German television "Tagesschau" (news) and "Tagesthemen" (current affairs). The commercial TV undertaking APF has its headquarters in Hamburg. Of considerable importance for the television and film industries is the privately run Studio Hamburg (cinema, films, TV productions, advertising films, video programmes, etc.), which is one of the largest undertakings of its kind on the Continent.

The Hamburger Film Bureau organisation has, since its foundation in 1979, supported numerous projects (plays, documentaries, experimental and video films) within the framework of a selective film promotion programme.

Advertising Agencies

In the field of publicity Hamburg is one of the leading places in the German advertising industry; some 300 relevant undertakings operate here. In addition there are institutes of market research and picture and text agencies. By far the largest German news agency, the Deutsche Presse-Agentur (dpa) has its headquarters in Hamburg.

Fairs, Congresses

With its centrally situated trade fair and exhibition site (Messegelände) and the modern Hamburg Congress Centre (CCH), Hamburg is among the favoured German venues for conventions and commercial exhibitions.

Trade and Industry

General

Originally the emphasis of Hamburg's economy lay in overseas trade, the city has in the meantime developed into the greatest industrial town of Germany. An important part is played by stock exchanges, insurance companies and banks, goods carriers, shipping, the wholesale and retail trade, building and construction and the provision of energy.
The fact that Hamburg, after New York, is the town with the largest number of consulates provides evidence of the international ramifications of the economic life of Hamburg.

Trade

Hamburg with its modern universal port (total annual turnover about 60 million tonnes) is still the German Tor zur Welt (Gateway to the World) and conducts the largest volume of foreign and transit trade in Germany. The port not only carries on trade with the countries of the Western World but is also a respected commercial partner of States in the Eastern Bloc. By far the most important area of trade continues to be with countries overseas, but European trade, both within the framework of the European Community (EEC) and also with countries belonging to the Council for Mutual Aid (Comecon), has recently been increased.

Industry

Three great industrial groups are represented in Hamburg, the processing of imports, industries concerned with shipping and those involved with consumer goods.
Among the branches of industry with an intensive turnover are: processing of mineral oil (refineries; the first petroleum terminal came into operation as early as 1876), electrotechnology, chemicals (especially consumer products), metal works (one of the largest copper plants in the West), engineering, oil-pressing (especially for the production of margarine), shipbuilding (Blohm+Voss, Howaldtswerke, Deutsche Werft, etc.), the processing of tea and coffee, production of cigarettes, the aviation and space industry (Messerschmitt-Bölkow-Blohm is co-operating in Finkenwerder with the wide-bodied "airbus" project; the technical base of the German Lufthansa at Fuhlsbüttel Airport), brewing and constructional engineering.

In the Stock Exchange

Blohm+Voss floating dock

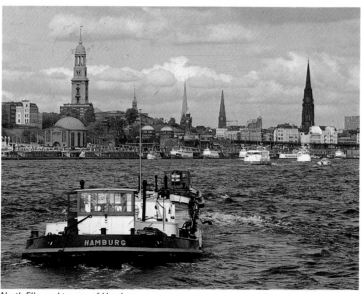

North Elbe and towers of Hamburg

Stock Exchanges, Insurance, Chamber of Commerce

Hamburg was one of the first places in the world to have a stock exchange (1558) and is the largest market for the insurance of shipping and merchandise in Germany (the first contract for building and shipping insurance dates from about 1590). The Chamber of Commerce, founded in 1665, represents over 30,000 registered firms.

Banks

The first German giro-bank was established in Hamburg in 1619. Flourishing overseas trade in the 19th c. led to the foundation of merchant banks and to the arrival of a number of foreign financial institutions. Now approximately one in every five foreign banks represented in the Federal Republic has its chief office in Hamburg. The Hamburg Savings Bank is the largest in Germany.

Wholesale Markets

Four wholesale markets – a cattle and meat centre (after Paris the largest meat market in Europe), a fruit and vegetable market (with the largest market-hall in Europe), a wholesale flower market (the largest in Germany) and a fish market in Altona, with one of the largest turnovers for fish, fish-products and, among other goods, frozen fish imports, and the largest for lobster, caviar, oysters and salmon in Europe – serve Hamburg and a wide area between the borders of Denmark and the Netherlands. Mention should also be made of the cultivation of fruit, vegetables, flowers and ornamental plants.

Tourism

In recent years the number of visitors to Hamburg has increased almost continuously. At the present time at least 1·5 million tourists visit Hamburg every year, including almost half a million from abroad. The greatest number come from Sweden followed by Great Britain, the USA, Denmark, Norway and Japan. To accommodate these visitors there are more than 18,000 beds in some 350 hotels and guest-houses available. The Hamburg information and tourist offices offer various programmes for short visits at attractive inclusive prices.

Famous People

Hans Albers
Actor
(1891–1960)

The popular actor Hans Albers was born in the Lange Reihe, the son of a butcher. He was apprenticed by his father, but in Frankfurt his long-cherished love of the theatre took over. His first part was in Kleist's "Der Zerbrochene Krug" (The Broken Jug). After appearing at several theatres, including the Schiller Theatre in Altona in 1913 and the Thalia Theatre in Hamburg, he went to Berlin, where Max Reinhardt cast him for the main role in Bruckner's "Verbrecher" (Criminal). His film career began with the "talkies" in 1929. On the screen he often portrayed the simplicity of a boy from the waterfront, especially typically in "Grosse Freihert Nr. 7" and in his last great film "Heart of St Pauli", with the song "In Hamburg, da bin ich zu Hause" (In Hamburg I am at home). However he finally he went to live in a house by the Starnberger Lake near Munich. A square in St Pauli was named after him.

St Ansgar
Archbishop of Hamburg-Bremen (*c.* 801–65)

The Benedictine monk Ansgar, the "Apostle of the North", was a missionary in Schleswig-Holstein from 826, and became the first Bishop of the see of Hamburg which was formed in 831. When the Vikings destroyed Hamburg in 845 Ansgar transferred the bishopric to Bremen. In 864 he became Archbishop of the newly formed archbishopric of Hamburg-Bremen.

Carl Philipp Emanuel Bach
Composer
(1714–88)

Carl Philipp Emanuel, the son of Johann Sebastian Bach, was born in Weimar and was first a pupil of his father. In 1740 he was appointed Chamber Harpsichordist at the Court of Frederick the Great at Potsdam. When Telemann died Bach was appointed to be his successor at Hamburg (1767), where he worked for 20 years. He had already published his instructional book "Essay on the true method of playing the piano". C. P. E. Bach, who had great influence on Haydn, completed the transition from the contrapuntal to the harmonic style.

Albert Ballin
Shipowner
(1857–1918)

From 1899 the shipowner Albert Ballin was Director General of HAPAG and was a confidant of Kaiser Wilhelm II. He recognised in good time the dangers of the naval policy of Admiral Tirpitz and endeavoured to effect a balanced position between the German and British fleets. During the First World War Ballin strove in vain for a negotiated peace. Probably disappointment about his failure was the cause of his suicide, although there are other versions of his end after an agitated conference with the Hamburg shipowners on Revolution Day. In honour of this 13th child of an immigrant agent of humble circumstances, the street previously known as the Alsterdamm his, since 1947, been called Ballindamm.

Ernst Barlach
Sculptor, Graphic Artist and Poet
(1870–1938)

Ernst Barlach, a pupil of the Dresden Academy of Art, resided for a time in Russia, which was decisive for his artistic development to become the leading Expressionist sculptor. He endeavoured to create forms as "yearning central figures between a 'whence' and a 'whither'". In the time of National Socialism the art of Ernst Barlach was considered "of a decadent, Eastern character". Barlach lived a withdrawn life in Gustrow (Mecklenburg), without caring about the acceptance or rejection of his work. A large number of his works are now in the Ernst-Barlach-Haus in Hamburg, including "The Russian Beggar Woman", "Moses" and "The Frieze of the Listeners".

Meister Bertram
Painter
(*c.* 1340–1414/15)

Bertram von Minden, called Meister Bertram, is considered to be the principal representative of North German art of the Late Gothic gentle style. He lived from 1367 to 1410 in Hamburg where he painted pictures with scenes from the Old and New Testaments on the wings of the altar in the Petrikirche (St Peter's Church). This altar, one of the most valuable treasures of the Hamburg Kunsthalle, is known as the Grabow Altar, because the citizens of Hamburg had presented the central shrine and two wings of the altar from the principal church in Grabow in Mecklenburg to the parish of St Peter's in 1734.

Wolfgang Borchert
Author
(1921–47)

Wolfgang Borchert, author of "Draussen vor der Tür" (The Man Outside), was born the son of a primary schoolteacher in Eppendorf. He was apprenticed to a bookseller but subsequently became an actor. While on his first engagement in Lüneburg he was conscripted into the army. In Russia he was brought before a military court accused of self-mutilation but

Albert Balin

Johannes Brahms

Matthias Claudius

was acquitted. Jaundice and typhus ruined his health after he was condemned by a military court for anti-Nazi utterances. In 1947 Borchert wrote the drama "Draussen vor der Tür" in a single week. On 21 November 1947, one day after Borchert's death in a Basle hospital, the first performances of his play was given in Ida Ehre's small theatre.

Johannes Brahms
Composer
(1833–97)

Hamburg looks upon the composer Johannes Brahms as a citizen, as he was born within the city, although he chose Vienna as his cultural home. Brahms was hailed as a child prodigy on the piano when he was only 10 years old, and embarked on concert tours. Following a short period in Detmold he settled in Vienna, after Hamburg had refused to appoint him conductor of the Philharmonic Society. North German reticence and Viennese tenderness are characteristic of his works which include four symphonies, two piano concertos, chamber music, the Academic Festival Overture and "A German Requiem".

Max Brauer
Local Government politician
(1887–1973)

Max Brauer was Bürgermeister of Altona in 1919 and Oberbürgermeister in 1924. After his dismissal by the National Socialists in 1933 he lived in exile, in Switzerland, China and in the USA. In 1946 he returned to Germany, joined the Social Democrats (SPD) and was First Bürgermeister of Hamburg from 1946 to 1953 and again from 1957 to 1960. During his time in office he contributed extensively to the reconstruction of the city.

Barthold Hinrich
Brockes
Poet
(1680–1747)

Barthold Hinrich Brockes is not only one of the most respected Baroque poets of his time, but he was also the representative of his native town between 1735 and 1741 in Ritzebüttel (now Cuxhaven) which was then part of Hamburg. He is still remembered by the Brockeswald (wood) on the edge of Cuxhaven. No poet of the time of transition from the Baroque to the Age of Enlightenment observed Nature so carefully and praised not only her beauty but also her uses. In this he even outshone Klopstock, for whom he was a kind of forerunner. In modern parlance he could be called the original ancestor of the Grünen (the "Green" party). In the St John Passion Johann Sebastian Bach used seven extracts from Brockes's nine-volume work "Irdisches Vergnügen in Gott" (Earthly Pleasure in God).

Johannes Bugenhagen Reformer (1485–1558)

Johannes Bugenhagen, fellow worker and confessor of Luther, drew up a liturgy for Hamburg in 1529 after the success of the Reformation. The fact that Hamburg was able to carry through the Reformation without serious internal upheaval – the conservative faction of the merchant class resisted the revolutionary movement – was due in no small measure to his considerable influence.

Julius Campe Publisher (1792–1867)

In 1823 Julius Campe took over the publishing house which had succeeded the booksellers G. B. Hoffmann and A. Campe. During the "Quarrelsome Life of the Publisher Julius Campe", the title of a biography of Campe, the firm of Hoffmann and Campe became the mouthpiece for the adherents of the Junges Deutschland (Youth of Germany) movement.

Matthias Claudius Poet (1740–1815)

Born in Reinfeld in Holstein, Claudius came in 1768 as a journalist to Hamburg via Copenhagen, and from 1771 to 1775 published in Wandsbek the celebrated "Wandsbeker Bothen" (Wandsbek Messenger). Afterwards he lived as a freelance writer. With his poem "Der Mond ist aufgegangen" (The Moon has risen) he created an immortal work. In 1814 Claudius, who had been banished by the French, settled with his son-in-law, the publisher Friedrich Christoph Perthes, in a corner house in the Grosse Bleichen where he died in the following year. Claudius was closely connected with the important poets of his time, such as Klopstock, Johann Heinrich Voss and Graf Stolberg. In his works he represents a Christian and earthy Realism.

Otto Ernst (really O. E. Schmidt) Author (1862–1926)

Although Otto Ernst does not belong to the "great" poets of Hamburg, this playwright, story-teller, lyricist and essayist had a considerable following in the first quarter of the 20th c. with his portrayals of the world of the lower middle class. His play "Flachsmann als Erzieher" (Flachsmann as Educator) appeared in 1901 and received many performances. A best-seller before the First World War was his book "Appelschnut", followed by "Heidede" in 1933, and even his autobiographical novel "Asmus Sempers Jugendland" (The youthful country of Asmus Semper) belongs to the literature of the Age of the German emperors.

Gorch Fock (Johann Kinau) Author (1880–1916)

Gorch Fock was actually named Johann Kinau, but he was known on the waterfront by his *nom de plume*. This writer, who was born in Finkenwerder, and who was employed as a book-keeper with the Hamburg-America Line, was killed on the cruiser "Wiesbaden" during a naval battle. He wrote humorous and lively seafaring stories, sometimes in Hamburg dialect, and in 1913 his "Seefahrt ist Not" had particular success. "Hein Godenwind", which appeared a year before, has also kept his memory alive.

Gustaf Gründgens Actor and Director (1899–1963)

Gustaf Gründgens appeared first – in 1923 – at the Hamburger Kammerspiele but in 1928 he moved to Berlin, where he held the position of General Manager of the Prussian State Theatre from 1934 until the end of the Second World War. From 1947 until 1955 he was General Manager of the Düsseldorf Civic Theatre. Then he returned to Hamburg, where his career had begun, and until 1963 he was General Manager of the Deutsches Schauspielhaus. Klaus Mann, in his novel "Mephisto", has given his former brother-in-law, whose most celebrated role was "Mephisto" in Goethe's "Faust", a literary memorial by tracing the career of von Höfgen-Gründgens from the middle of the 1920s in the Hamburg Artists Theatre until the beginning of the Nazi epoch.

Friedrich von Hagedorn
Poet
(1708–54)

Friedrich von Hagedorn remained attached to Hamburg for the whole of his life. The leading poet of the anacreontic manner, he wrote odes, ballads and fables and "Johann, der muntere Seifen sieder" (John the jolly soapmaker). From 1733, after a short sojourn in London, he was a business employee in Hamburg.

Carl Hagenbeck
Animal-dealer
(1844–1913)

Carl Hagenbeck personifies part of Hamburg. His father was an animal-dealer, but Carl extended the business considerably and in 1907 founded the Zoo in Stellingen which became the model for many others. His principle was to exhibit animals not only behind bars but also in open-air enclosures. Hagenbeck arranged animal-catching expeditions, chiefly in Africa, and organised ethnological exhibitions in association with the zoo. A circus also bears his name.

Christian Frederik Hansen
Architect
(1756–1845)

The architect Christian Frederik Hansen was born in Copenhagen but lived from 1784 in Altona; between Altona and Blakenese he designed a series of imposing classicistic country houses. Together with his nephew, Matthias Hansen, he made the avenue of Palmaille into a masterpiece of Classicism. His buildings gave the Elbchaussee a character which has to a great extent lasted until today. In 1804 Hansen returned to Copenhagen, where he became the Director of the Academy.

Heinrich Heine (originally Harry Heine)
Poet
(1797–1856)

After Heinrich Heine left the Düsseldorf Lyceum in 1815 without a leaving diploma, he took an apprenticeship in the Hamburg banking business of his uncle, Salomon Heine, on whom he was financially dependent for the rest of his life. In 1817 Heine's first poems appeared under the pseudonym of Freudholf Riesenharf. In 1819 he became bankrupt as a result of a commission business financed by his uncle, and he moved to Bonn, where his uncle paid for him to study law. Periods spent in Hamburg and Nordeney in 1825 gave rise to the "Reisebilder" (Part 1). In 1831 Heine went to Paris as correspondent for the Augsburg newspaper, the "Algemeine Zeitung". He only returned to Germany in 1843 and 1844, when he again visited Hamburg. The literary result of these visits were "Deutschland, ein Wintermärchen" (Germany, a winter's tale).

Heinrich Rudolf Hertz
Physicist
(1857–94)

Heinrich Rudolf Hertz, who was born in Hamburg, was Professor of Physics at the Universities of Bonn and Karlsruhe. He confirmed Maxwell's theory of light and by the discovery of electromagnetic waves made a great contribution to the development of modern broadcasting. In his short life he made other important discoveries. Hamburg's television tower bears his name.

Fritz Höger
Architect
(1877–1949)

Fritz Höger, builder of the Chilehaus and the Sprinkenhof, was the son of a master carpenter from Steinburg who came to Hamburg as an apprentice carpenter. The splendid façade of the Chilehaus made him the Classicist of modern Hamburg architecture. At the same time he succeeded in temporarily reviving the brick architecture of North Germany. From 1905 he practised as an independent architect in Hamburg, construct-

Gorch Fock

Heinrich Heine

F. Medelssohn-Bartholdy

ing powerfully articulated office buildings, in which colourful brick and unpretentious ornamentation determine the style.

Hans Henny Jahnn
Writer and Organ-builder
(1894–1959)

Hans Henny Jahnn, who was born in Stellingen now a part of Hamburg, came from a family of shipwrights and organ-builders. From 1915 until 1918 he lived in exile in Norway as a convinced pacifist. In 1919 after his return he made an artistic breakthrough with his drama "Pastor Ephraim Magnus". At the same time Jahnn was a leading representative of a movement concerned with the art of organ-building, a movement which had spread into Germany from Switzerland after the First World War. The adherents of the movement wanted to restore the art of organ-building to the form which had existed before 1750, and Jahnn had built more than 100 organs himself.
In 1920, as a protest against civilisation and convention, Jahnn founded the Glaubensgemeinschaft Ugrino (Community of Belief) which propagated a new heathen realm. After Hitler came to power Jahnn went into exile on the island of Bornholm and devoted himself to agriculture, horse-breeding and research into hormones. At the end of the Second World War he returned to Germany and in 1950 became President of the Free Academy of Art in Hamburg.

Joachim Jungius
Naturalist and Philosopher
(1587–1657)

Joachim Jungius, mathematician and Professor of Medicine, settled in Hamburg where he was for a time Head of the Johanneum (classical school) and also taught Logic and Physics at the Akademisches Gymnasium (grammar school). One of his major works is the "Logica Hamburgensis" which contributed in no small measure to the revival of Logic.

Friedrich Gottlieb Klopstock
Poet
(1724–1803)

Klopstock, who was born in Quedlinburg in the Harz, was so impressed, while a pupil at the Gymnasium of Schulpforta, with ancient poetry that he personally resolved to create a great epic. During his subsequent theological course in Jena he began the "Messiade", part of which was published in 1748 and brought him to notice. After employment as a private tutor and a stay in Zürich and Copenhagen, he first came to Hamburg in 1754, only to leave the city in 1758 after the death of his wife. He did not return until 1771, his life's work the "Messiade" being completed two years later.

With Klopstock's "Poesie des Herzens und der Empfindung" (Poetry of the Heart and Senses) there began a new era of German poetry which is particularly associated with the beginnings of the "Messiah", although in the second half of his life Klopstock became less prominent on account of the emergence of new literary movements. He is buried in Ottensen (Altona).

Karl Ferdinand Laeisz
Shipowner
(1853–1900)

The Hamburg shipowner Laeisz was especially well known for the so-called P-ships, the names of which all began with P: "Pamir", "Passat", "Preussen", etc. The "flying" P-ships took a bare 80 days between Hamburg and Valparaiso and were mainly employed in bringing saltpetre from Chile in voyages round Cape Horn.

Hans Leip
Author, Illustrator and Painter
(1893–1983)

The son of a port worker and seaman, Hans Leip was born in Hamburg, became a teacher and then worked as a journalist and illustrator. He was severely wounded in the First World War. The extensive field of his literary output embraces stories, novels, poems, religious and secular drama, plays for radio and television, film scripts as well as souvenir books and autobiographical work. As an illustrator Leip worked for a time on the satirical magazine "Simplicissimus" and illustrated some of his own work. Leip preferred subjects connected with the sea, shipping and the port, as well as writing about coastal dwellers and seamen.
As an author Hans Leip is known for his prize-winning book "Godekes Knecht" (1925) which was praised by Thomas Mann and which told of the life of the pirate, Klaus Störtebeker. Other major works are the lively novel "Jan Himp und die kleine Brise" (Jan Himp and the light breeze) which appeared in 1933 and the medieval family chronicle "Das Muschelhorn" (1940). Besides novels and stories Leip composed very many poems, ranging in subject-matter from dry humour and sentimentality to highly demanding lyrical art. His best-known poem is "Lili Marleen" which he wrote in 1915 when he was a soldier. Set to music by Norbert Schulze and sung by Lale Andersen, Leip's verses became probably the most famous war song on both sides of the front, after it had been broadcast in August 1941 by the military radio station in occupied Belgrade.

Gotthold Ephraim Lessing
Writer and Philosopher
(1729–81)

Although Lessing only spent three years in Hamburg, he nevertheless perpetuated the city's leading position in the literary field with his "Hamburgische Dramaturgie" which originated as a theatrical publication. Born in Kamenz (Lausitz) the son of a parson, he was educated in the princely school in Meissen and then studied in Leipzig, where he came into contact with the theatre; here his first play "Der neue Gelehrte" (The new Scholar) was produced by the Neuber company. After visiting Berlin and going on several journeys, Lessing went to Breslau, where he began his most important literary work with "Laokoon' and "Minna von Barnhelm". Lessing came to Hamburg to play an active part in the foundation of a national theatre. The theatre did not achieve its expected success, and Lessing finally accepted the position of a librarian in Wolfenbüttel, from where he carried on his literary battle with Goeze, the leading Hamburg clergyman. After "Minna von Barnhelm" had received its first performance in Hamburg, "Nathan der Weise" appeared in 1779.

Alfred Lichtwark
Art historian
(1852–1914)

Lichtwark, who was Director of the Kunsthalle (museum of art) in Hamburg from 1886 until 1914, was the son of a miller in the Vierlande. His primary schoolteacher helped him to become a teacher and subsequently to study the History of Art.
In spite of restricted funds Lichtwark succeeded in obtaining for the Kunsthalle the altar-paintings of Meister Bertram and Francke as well as the works of the Romanticist, Philipp Otto Runge. Later he also acquired important works by Caspar David Friedrich and Max Liebermann. He became a kind of guardian of art and culture, so that it was said that "he did not preach culture, he possessed it'. Lichtwark was the leader of a movement for art education which found its expression in 1886 with the foundation of the Gesellschaft der Hamburger Kunstfreunde (Society of the Friends of Art in Hamburg).

Detlev von Liliencron
Poet
(1844–1909)

Detlev von Liliencron, born in Kiel, took part in the campaigns of 1866 and 1870–71 as an officer; then he went to America and after his return lived as a District Governor at Pellworm then from 1889 in Altona and from 1901 in Rahlstedt, where he is buried. Liliencron was only able to avoid poverty by giving occasional piano lessons and through an annual allowance given to him on his 60th birthday by Kaiser Wilhelm II.
Liliencron is one of the leading lyric Impressionist poets. His "Poggfred" was written in House No. 5 in the Palmaille in Altona.

Felix Mendelssohn-Bartholdy
Composer
(1809–47)

Felix Mendelssohn, born in Hamburg, was the grandson of the philosopher, Moses Mendelssohn. His father, a banker, had taken the name of his brother-in-law, Bartholdy, in order to distinguish himself from Moses. Felix received a diligent musical education, and appeared as a pianist at the early age of 9. When he was 11 he began to compose, and was being hailed as a child prodigy when he met Johann Wolfgang von Goethe, Carl Maria von Weber and Luigi Cherubini. When he was 17 he wrote the Overture to "A Midsummer Night's Dream", one of his greatest works. Felix Mendelssohn-Bartholdy died at the early age of 38, but left to posterity musical works of many different kinds.

Richard Ohnsorg
Actor and Drama critic
(1876–1947)

Born in Hamburg, Richard Ohnsorg was first librarian then actor, but he finally found his true calling when in 1920 he revived the Hamburg Low-German Theatre which had been founded by enthusiasts in 1902. This theatre became the model for all Low-German amateur theatrical companies. The Ohnsorg theatre owes its fame to television, even though the Low-German popular plays had to be adapted into High German for the benefit of viewers.

Carl von Ossietzky
(1889–1938)

Born in Hamburg, Carl von Ossietzky was a convinced pacifist and from 1919 he worked for the German Peace Society. After journalistic experience on the "Beliner Volks-Zeitung" (1920–22) and on the magazine "Das Tagebuch" (The Diary) from 1924 to 1926; he edited from 1927 to 1933 the political weekly "Die Weltbühne" (The World Stage).
In 1931 he was accused of treachery and at the end of the so-called Weltbühne Trial was sentenced to 18 months' imprisonment but was granted an amnesty at the end of 1932. After the Reichstag fire in 1933 he was arrested by the Nazi authorities and in 1934 sent to the Esterwegen concentration camp in Emsland. In 1935 he was awarded the Nobel Prize for Freedom

which the Nazis tried to prevent him accepting. After removal to a Berlin hospital in 1936 Ossietzky died at the beginning of May 1938 from the effects of his imprisonment.

Friedrich Christoph Perthes
Bookseller and Publisher
(1772–1843)

Friedrich Christoph Perthes was the nephew of Justus Perthes, who in 1785 had founded the geographical publishing house in Gotha (now in Darmstadt) which bears his name. The bookshop set up in Hamburg in 1796 by Friedrich Christoph Perthes is thought to be the oldest retail bookseller in Germany. After the upheaval of the War of Liberation against Napoleon I, when he was in exile in Denmark and in Great Britain, Perthes gave up his Hamburg bookshop and moved to Gotha.

Philipp Otto Runge
Painter and Writer
(1777–1810)

The Early Romanticist Philipp Otto Runge came to Hamburg in 1795 as an apprentice. He became acquainted with such distinguished men as the poet Matthias Claudius and the bookseller Friedrich Christoph Perthes, was accepted into artistic circles and took lessons in drawing. After studies in Copenhagen and Dresden he returned to 1803 to Hamburg and remained there for the rest of his life.

Arp Schnitger
Organ-builder
(1648–1719)

Arp Schnitger, who lived in Hamburg from 1682, was the most famous organ-builder in North Germany. Of about 160 instruments which he created the largest, the organ of the Nikolaikirche, has not survived. This had 4 manuals and 67 stops. The organ in the Jocobikirche, which was restored by Hans Henny Jahnn and Emanuel Kemper in 1919 has survived.

Fritz Schumacher
Architect
(1869–1947)

Fritz Schumacher, who was born in Bremen, has embellished the townscape of Hamburg with distinguished buildings. From 1899 until 1908 he was a Professor at the Technical University in Dresden and was appointed City Architect of Hamburg in 1909. Schumacher's hope of giving Hamburg a new look after destruction in the war was not, however, fulfilled.
His dream was a Stadt im Grünen (a city of parks and gardens), and he was the creator of the Stadtpark which was begun in 1910. The first section was completed in 1914 and the second – the work of the Horticultural Director Linne – dates from 1923. The "green island" in the city remains Schumacher's bequest to Hamburg.

Ernst Georg Sonnin
Architect
(1713–94)

Born in 1713 the son of a parson in Perleberg, Ernst Georg Sonnin lived permanently in Hamburg from 1737 where he was engaged as an architect. He is chiefly renowned for rebuilding the "Michel", the tower of St Michael's Church, which had been destroyed by lightning in 1750. The church had been rebuilt by 1762, but there were not sufficient funds for the tower, and Sonnin was only able to complete it between 1776 and 1786. By restoring the "Michel" Sonnin has not only built the most celebrated Protestant church in the whole of North Germany, but he has also created the acknowledged symbol of Hamburg.

Georg Philipp Telemann
Composer
(1681–1767)

Georg Philipp Telemann, born in Magdeburg, worked in Leipzig, Sorau, Eisenach and Frankfurt am Main before coming to Hamburg in 1721 as Director of Music for the five principal churches and Choirmaster at the Johanneum. A year later he was also appointed Director of the Opera. In the 18th c. Telemann was one of the leading musicians in Europe and a precursor of Classicism.

In the light of the social problems of a growing industrial society, Johann Hinrich Wichern felt a call to direct Church work towards social needs and to devote his life to charity. In 1833 he founded in Hamburg the Rauhes Haus, a welfare home for neglected and endangered children and young people. Wichern's method of teaching children in groups, as if they were a family, became the generally accepted model for welfare education.

Johann Hinrich Wichern
Protestant theologian
(1808–81)

History of Hamburg

4th c.

Evidence of a Saxon settlement in the territory of modern Hamburg goes back to the 4th c. A.D.; the oldest remains of buildings yet discovered have been dated to the 5th–6th c. At the beginning of the 9th c. the Franks press northwards to the Elbe. Probably about 810 they establish at the village of Hamm, near the mouth of the Alster, a fortified base for missionary work in the north (Schleswig-Holstein, Denmark), and this base is first mentioned in 834 as "Hammaburg".

845

Ansgar, the first Archbishop, is not in office very long. In 845 Danish Vikings arrive and destroy the fortification, so that the Bishop has to withdraw to Bremen. An archbishopric founded in 848 is now called Hamburg-Bremen.

937–83

At first craftsmen and tradesmen settle; Archbishop Aldag, however, restores a fortified archbishopric. Hamburg even has a Pope within its walls in the 10th c.; the deposed Benedict V takes refuge here until his death in 965 and is buried in the choir of the cathedral; his remains are transferred to Rome in 999. About the year 950 Hamburg has some 500 inhabitants. Trade which had been slowly increasing is destroyed by an Obotrite attack in 983. The settlement with its school, church and monastery is burnt down.

about 1035

Gradually building gets under way. About 1035 the archbishops put up new buildings and establish a circular archiepiscopal Old Town. The Petrikirche is founded as the market church. About 1050 Hamburg has 800–900 inhabitants, half clergy, half laity. In the course of the 11th c. rivalry about precedence arises between the archbishops and the Saxon dukes and this expresses itself by the erection of castles by both factions. Adalbert von Bremen wishes to make Hamburg the fulcrum of Christendom for the whole of the north.

1066–72

When Adalbert is overthrown in 1066 the Wendish Obotrites take the opportunity of attacking and destroying Hamburg on two occasions (1066 and 1072). In the future the archbishops only reside in Bremen.

1111–89

Lothar, Duke of Saxony (later Emperor), confers the Dukedoms of Holstein, Wagrien and Stormarn – and therefore Hamburg – on the Dukes of Schauenburg who come from the Weser near Rinteln. They bring in settlers from the west. There is an accord with the Slavs who are Christianised and assimiliated. Dikes are built to protect the marshes along the Elbe. Under Count Adolf III a merchants' settlement is established and the first harbour on the Alster is laid out. On 7 May 1189 a charter from Barbarossa grants privileges which secure trade and freedom for the citizens of Hamburg.

1190–1292 The absence of the Count on the Third Crusade enables the citizens of Hamburg to escape from his tutelage. Both parts of the town – the former archbishopric and the ducal new town (in all 1000–1500 people) – elect an aristocratic council in 1190, and about the year 1200 two town halls are built. During Danish domination between 1202 and 1225 (Waldemar II) both parts of the town work closely together; from 1216 the united town has a council, a town hall, independent law courts, which after the end of Danish rule is systematically maintained against the Dukes. From 1292 the council has legislative powers. Until 1459 the Schauenburg rulers have only symbolic significance.

13th–14th c. From 1240 the Hamburgers set up a new defence line with walls, ditches and gates, and these are commemorated in the present names of streets: Glockengiesserwall, Alstertor, Millerntor, etc. By 1300 the population increases to 5000, craftsmen, sailors, tradesmen and clergy. In the council the rich merchants prevail and at the same time extend trade, in which at first Lübeck (Salzstrasse) leads the way. In the middle of the 14th c. Hamburg becomes a member of the Handelsstädtebund (trading towns association) of the Hanse. Now there are already 7000–8000 Hamburgers.

14th–15th c. Following the rapid increase in population (by 1450 there are nearly 15,000 inhabitants) the present-day outer districts of Bergedorf and Ritzebüttel (= Cuxhaven) are added to Hamburg. In the 14th c. the following suburbs become part of Hamburg: Gross Borstel, Elmsbüttel, Eppendorf, Winterhude, Ohlsdorf, Langenhorn, Klein Borstel, Horn, Hammerbrook, Billwerder, Fuhlsbüttel, Eilbek, in addition Glindesmoor, Ochsenwerder and Moorwerder and, in the 15th century, Nordfinkenwerder. The northern Elbe becomes an important highway leading to Hamburg.

1400–1525 From the end of the 14th c. the activities of pirates grow alarmingly. Under the names of Vitalienbrüder (= Brothers of Provisions) or Likendeeler (= Equal Distributors) they plunder Hamburg merchant ships. Therefore the council is forced to proceed continually against the pirates –Godeke Michels and Klaus Störtebeker are the best known. About 1400 the pirates are vanquished on the open sea and subsequently beheaded in Hamburg. In 1525 Klaus Kniphof is the last pirate to be executed.

from 1460 In the course of the 15th c., and in the first half of the 16th c., the defences are constructed which are commemorated today in the Alter and Neuer Wall and the Baumwall. When, after the death of the last Schauenburg Duke in 1469 the aristocracy of Schleswig and Holstein chooses the Danish King, Christian I, as his successor, Hamburg also passes into his sovereignty until 1768. However the Hamburg Bürgermeister, Detlev Bremer, succeeds in avoiding taking the oath of allegiance and thus ensuring the privileges of the city. So it comes about that Hamburg, although part of the *Land* of Stormarn and thus a town in Holstein, is able, however, in all respects to be practically independent.

1517–29

Although opposed at first by the council, preachers spread the new teaching which has become known through Luther's theses of 1517. In a public debate in the town hall between Evangelical and Catholic priests, the new beliefs prevail. Through Luther's friend Johann Bugenhagen, who is invited from Wittenberg by the council, the Hamburg liturgy is created with a Superintendent at its head. The educational system is also revised.

1546–1648

In the War of the League of Schmalkalden in 1546 Hamburg declares itself as a champion of Protestantism in the north until the Peace of Augsburg in 1555 facilitates the co-existence of both religions. As a consequence of the religious wars in the Spanish Netherlands many Dutch refugees flee to Hamburg so that the population doubles to 40,000 between 1550 and 1600. Once more Hamburg strengthens its defences in good time so that the Thirty Years War merely brings sieges but not occupation with all its consequences. In the first half of the 17th c. Jews from Portugal, Spain and parts of Germany come to Hamburg.

16th–17th c.

With the great discoveries at the end of the 15th c. the commercial interests of Hamburg were extended from the Baltic and Mediterranean to the Atlantic. By the regulation of the northern Elbe the town on the Alster becomes a river port which, after the decline of the Hansa, seeks its fortune in the North Sea and the Atlantic. At the end of the 16th c. Hamburg is the most important port for the export of grain to west and north Europe as well as to Italy. The Elbe becomes Hamburg's lifeline. From 1607 pilots navigate the ships.

1664–1768

Hamburg and Denmark come into opposition. Whereas the Danish King Christian IV endeavours to control shipping on the Elbe by founding Glückstadt (1616), his successor, Freidrich III, promotes Altona as a rival to Hamburg. In 1536 Altona is mentioned as a small fishing village. In 1664 the Danish King makes it a town and the first free port of northern Europe. Thereupon the Hamburgers fortify their suburbs of St Georg and the later St Pauli with the Neues Werk from the Alster to the Bille. In 1686 Christian V takes advantage of dissension in the town to appear with an army outside Hamburg. The war, which is catastrophic for the Danes, ends in favour of Hamburg but since the quarrels continued, eventually in 1768 the Gottorper Vergleich is concluded between Hamburg and the House of Holstein. Hamburg renounces the repayment of Danish loans and is eventually recognised as an Imperial Free City independent of Holstein. In addition Hamburg receives the islands in the Elbe (important for the extension of the port).

Hamburg in 1681 (painting in the Jacobikirche)

1806–14

Following the French Revolution many French refugees flee to Hamburg and give a new aspect to life in the town which about 1800 numbers some 130,000 inhabitants. From the end of the old German Reich (1806), Hamburg calls itself a Free Hansa Town. Shortly afterwards, following the victories at Jena and Auerstedt French troops move into Hamburg. The ensuing blockade affects Hamburg severely. After the fall of Napoleon in 1814 the French leave the town.

1815–66 After the defeat of Napoleon the defences of Hamburg are removed. Hamburg becomes a member of the German Federation and from 1819 takes the name of the Freie und Hansestadt Hamburg. In the period of new prosperity Hamburg is severely ravaged by the Great Fire which rages between 5 and 8 May 1842. More than a quarter of the inner city is destroyed. Some 20,000 people are homeless since more than 4200 dwellings have been destroyed. In the following years systematic reconstruction follows and the population numbers 170,000. Boats on the Alster operate from 1859 and from 1866 there are horse-drawn trams. In 1860 Hamburg grants itself a constitution in which, in the place of a council, a senate is created.

1867–71 After the German War (1866) Hamburg joins the North German Confederation in 1867, in which Prussia plays a leading part. Thereby the town loses a number of privileges (e.g. ships are no longer permitted to fly the Hamburg standard).

1871–1918 It is not easy for Hamburg to find its rightful place in the new German Reich. Although it is now in the German customs area, the creation of a Free Port facilitates overseas trade. With the Customs Union of 1888 Hamburg becomes the largest port in the German Reich and Germany's "Gateway to the World". The port is extensively developed. Shipbuilding and industry thrive. In 1913 Hamburg has a population of 1 million.

The formative years also leave their mark on Hamburg. Only the epidemic of cholera in the summer of 1892, when there are 8600 deaths, causes a setback. Shipping companies such as Ballin coin the expression "Mein Feld ist die Welt" (The world is my oyster). In 1897 the new City Hall is opened as an expression of Hanseatic self-confidence.

The First World War causes 40,000 deaths in Hamburg. The port and the economy have to pay dearly for the consequences of the war.

1919–33 Following the November Revolution of 1918 Hamburg receives in 1921 its first democratic constitution. In 1919 the university and the world-economic archive are opened. New buildings, such as the Chilehaus and the building up of a new merchant fleet follow in the 1920s.

1933–45 The Greater Hamburg Measure of 1937 brings Altona, Harburg-Wilhelmsburg and Wandsbek into the city of Hamburg. But even Hamburg's independence is set aside. In the place of the Senate a city council and a Reichsstadthalter (government overlord) come into power. The only ray of light during this period is the opening in 1935 of the park called Planten un Blomen (plants and flowers). Nevertheless more than other *Länder* Hamburg retains its characteristic growth and reaches 1·7 million inhabitants.

Between 1943 and 1945 during the Second World War Hamburg is destroyed by numerous bombing attacks. Fifty per cent of the houses, and 80 per cent of the port installation are destroyed. Some 55,000 persons are killed in the air raids. In 1945 Hamburg has only 800,000 inhabitants.

1945–70 On 3 May 1945 Hamburg is occupied by British troops and reconstruction begins. In 1952 the Freie und Hansestadt Hamburg receives a new constitution as an autonomous *Land* of the German Federal Republic. In 1962 severe flooding causes the death of over 300 people and enormous damage. Numerous new buildings give the city a modern image, the Exhibition Buildings (Messehallen 1952), the commercial quarter City Nord (1962), the State Opera, the Volkspark stadium, the motorways. In 1964 Hamburg attains its greatest population figure with 1·9 million inhabitants (subsequently this has dropped to 1·6 million).

As in 1953 and 1963 the International Horticultural Show (IGA) takes place in 1973 in Hamburg, and in Planten un Blomen the Hamburg Congress Centre begins to operate. In 1974 traffic begins to use the Köhlbrand Bridge and in the following year the New Elbe Tunnel comes into use. 1973–75

Container traffic in the Port of Hamburg in 1980 accounts for over 30 per cent, and in 1983 44 per cent of the total turnover of consignments. 1980–84
From 18 June to 27 July 1984 the International Postal Congress meets in Hamburg.
On the evening of 2 October 1984 19 people lose their lives when the port launch "Martina" sinks in the North Elbe after a collision with a dredging barge.

Hamburg from A to Z

Ahrensburg

Location
about 25 km (15·5 miles)
NE from centre of Hamburg

Land
Schleswig-Holstein

S-Bahn station
Ahrensburg (S 4)

U-Bahn station
Ahrensburg-West
Ahrensburg-Ost
(both U 1)

Access
Bundesautobahn A 1 (E 4)
Bundesstrasse B 75

The town of Ahrensburg (pop. 27,000; printing, tobacco, etc.) is in the Schleswig-Holstein district of Stormarn; it is easily accessible from Hamburg and, since the Second World War, has developed into a convenient dormitory for many Hamburg commuters.

*Castle

The most important feature of the town is Schloss Ahrensburg, now a museum of domestic culture of the Holstein nobility. The magnificent Renaissance castle, situated in a park, was erected between 1594 and 1598 by Count Peter Rantzau "in honour of his family and the Fatherland". The whitewashed brick building was modelled on the moated Castle of Glücksburg near Flensburg; the builder is unknown. In 1759 Schloss Ahrensburg was acquired by the merchant and financier Heinrich Carl Schimmelmann who carried out extensive reconstruction of the interior. Further alterations to the inside of the castle were made in 1855–56.
There are conducted tours Tuesday to Sunday 10–11.45 a.m. and 1.30–4.45 p.m. An entrance fee is payable.

Castle Church

The church "zu Woldenhorn", belonging to the castle was built between 1594 and 1596; the west tower was not completed until 1773. The church stands between two rows of 12 almshouses – Gottesbuden (God's cottages).

Bredenbeker Teich

On the western outskirts of Ahrensburg lies the pretty Bredenbeker Teich, a lake with a bathing beach, camp site and extensive golf-course.

*Stone Age finds

To the south of Ahrensburg the Hamburg expert in prehistory, Alfred Rust, has excavated hunting and dwelling sites, chiefly at Meiendorf and Stellmoor. The finds of the Ahrensburg culture provide conclusive evidence of the mode of life of the Late Ice-Age reindeer-hunters in north-west Germany (9th c. B.C.)

Airport (Hamburg Airport in Fulhsbüttel)

Location
in the district of Fuhlsbüttel
about 10 km (6 miles) north
from the centre of Hamburg
HH 62

S-Bahn station
Ohlsdorf (S 1, S 11)
then by Airport Express
bus 110

Buses
109, 110, 172, 292

Hamburg Airport, founded in 1911 as an airship base, is the air traffic centre for the whole of North Germany. Its location in the district of Fuhlsbüttel near the city is certainly advantageous for passengers, but, because of noise and pollution, has disadvantages for the heavily populated surroundings. Plans to create a new major airport to the north of Hamburg near Kaltenkirchen are not at present being pursued.
Hamburg Airport has two runways, 3250 m (3556 yd) and 3665 (4010 yd) in length. As they intersect at approximately right angles, aircraft have four directions for take off and landing and thus problems of wind direction are practically eliminated.

With more than 4·5 million passengers annually Hamburg Airport is in fourth place in Germany behind Frankfurt am Main, Düsseldorf and Munich. At the beginning of the 1920s regular services began in Fuhlsbüttel and today 15 airlines and more than 70 charter flight companies are represented here. In addition there are services to North Sea resorts, and supplementary and air-taxi services.

U-Bahn station
Ohlsdorf (U 1)
then by Airport Express bus 110

Plan of Airport
see Practical Information – Airport

Passenger areas

The layout for passengers is in three parts: the main concourse is reserved for international flights and services to Berlin.
Flights within the Federal Republic of Germany are catered for in a special terminal linked to the main building. Charter traffic is dealt with in a building separate from the main terminal. It goes without saying that all the usual services of an international airport are available, including banks and post office, tourist information, left luggage, car hire, restaurants, newspaper kiosks and souvenir shops, etc.
Adjoining the passenger terminal on the south is the air-freight area with the airmail office.

Lufthansa workshops

On the southern boundary of the airport are the extensive workshops of the Lufthansa Company (4 huge aircraft hangars with another planned and over 6000 employees) with the technical base of the German Lufthansa which was founded on 6 January 1926 in Fuhlsbüttel. Here Lufthansa aircraft are serviced, overhauled and repaired (including the engines).

Sightseeing

From an observation garden visitors can watch aircraft taking off, landing and being serviced on the ground.

Model of Airport

By means of an instructive model layout the working of the airport is demonstrated daily at 10 a.m., midday and 2 and 4 p.m. In addition slides and film shows illustrate the working and history of air transport.

Pleasure flights and flights to North Sea resorts

See Practical Information – Airport

**Alster L–N4–9

The centre of Hamburg is unmistakably characterised by the Alster. The waters of the Inner and Outer Alster are a most charming feature of the townscape of the North German metropolis.

Course of the river

The Alster is a tributary on the right bank of the Elbe (see entry); it rises in the Henstedter Moor in Schleswig-Holstein, 25 km (16 miles) north of the city centre. It winds its way through the north of Hamburg (see Alster Valley) and then is canalised in the inner city being dammed up to form the Outer and Inner Alster and the Kleine Alster (Little Alster); finally it flows in Fleete (see entry) and through locks into the inner harbour and thence into the northern Elbe.

Outer Alster

Almost entirely surrounded by greensward and gardens (including the Alsterpark extending over 70 ha (173 acres) on the north-west bank) the Outer Alster (Aussenalster) has an area of about 160 ha (395 acres) with a maximum depth of 2·5 m (8 ft). On its west bank are the elegant districts of

Outer Alster

Inner Alster

Rotherbaum and Harvestehude (with Pöseldorf, see entry); on the east lie Uhlenhorst, Hohenfelde and St Georg (see entry). Several tributaries, all of which are canalised and navigable, flow into the Outer Alster. A trip in one of the flat-bottomed motor-boats, still called Alsterdampfer (Alster steamships) is well worth while. There are two routes as well as canal and special trips from the landing-stage at the Jungfernstieg.
From the north-east bank in the district of Uhlenhorst, a favoured residential quarter with fine villas, there is the best view across the Outer Alster to the tall buildings of the city. Here, until it was destroyed in the Second World War, stood the Uhlenhorster Fährhaus, a ferry house and popular meeting-place; today there are only lawns and a landing-stage for the Alster boats; not far to the east stands a mosque (Iranian-Shi'ite rite), built in 1960, flanked by two minarets. In this district the bronze sculpture 'Drei Männer im Boot' ('Three men in a boat') by Edwin Scharff, can be seen at the widest point of the Outer Alster (Schwanenwik). The broad boulevard in the district of St Georg (see entry), called An der Alster (along the Alster) leads from the Schwanenwik to the Kennedybrücke (see Lombardsbrücke). At Nos. 72–79 stands the elegant Atlantic Hotel; entrance on the Holzdamm.

Inner Alster

The almost square basin of the Inner Alster (Binnenalster), about 18 ha (45 acres) in extent, was separated from the Outer Alster by a ring of defences in the 17th c. It is surrounded by 3 promenades, Jungfernstieg (see entry), Neuer Jungfernstieg and Ballindamm as well as by the Lombardsbrücke (see entry). A walk round the Inner Alster takes approximately 30 minutes. The S-Bahn runs beneath the bed of the lake. The Inner Alster, lying entirely in the central part of the city, gives the area an especially attractive appearance, probably unmatched by any other large German town.

Kleine Alster

Alsterwasser is the name given to a refreshing drink of Bier und Brause (beer and fizzy lemonade). The actual waters of the Alster, however, leave the inner Alster at its southern end under the Reesendammbrücke, where the Jungfernstieg (see entry) begins (the extensive S- and U-Bahn junction Jungfernstieg lies below ground). Between here and the nearby locks it forms the so-called Kleine Alster, a rectangular basin (originally a mill-pond), bordered on the north by the elegant arches of the Alster Arcades (see Passages) and on the south by the broad cascades of the Ressendamm which in turn leads to the newly laid-out pedestrian precinct of the Rathausmarkt (see entry).

Alsterfleet

On the far side of the Schleusenbrücke, below which is a lock, begins the Alsterfleet which is crossed by 6 bridges and finally flows into the inner harbour. Originally the Alster in the old town followed the Nikolaifleet (see entry) where the first port was situated. The waters of the Alster also flow through the Bleichenfleet, running parallel to the Alsterfleet and the adjoining Herrengrabenfleet.

Alster Arcades

See Passages

Kleine Alster and Alster Arcades

*Alster Pavilion M5

Address
Jungfernstieg 54
HH 36

S-Bahn station
Jungfernstieg (S 2, S 2, S 3)

U-Bahn station
Jungfernstieg (U 1, U 2)

Buses
34, 36, 38, 102, 109

Alster boats
(only in summer)
Jungfernstieg landing-stage

The Alster Pavilion ranks as Hamburg's best-known café and restaurant (open daily 10 a.m.–11 p.m.; light music), and is a favourite meeting-place in the city. It is situated at the south-west corner of the Inner Alster and from it the visitor has a fine view over the water as far as the Lombardsbrücke (see entry), with the landing-stage of the Alster boats near by, as well as the activity of the Jungfernstieg (see entry). In fine weather the palm-fringed terrace outside the pavilion is an excellent resting-place after an exploration of the town. This Hamburg "institution" dates back to 1799 and has been rebuilt no fewer than six times; it was destroyed in the Great Fire of 1842 and again in the Second World War. Heinrich Heine was one of the well-known personalities who liked to sit here drinking coffee and watching the girls go by.

Alster Valley

Location
10–20 km (6–12 miles)
NE from the centre of
Hamburg

S-Bahn stations
Kornweg, Hoheneichen,
Wellingsbüttel, Poppenbüttel
(all S 1 and S 11)

The northern Hamburg residential district of Wellingsbüttel and Poppenbüttel, together with places in the immediate neighbourhood, comprise the Alster Valley. Until the beginning of the 20th c. there was waterborne trade between Kayhude in Schleswig-Holstein and Hamburg (boats were towed upstream). A few locks and weirs remain from this period and these also serve to control the water-level.

Footpath

The Alster footpath follows the whole course of the river from its source on the Henstedter Moor through the pastures in the Valley of the Upper Alster (Nature Park) and the territory of Hamburg itself right up to its junction with the Elbe.
The scenery of the Alster Valley between Rade in Holstein (see Rade Museum) and the Hamburg suburb of Klein Borstel, on the northern side of the Ohlsdorf Cemetery (see entry), is particularly attractive. The footpath passes the Mellingburg Lock with a 16th c. lock-keeper's house, now an inn, the attractive Henneberg Park and the modern Alster Valley shopping centre by the S-bahn station of Poppenbüttel, as well as the Alster Valley Museum in Wellingsbüttel which specialises in cultural history (Wellingsbütteler Weg 79g–h, Torhaus; open Saturday and Sunday 11 a.m.–1 p.m. and 3–5 p.m.)

Alte Post

L4/5

Address
Poststrasse 11
HH 36

S-Bahn station
Jungfernstieg (S 1, S 2, S 3)

U-Bahn station
Jungfernstieg (U 1, U 2)
Rathaus (U 3)

Alster boats
(only in summer)
Jungfernstieg landing-stage

On the north-west side of the Bleichenfleet stands the brick building erected by Alexis de Chateauneuf in 1845–47 in the style of the Tuscan Renaissance. Its octagonal tower was originally used for the optical telegraph between Hamburg, Cuxhaven and Bremen. Before the Great Fire of 1842 there were post offices situated in various parts of the town belonging to the Hamburg (Free City) Post, the Thurn and Taxis Post, the Royal Hanover Post and the Royal Swedish Post which were amalgamated in this building; their coats of arms and emblems can be seen on the entrances. Until the opening of the main office on Stephansplatz (1887) the building was utilised by the postal service and subsequently

Alte Post

In the Altes Land

used for administration and the housing of archives. From 1968 to 1971 the Alte Post was restored and converted for business and commercial purposes (including the headquarters of the Hamburg Adult Education Institute) with shopping arcades (see Passages) on the ground floor; the historic façade, however, has been retained.

*Altes Land

Location
10–30 km (6–18 miles) SW from the centre of Hamburg

Land
Hamburg and Lower Saxony

Access
Bundesstrasse 73 westwards from HH-Harburg

Elbe Ferries
HH-Blankenese–Cranz
Wedel-Schulau–Lühe

The Altes Land is a broad strip of marshy land, about 30 km (19 miles) long and 7 km (4 miles) wide, extending from Hamburg along the south bank of the Elbe as far as the town of Stade in Lower Saxony. This fertile region, criss-crossed by drainage canals and traversed by the rivers Este and Lühe, is the most northerly area in the world entirely devoted to fruit-growing. The principal fruits grown are apples and cherries and at blossom time a visit to the Altes Land is very popular with the citizens of Hamburg.
The Altes Land was settled in the 12th and 13th c. by incomers from the Netherlands, and from 1832 it had its own constitution. The imposing Altland farmhouses with their artistically furnished and decorated doorways provide evidence of rural prosperity.

Neuenfeld

At one time the Southern Elbe joined the main stream, which is nearly 3 km (2 miles) wide at this point, near the rural Hamburg suburb of Neuenfelde. Today the old Southern Elbe terminates in a dead end at the Neuenfelde Hauptdeich; the water from the Southern Elbe flows from Harburg Harbour through the Köhlbrand into the Lower Elbe.
In the Baroque Church of St Pancras, which is visible from afar, there are a painted wooden barrel roof, an altar of 1688 and a fine organ (1689–91), by the famous organ-builder Arp Schnitger (1648–1719) who had a farm here and is buried in the church.

Jork

Jork (pop. 10,000; Estehof Inn) lies in the centre of the Altes Land in Lower Saxony. Not far to the east the Este joins the Elbe. Jork is the headquarters of a fruit-growing research institute and boasts a number of fine old farmhouses and a church of 1709. In the parish of Borstel stands an old windmill.

Stade

The Lower Saxon county town of Stade (pop. 45,000), once an important member of the Hanseatic League, is situated at the west end of the Altes Land on the River Schwinge, a tributary of the Elbe on the left bank. The old town surrounded by a rampart is worth seeing; there are pretty half-timbered houses and the Church of St Cosmae, originally Romanesque which has an Arp Schnitger organ. To the south-west on an island is an open-air museum with old buildings from the region.

Altona H/J4/5

Location
about 4 km (2·5 miles) W from the centre of Hamburg

Until 1937 when Greater Hamburg was created, Altona was an independent town which originated in a fishing settlement of the early 16th c. It then belonged to the Count of Pinneberg

Altona Town Hall and Platz der Rububl̲ik

S-Bahn stations
Altona
(S 1, S 2, S 3, S 5, S 11, S 31)
Konigstrasse
(S 1, S 2, S 3)

and, from 1640 to Denmark, becoming Prussian in 1867. The name is said to indicate "all to nah" ("all too near" to Hamburg).
Historically there was great rivalry between Altona and the Hansastadt of Hamburg. Air attacks in the Second World War caused considerable devastation in Altona especially in the centre of the town.

Altona Harbour

The harbour of Altona, confined by the steep bank of the Elbe, now serves as the fishing port of Hamburg.

Altona Station

Altona Station has particular importance for railway traffic (motorail terminus and S-Bahn station). The former main building was replaced between 1975 and 1979.

Altona Town Hall

Altona Town Hall, now the headquarters of the district of Altona, goes back to the period between 1896 and 1898 when the buildings of the former station on this site were converted; the relief on the gable is the work of Karl Garber assisted by Ernst Barlach. The Town Hall is an effective terminus to the extensive Platz der Republik.

Altona Museum

About half-way between the Town Hall and the station lies the Altona Museum.

Christianskirche

In Ottensen, a neighbouring part of Altona not far west of the Town Hall, stands the Christianskirche, an Evangelical church built between 1735 and 1738. It is named after the Danish King Christian IV (1577–1648) who was responsible for building a great deal of Altona. The Baroque hall-church was damaged in the Second World War and restored between 1946 and 1952.

Grave of Klopstock

In the churchyard, which was laid out in 1758 and converted into a park in 1954, can be found the grave of the poet F. G. Klopstock (1724–1803).

Altona Balcony

South of Altona Town Hall an attractive unspoiled pathway known as the Altona Balcony extends along the bank of the Elbe. From here there is an impressive view over the port of Hamburg including the extensive span of the Köhlbrand Bridge (see entry).

Palmaille

Palmaille, Altona's prestigious street, between the squares to the south of the Town Hall and the commencement of the Breite Strasse, is named after a ball game (Palla a maglio) which Count Otto V of Holstein-Schauenburg set up here in 1638–39 with three courts each 647 m (707 yd) long. However, they later became derelict and in the 18th c. were widened to form a roadway and planted with lime trees. Between 1786 and 1825 the Danish architect Christian Frederik Hansen and his nephew Matthias Hansen built up the road with fine houses in the Classical style. A great number were destroyed in the Second World War; a few, however, are still in existence (Nos. 49–71 and 108–120) some having been rebuilt (Nos. 73–79) and still provide an impression of the unique elegance of the original buildings.

Trinity Church

The first church was originally built in 1650 and gradually added to until the Baroque building of the Evangelical Church of the Holy Trinity on the corner of Königstrasse and Kirchenstrasse was completed in 1743. In the Second World War the building was destroyed apart from the walls and the base of the tower. Between 1954 and 1969 it was faithfully reconstructed and refurnished. The tower, which had been in existence in 1690 was also rebuilt with two Italian domes and a lantern, providing once again a fine landmark.

Jewish Cemetery

To the north of the Church of the Holy Trinity on the far side of Königstrasse lies the Jewish Cemetery, laid out at the beginning of the 17th c. It contains several thousand graves, including those of numerous Portuguese Jews.

Altona Volkspark

See Volkspark

Elbchaussee

See Elbchaussee and Elbuferweg

*Altona Museum in Hamburg (North German Provincial Museum) H4

Address
Museumstrasse 23
HH 50 (Altona)

S-Bahn station
Altona (S 1, S 2, S 3, S 5. S 11, S 31)

Buses
36, 37, 112, 113, 115, 150, 183, 187, 188, 250

Opening times
Tue.–Sun. 10 a.m.–5 p.m.
Closed Mon.

Entrance fee

The "Public Museum in Altona" was opened in 1863 by a private museum company in one of the houses in Palmaille built by the Danish architect C. F. Hansen; in 1888 the collections passed to the town of Altona which was then in Schleswig-Holstein. In 1901 a new museum building was completed in Museumstrasse and was enlarged between 1912 and 1914. After the incorporation of Altona in Greater Hamburg (1937) the museum passed into the possession of the Free Hansa City of Hamburg. In the last year of the Second World War (1945) about two-thirds of the building and about a third of the collections were destroyed. In the course of reconstruction two new buildings were added, one in 1955 and another in 1967. In 1980 a serious fire caused further heavy damage anbd part of the collection has been rearranged and will be housed separately until about 1985.

Model ship

Ship's figurehead

The Altona Museum deals with the cultural and regional history of the whole of North Germany; covering the fields of art and craft, ethnology and tradition, shipping, fishing, geology and not least the history of toys. Of particular interest are the Vierländer Kate (an original furnished farmhouse of 1745; inn), the numerous rural rooms, models of farmhouses, pottery, models of ships and wharves, ship's carpenter's workshop and a ropemaker's, figureheads, nautical apparatus as well as dolls, dolls' houses and other toys. The art collection contains North German landscapes from the 18th c. to the present day (Schmidt-Rottluff, Pechstein, Feiniger, etc.).

Exhibits

Associated with the Altona Museum are the Vierländer Open-air Museum, Rieck Haus (see Vierlande and Marschlande) and the Jenisch Haus (see Jenisch Park).

Associated Museums

Aussenalster

See Alster

Barlach Haus

See Jenisch Park

Bergedorf

Location
15–20 km (9–12 miles) SE from the centre of Hamburg

S-Bahn station
Bergedorf (S 2, S 21)

Access
Bundesautobahn A 25
Bundesstrasse B 5

The Hamburg suburb of Bergedorf in the south-east of the metropolis is the second largest district of the city but from the standpoint of population it is the smallest. This popular residential quarter with its green open spaces is in the region of Vierlande (see entry) and Marschlande and lies on the Bille, a tributary on the right bank of the Elbe.
Originally a seat of the Count of Orlamünde, the Castle of Bergedorf came into the combined jurisdiction of the Hansa towns of Hamburg and Lübeck in the year 1420. It was not until 1863 that Hamburg acquired control of the administration of the whole of Bergedorf with a payment of 200,000 Prussian thaler. But even today the citizens of Bergedorf value their independence.

Castle

The moated castle, built in the early 13th c. was later converted by the Dukes of Lauenburg into a frontier strongpoint against Hamburg. In 1420 it was taken by storm by the combined troops of Hamburg and Lübeck. After being rebuilt several times the castle losts its protective earthworks and moat in the early 19th c. and was surrounded by a park. It now houses the

Museum of Bergedorf and the Vierlande

Museum of Bergedorf, a collection of exhibits illustrating rural and middle-class culture (open Tuesday, Thursday and Sunday 10 a.m.–5 p.m.; entrance fee).

St Peter and Paul

The Church of St Peter and Paul (St Petri und Pauli) was first mentioned in 1162, the present building dating mainly from about 1500. Of interest inside the brick and timber building are

Bergedorf Castle, now a museum

the pulpit of 1583 and various 16th c. wooden reliefs. In the Verger's House is a memorial tablet to the extremely prolific composer Johann Adolf Hasse (1699–1783) who was the son of a Bergedorf organist.

The Stadt Hamburg Inn

The Gasthof Stadt Hamburg is the finest of the half-timbered houses of Bergedorf and also the oldest surviving secular building in the whole of Hamburg. There is elaborate ornamental carving on this corner building which dates from about 1550. In 1958–59 the house was moved a short distance for traffic reasons and the opportunity was taken for restoration.

Windmill

North of the centre of Bergedorf by the Chrysanderstrasse stands a windmill erected in 1831, a representative of Dutch Gallery type (Galerie-Holländers) which was formerly common in north-west Germany.

Old station

The old station in the south of Bergedorf was built for the railway line constructed in 1842 between Hamburg and Bergedorf. It is the oldest remaining station building in the Federal Republic. From time to time trips with an old-time steam locomotive operate to Geesthacht.

Observatory

In the south-east of Bergedorf (Gojenbergsweg 112) stands the Hamburg Observatory. It was founded in 1802 and until 1912 was situated in the Wallanlagen at Millerntor (see Museum of Hamburg History). But since the clarity of the air in the town centre was becoming impaired the observatory was moved to its present site. B. V. Schmidt (1879–1935), who worked at the observatory, developed a valuable mirror telescope which is named after him.

Binnenalster

See Alster

Bischofsburg (Excavation) M4

When excavating for the present Parish House of St Peter (St Petri; see St Peter's Church) in 1962, one of the most important archaeological discoveries of the old town of Hamburg was made. About 3 m (10 ft) below the present road level a huge circular stone foundation was uncovered. Rough blocks of stone form a 4 m (13 ft) thick stone ring with an external diameter of 19 m (62 ft) and an internal diameter of 11 m (36 ft), clearly articulated into an external and internal bowl between which on a bed of boulders small pebbles had been tipped. To the west of the main circle a smaller stone circle with a diameter of 4·5 m (15 ft) had been added (former shaft of a well). This was the foundation of a round tower of the mid 11th c., part of the stone house of the Archbishop Bezelin-Alebrand (1035–43) which stood on the highest point of Hamburg at that time. This stone foundation is the remains of the oldest secular stone building in Hamburg and also of the earliest known stone fortress north of the Elbe.

Address
Kreuslerstrasse 4 (corner of Speersort)
HH 1

U-Bahn station
Rathaus (U 3)

Buses
31, 34, 35, 36, 37, 38, 102, 108, 109

Opening times
Mon.–Fri. 10 a.m.–1 p.m. and 3–5 p.m. Sat. 10 a.m.–1 p.m. Closed Sun.

Cellar Room

The excavation site can be seen from a room in the cellar.

Hammaburg

To the south immediately adjoining the Bischofsburg (Bishop's Fortress) lay the zone of immunity in the jurisdiction of the Bishop which coincided with the area of the Hammaburg (see entry).

Bismarck Monument K4

Location
at Millerntor
HH 4

U-Bahn station
St Pauli (U 3)

Buses
36, 37, 112

On the site of a former bastion of the 17th c. town defences rises a sandy hill on which stands the enormous Bismarck Monument which is visible for miles around. It was built between 1903 and 1906 (picture p. 20). On a huge round plinth, 19 m (62 ft) high with reliefs of German tribes, towers the 14·8 m (49 ft) high colossal statue of Chancellor Bismarck, stylised as a "Roland figure". The statue, which consists of hewn blocks of granite, was created by the sculptor Hugo Lederer; it is meant to symbolise the protection of the German Reich for Hamburg's international trade.

Stintfang

Port

Not far south of the Bismarck Monument on the Stintfang, the last hillock on the shore, stands Hamburg's youth hostel (Haus der Jugend). From here there is a fine view of the port (see entry).

Bismarck Mausoleum and Bismarck Museum

See Sachsenwald

*Blankenese (District of Hamburg)

Location
14 km (9 miles) W from the centre of Hamburg

S-Bahn station
Blankenese (S 1, S 11)

Buses
36, 48, 189, 286

The original fishing settlement of Blankenese (the name is derived from the Low German "blanke Nees" = "light nose"), was first mentioned at the beginning of the 14th c. as a ferry point on the Elbe. Towards the end of the 18th c., and especially in the 19th c., Hamburg merchants built their imposing country houses in this area. Nevertheless the old centre of the place on the steep sandy slopes with its stepped pathways and little houses has retained its original, almost southerly character. Many people consider Blankenese, which was only incorporated in Hamburg in 1927 (until 1864 it was Danish), to be the most beautiful suburb of Hamburg.
The brick fisherman's houses, often thatched, were mostly built in the 18 th c. A few mansions (for instance Elbchaussee 547 or Blankeneser Landstrasse 34) were constructed from plans by the Danish architect Frederik Hansen. The Haus Michaelsen (Grotiusweg 55) in the style of Neue Sachlichkeit (New Objectivity) is a good example of modern architecture.

Villas crowding the steep bank of the Elbe at Blankenese ▶

River path

From the river path, which forms a kind of terrace and where there are numerous inns and restaurants, fine views across the broad and busy River Elbe can be enjoyed, for instance over the island known as Schweinesand as far as the Altes Land (see entry). From the river-bank picturesque paths and steps lead up to the Blankeneser Landstrasse with its modern shops and businesses.

Süllberg

Above Blankenese rises the 86 m (282 ft) high Süllberg with a popular restaurant which is often crowded in summer and from which there are fine views.
Westwards along the Falkenstein bank and the Rissen bank of the river it is possible to walk to Wedel and the Schulau Fährhaus (ferry house) with the ship's greeting point (see Willkommhöft). In an easterly direction the well-known river walk Elbchaussee (see entry) leads to Altona (see entry).

* Börse

See Stock Exchange

* Botanical Gardens

Old Botanical Gardens L5

Main Entrance
Stephensplatz HH 36

S-Bahn station
Dammtor (S 11, S 21, S 31)

U-Bahn station
Stephensplatz (U 1)

Buses
34, 36, 38, 102, 112

Opening Times
Daily
Summer 7 a.m.–10 p.m.
Winter 7 a.m.–8 p.m.

Hothouses
Summer 9 a.m.–6 p.m
Winter 9 a.m.–4 p.m.

The Old Botanical Garden at the Dammtor was laid out in 1821 for the then existing Academic Museum. The chosen site was a part of the town defences and moat which had been razed a short time beforehand; the course of the moat can still be traced by the lake in the gardens. Lack of space, the ageing of trees and environmental conditions necessitated the creation of the New Botanical Garden in Flottbek (see p. 54); the hothouses are located in the Old Garden which is now part of the Wallringpark (see entry).

The hothouses (open to the public) comprise a total area of 2800 sq. m (30,140 sq. ft), of which 2450 sq. m (26,372 sq ft) are under glass. They are grouped round an open space with pools containing aquatic plants.
The visit begins with the large Tropical House where banana bushes, mangroves, sugar-cane, bamboos, palms, tropical ferns, etc. thrive. The adjoining Cycad House contains the so-called palm-ferns, an original group of gymnosperms which grow slowly and can live to an extremely old age.
The stock of the Sub-tropical House is arranged from a geographical standpoint (Mediterranean, Africa, Australia, Asia, America); here there are many well-known useful plants such as olives, laurel, fig trees, coffee and tea bushes, citrus plants, etc. Passing through the Fern House one comes to the Succulent House. Succulents are plants belonging to different systems but which all possess the ability of storing large quantities of water and are, therefore, able to exist in periods of extreme drought.

New Botanical Garden
'System'

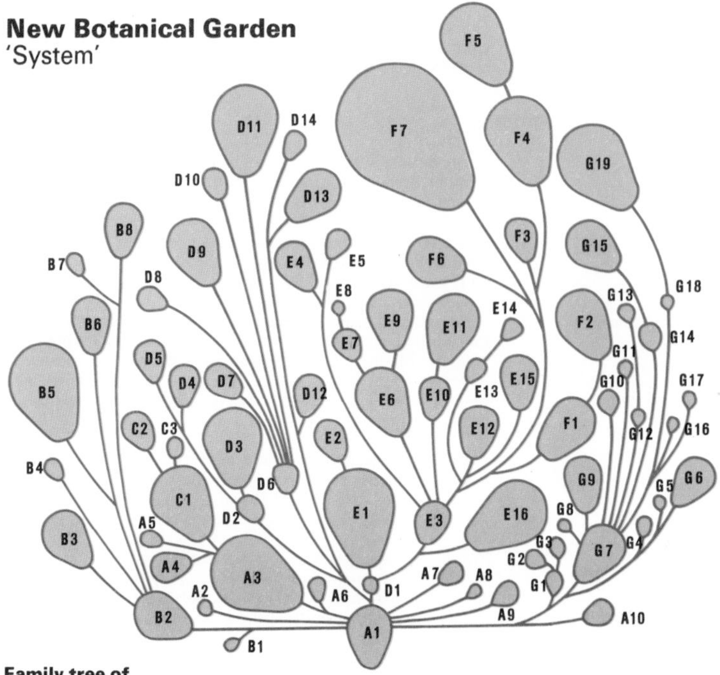

Family tree of flowering plants (Angiospermea)

A1 Magnoliales (tulip tree, magnolia)
A2 Nelumbonales
A3 Ranales (anemone, achillea, berberis)
A4 Papaverales (poppy)
A5 Sarraceniales
A6 Illiciales
A7 Aristolochiales
A8 Piperales (pepper)
A9 Laurales (laurel)
A10 Nymphaeales (water lilies)

B1 Troachodendrales
B2 Hamamelidales (plane tree)
B3 Urticales (stinging nettle, fig, elm)
B4 Casuarinales
B5 Fagales (oak, beech, chestnut)
B6 Betulales (birch, hazel, alder)
B7 Myricales
B8 Juglandales (walnut)

C1 Caryophylliales (carnation, orache, cactus)
C2 Polygonales
C3 Plumbaginales

D1 Dilleniales (peony)
D2 Theales
D3 Ericales (rhododendron, heather)
D4 Ebenales
D5 Primulales
D6 Cistales (violets)
D7 Passiflorales
D8 Datiscales (begonia)
D9 Capparidales
D10 Tamaricales
D11 Salicales (willow, poplar)
D12 Malvales (lime, mallow)
D13 Euphorbiales
D14 Thymelaeales (mezereon)

E1 Rosales (rose, apple, cherry, strawberry)
E2 Saxifragales
E3 Cunoniales (gooseberry, hydrangea)
E4 Myrtales (evening primrose, eucalyptus)
E5 Haloragales
E6 Rutales (lemon)
E7 Geraniales
E8 Polygalales
E9 Sapindales (maple, red chestnut)
E10 Cornales
E11 Araliales (ivy)
E12 Celastrales (holly)
E13 Santalales (mistletoe)
E14 Proteales
E15 Rhamnales (vines)
E16 Fabales (beans, clover, broom, acacia)

F1 Gentianales (gentian, ash, forsythia)
F2 Rubiales (valerian, woodruff, elder)
F3 Polemoniales (phlox, forget-me-not)
F4 Scrophulariales (plantain, tomato, antirrhinum)
F5 Lamiales (dead nettle, sage, marjoram)
F6 Campanulales (campanula)
F7 Asterales (sunflower, dandelion, edelweiss, thistle)

G1–3 Helobiae
G4 Arecales (palm)
G5 Pandanales
G6 Arales (arum, duck-weed)
G7 Liliales (narcissus, asparagus, tulip)
G8 Bromeliales (pineapple)
G9 Iridales (iris)
G10 Dioscoreales
G11 Zingiberales (cane)
G12 Haemodorales
G13 Ochidales
G14 Juncales (rushes)
G15 Cyperales
G16 Commelinales
G17 Eriocaulales
G18 Restionales
G19 Poales (grasses, cereals, bamboos)

Instructional Collection

The collection belongs to the Institute of Applied Botany (Marseiller Strasse 7; Mon.–Fri. 9 a.m.–3.30 p.m.) and exhibits products from tropical and sub-tropical plants.

New Botanical Garden E5/6

Address
Hesten 10
HH 52

S-Bahn station
Klein Flottbek (Botanical Garden; S 1, S 11)

In September 1970 a decision was made to lay out in Klein Flottbek a new botanical garden which would meet the more demanding requirements of science. At the same time it serves as a public open space for relaxation. In 1979 the first section was opened; work is still proceeding on other sections. The New Botanic Garden is open daily from 10 a.m. to 7 p.m. (in winter from 9 a.m. to 3.30 p.m.).

Thematic Gardens

Large parts of the new layout are arranged thematically. Near the entrance are useful plants, allotments, poisonous plants as well as Mediterranean plants; circulating in a clockwise direction there follow a rural garden and a medicinal herb garden, conifers, a spring garden, heathers and rhododendrons.

Habitat

The next main division the visitor comes to includes the following sections: German forest, flora of heath, moor and shore, steppes, the flora of China, a Japanese garden, North American plants; in the Alpinum plants of the high mountains.

System

The so-called system is the nucleus of the New Botanical Garden. As the name implies this range is constructed in the form of a systematic family tree which clarifies the developments and relations of the various groups of plants (schematic plan, see p. 53).

Brahms Commemorative Rooms

See Peterstrasse

*Chile House M4

Location
Between Burchardplatz and Messberg
HH 1

U-Bahn station
Messberg (U 1)

Bus
111

With its unconventional shape the mighty elongated Chilehaus (picture p. 20) is probably the best-known building in the Hamburg business quarter. It was erected in 1922–24 from plans by Fritz Höger for Henry B. Sloman, who had a successful trade in saltpetre with Chile. It is considered the most representative example of the more modern North German clinker-brick architecture. The most impressive view of this monumental 10-storey building, at the corner of Burchardstrasse and Pumpen, with its façades meeting at a sharp angle like a ship's prow is from the east. By restrictions applied to the nearby buildings on either side the Oberbaudirektor (Director of Buildings) of that time, Fritz Schumacher, succeeded in creating for the Chilehaus an effect unique in civic architecture. Also notable is the ceramic wall decoration by Richard Kuöhl. Visitors should look at the entrance halls and staircases on the longer sides.

**City Hall (Rathaus)

M4

Location
in the city centre at the Rathausmarkt
HH 1

S-Bahn station
Jungfernstieg (S 1, S 2, S 3)

U-Bahn station
Jungfernstieg (U 1, U 2)

Buses
31, 34, 36, 37, 38, 102, 108, 109

Alster boats
(only in summer)
Jungfernstieg landing-stage

The mighty Hamburg City Hall (Rathaus) is no old historic building but dates from the end of the 19th c., being in the style of the Nordic Renaissance. It is the work of 7 architects led by Martin Haller. Artists from all over Germany were engaged in the ornamentation of the façades and in the rich internal furnishings. The Free Hanseatic City of Hamburg is very conscious of its traditions, a spirit which is manifested in this impressive edifice. The City Hall is the seat of the Senate (Landesregierung = provincial government) and of the Bürgerschaft (Landesparliament); it also contains the official civic apartments of the First Bürgermeister, the rooms of the political parties and a series of magnificently furnished function rooms. In all there are said to be 647 rooms in the City Hall.
The present City Hall is the sixth. Little is known of the first two, except that they both existed at the same time. Shortly after the foundation of the New Town on the Alster Harbour near the Nikolaikirche in the year 1189, the first Rathaus would probably have been built. It was a modest stone building on the site of the present Hopfenmarkt. Then a town hall was also built in the archiepiscopal Old Town on the north side of the old fish market.

History of the City Hall

In 1216 the two towns joined together, and on the corner of Dornbusch and Kleine Johannisstrasse the third Hamburg City Hall was built. It consisted only of a narrow hall, approached by an arcaded staircase and in 1284 it was destroyed in a fire. The fourth City Hall existed on the Ness and by the Trostbrücke, where today stands the building of the Patriotische Gesellschaft (see entry). It was an ideal site at the crossing between the Old and the New Towns. Once again there was a hall with an arcade, this time, however, in notable dimensions (26 × 18 m (85 × 59 ft)). Around the Rathaus were grouped the Lower Court, the crane, scales and customs house for the trading centre of the town. This building was the actual historic City Hall, for it was to fulfil its purpose for more than 500 years, even if repeatedly in a different and extended form.
In the night of 5/6 May 1842 when the Great Fire had already raged for 24 hours, the council resolved to blow up the already dilapidated building in order to prevent the fire spreading. On the very day after the end of the fourth Rathaus, a fifth, although not yet built, had already been found; the Senate moved temporarily to the orphanage in the Admiralitätsstrasse; a move which was to last 55 years! The Parliament (Bürgerschaft) at first met in the orphanage church but from 1859 in the new building of the Patriotische Gesellschaft, which had risen on the site of the old Rathaus.
After protracted discussions about the future site and appearance of the new City Hall, as well as two international competitions, the foundation-stone for the sixth Hamburg City Hall was laid on the 6 May 1866. The consortium for the present building, under the direction of Martin Haller included the architects Johannes Grotjan, Bernhard Hanssen, Wilhelm Hauers, Emil Meerwein, Hugo Stammann and Gustav Zinnow. Topping out was on 6 May 1892 and on 26 October 1897 the present City Hall was dedicated with enthusiastic popular support (total building costs amounted to 11 million gold marks). As if by a miracle it survived the catastrophic aerial

City Hall (Rathaus)
(built 1886–97)

MAIN FLOOR
(FIRST FLOOR)

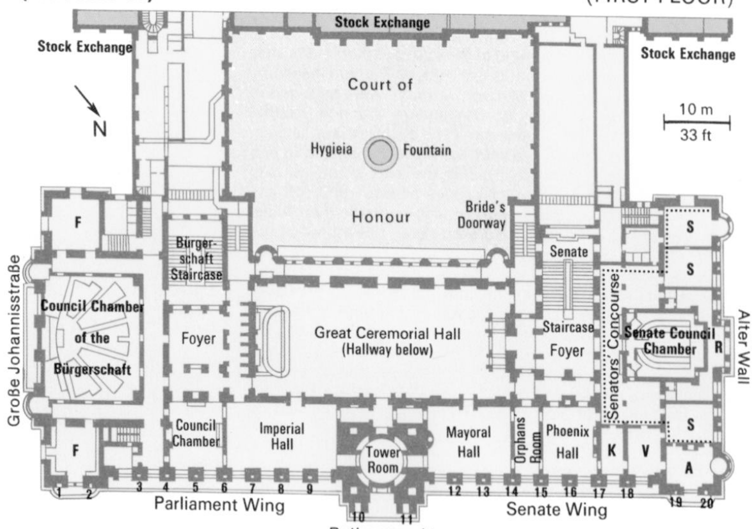

A Bürgermeister's Office
R Council Corridor

F Party Rooms
S Committee Rooms

K Conference Room
V Bürgermeister's Ante-room

STATUES OF EMPERORS on the main façade

1 Lothar III of Saxony (1125–37)
2 Heinrich III (1039–56)
3 Konrad II (1024–39)
4 Otto II (973–983)
5 Otto the Great (936–973)
6 Heinrich I (919–936)
7 Konrad I (911–918)
8 Ludwig the German (843–876)
9 Ludwig the Pious (814–840)
10 Charles the Great (768–814)
11 Friedrich I Barbarossa (1152–90)
12 Heinrich VI (1190–97)
13 Friedrich II (1212–50)
14 Rudolf von Habsburg (1273–91)
15 Karl IV (1346–78)
16 Maximilian I (1493–1519)
17 Karl V (1519–56)
18 Maximilian II (1564–76)
19 Joseph II (1765–90)
20 Franz II (1792–1806)

attacks of the Second World War without fundamental damage.

Outside

Because of the marshy nature of the subsoil, the City Hall is supported by 4000 piles driven into the ground. The monumental 4-storeyed building with a copper saddle-roof measures 111 × 70 m (364 × 230 ft); the dominating central tower rises to a height of 112 m (368 ft).
The façade facing the Rathausmarkt (see entry) is ornamented with numerous figures, including, between the windows of the main storey, statues of German Emperors.
At the rear two relatively narrow wings link the building to the Stock Exchange (see entry). In the internal courtyard (Courtyard of Honour) where occasional concerts are given, stands a large fountain with allegorical bronze figures (at the top can be seen Hygieia, the embodiment of health and pure water), a reminder of the devastating cholera epidemic of 1892 when in 71 days there were 8605 deaths.

City Hall by night

Council Chamber

Interior

On the ground floor is the great Rathausdiele, a hall supported by 16 squat sandstone pillars (starting-point for City Hall tours; frequent exhibitions); on the right is the magnificent staircase to the Senate Wing, on the left the more modest entrance to the Parliament Wing (every second Tuesday from 4 p.m. a public sitting in the plenary hall).
On the first floor, actually the main floor of the City Hall, on the side facing the Rathausmarkt, are the massive state rooms: the Bürgersaal (Council Chamber), the Kaisersaal (Imperial Hall), Turmsaal (Tower Room), Bürgermeistersaal (Mayoral Hall), Waisenzimmer (Orphans' Room), and Phönixsaal (Phoenix Hall); adjoining are the rooms of the Bürgermeister (in his office the Golden Book of the City).
On the Alter Wall side, in the Senators' Concourse (bronze lattice-work on the stairwell) is the Ratsstube (the Senate Council Chamber).
In the Great Ceremonial Hall (46·6 m (153 ft) long, 18 m (59 ft) wide, 15 m (49 ft) high; paintings by Hugo Vogel, 1902–07) above the Rathausdiele, there takes place annually on 24 February the traditional Matthiae-Mahlzeit (St Matthias's Banquet) for about 300 invited guests.

Ratsweinkeller (Wine Cellar)

Only the figure of Bacchus swinging his beaker at the entrance in the Grosse Johannisstrasse reminds us of the former Ratsweinkeller. The larger than life figure came from the Swedish sculptor, J. W. Manstadt, who had created it for his Eimsbecksche Haus, an inn well known in its time where Einbeck ale could be obtained. The inn was destroyed in the

Great Fire of 1842. The present Ratsweinkeller (good medium-priced restaurant) comprises a bar with several model ships, the Grundsteinkeller, where the City Hall foundation-stone of 6 May 1886 can be seen, the Great Hall and a domed room known as the Rose.

City Nord N9

Location
about 7 km (4 miles) N from centre of Hamburg

S-Bahn station
Rübenkamp (City Nord; S 1, S 11)

U-Bahn station
Sengelmannstrasse (City Nord), Alsterdorf (both U 1)

Buses
E 17, 117, 118, 179, 217

From 1962 an administration centre for private and public undertakings was laid out in the north on the far side of the Stadtpark (see entry). It was called City Nord or Geschäftsstadt Nord and was built according to the proposals of the Director of Building, Werner Hebebrand.
Within the Überseering, a semi-elliptical ring of roads stand more than 20 office buildings in differing architectural styles. In addition to the Headquarters of the Hamburg Post Office and the Hamburg Electricity Works (HEW) the multi-national oil companies of Shell, Esso, BP and Texaco together with large firms such as IBM, Hoechst, Edeka and Tchibo have their administrative offices here. There are also a number of shops and restaurants as well as an hotel. In this "office town in the country" more than 20,000 people are employed, and they have at their disposal the adjoining Stadtpark (see entry) where they can relax during breaks from work.

Colonnades

See Passages

Communication Centre

See Fabrik

Congress Centre of Hamburg (CCH) L5/6

Address
at the Dammtor/Marseiller Strasse, HH 36

S-Bahn station
Dammtor (S 11, S 21, S 31)

U-Bahn station
Stephansplatz (U 1)

Bus
34

The Congress Centre of Hamburg (CCH; see pictures on pp. 8 and 138) was opened in 1973 in the north-east corner of the park Planten un Blomen (see Wallringpark) not far from the Exhibition Grounds (see entry) and only a few steps from Dammtor Station. The huge spaciously laid-out complex comprises 17 conference and reception rooms which can also be used for concerts and entertainment of various kinds, with an effective floor space of between 50 sq. m (538 sq. ft) and 2800 sq. m (30,140 sq. ft), a restaurant and a two-storey underground garage with nearly 850 parking spaces. Among the modern technical facilities provided are large projectors for

Modern administration buildings are a feature of the City Nord ▶

Hamburg Congress Centre

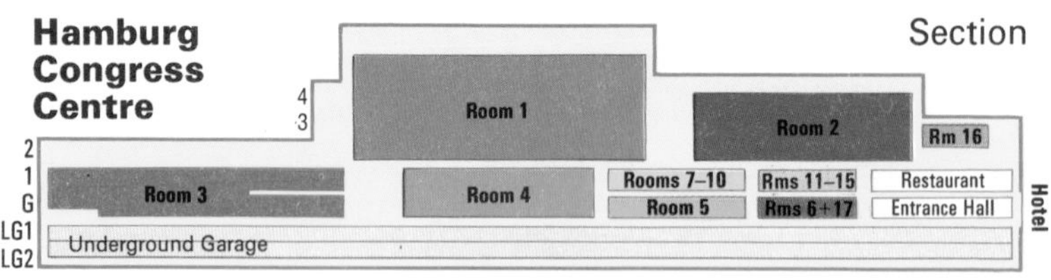

ROOMS/AREA/CAPACITY

Room No.	Floor	Area in sq. m.	Area in sq. ft.	Seating in rows	Seating in conference order	Room No.	Floor	Area in sq. m.	Area in sq. ft.	Seating in rows	Seating in conference order
1	2–4	2600	27981	3000	1400	13	1	80	861	90	35
2	2–4	1570	16899	1500	750	14	1	60	646	75	25
3	G	2800	30139	2300	1350	13+14	1	140	1507	156	72
4	G	700	7535	800	375	15	1	60	646	85	35
5	G	950	10225	780	390	16	3	80	861	110	45
6	G	380	4090	400	200	17	G	75	807	80	40
7	1	110	1184	120	65	Restaurant	1	900	9688	480 places	
8	1	235	2530	285	110	Terrace	1	314	3380	150 places	
9	1	60	646	80	40	Underground					
10	1	50	538	55	30	Garage	LG1	11850	127553	408 places	
11	1	50	538	55	20	Underground					
12	1	60	646	50	35	Garage	LG2	12100	130244	436 places	

films and television, interpreting and audio translation equipment, etc.
In association with the Hamburg Congress Centre is the striking Hamburg Plaza, an hotel of 32 storeys.

Cremon

L4

Location
between Nikolaifleet and the Inner Harbour

U-Bahn station
Rödingsmarkt (U 3)

Bus
111

As early as the 12th c. Friesian and Dutch incomers had built a dike round the little island of "Cremon" between the Nikolaifleet (see entry) and the Steckelhörnfleet which no longer exists. As in the nearby Deichstrasse (see entry) storehouses and dwellings were built here with one side facing the street and the other the Fleet, so that goods could be transported by land or by water. Nos. 33–36 are the last remaining storehouses.

Cremon Bridge

See Deichstrasse

Neuer Krahn

The road called Cremon leads south to the Inner Harbour. Here stands the green so-called Neuer Krahn of 1858, which replaced a wooden crane of 1657. When the first New Crane was set up in 1352, handling of cargoes of larger ships was already beginning to be moved from the old Alster port to the new port on the Elbe (see Port).
From the Neuer Krahn it is only a few steps westwards along the Inner Harbour, on the far side of which lies the Speicherstadt (see entry), to the Hohe Brücke (see Deichstrasse) over the Nikolaifleet (see entry) which here flows into the Inner Harbour; there is an extensive view from the bridge.

Remierstwiete

Not far from the Katharinenkirche (see entry), Reimerstwiete, which runs between Katherinenstrasse and the Zollkanal, originally linked two main roads on the former Cremon Island.

The narrow Twiete (= alley) was a characteristic thoroughfare in the residential part of Old Hamburg. A row of fairly small half-timbered storehouses of the second half of the 18th c., the "Five Sisters" (Nos. 17–21), has been restored in the original form.

Dammtor Station

L5

The area between Stephansplatz and Moorweide is usually called Dammtor. From 1622 until 1807 the actual Dammtor Gate stood on the site now occupied by the "beer palace" on the Dammtordamm; then it was replaced by the first Dammtor Station.
Not far north-west of the old station the present Dammtor-bahnhof was completed in 1903. The elevated building was covered with a steel and glass roof, below which was the booking hall in Art Nouveau style which has been recently renovated and is now a protected building. Today, on account of the proximity of the Hamburg Congress Centre (see entry), the station is also called the Kongressbahnhof and with the Main and Altona stations is an important stop both for long-distance and local trains.

Location
between Theodor-Heuss-Platz and Dag-Hammarskjöld-Platz
HH 36

S-Bahn station
Dammtor (S 11, S 21, S 31)

U-Bahn station
Stephansplatz (U 1)

Buses
34, 38, 102, 109

Monuments at the Dammtor

On the western side of the Dammtor Dam stands the monument, designed by Richard Kuöhl and dedicated in 1936 to the 76th Hanseatic Infantry Regiment of Hamburg. The Muschelkalk block encircled by reliefs of soldiers, is to be completed by five anti-Fascist "ante-memorials" by Alfred Hrdlicka (a bronze "Fire-storm of Hamburg", unveiled on 8th May 1985).
Opposite in the Dammtorpark stands a memorial to Schiller (1866). North of the Dammtor Station in the park of Rothenbaumchaussee and Edmund Siemers Allee, the monument to the mathematician and economist Johann Georg Büsch (1728–1800), which was erected in 1802 near the Lombardsbrücke (see entry), has recently been removed. Busch was a founder-member of the Patriotic Society of 1765 (see entry). Mention should also be made of the modern sculptures of Ulrich Rückriem, one a monument to deportees (1983) at the eastern end of Moorweidenstrasse, the other a stone relief at the north end of Moorweider (1984).

Davidswache

See Reeperbahn

*Deichstrasse

L4

The Deichstrasse is first mentioned in 1304. It follows the Nikolaifleet (see entry), the old course of the River Alster and the first Hamburg port, on the dike which protected the settlement on the Rödingsmarkt in the 13th c. Originally the

Location
between Ost-West-Strasse and Hohe Brücke
HH 11

U-Bahn station
Rödingsmarkt (U 3)

Bus
111

houses stood on the landward side of the street; the waterfront was built up from the 15th c. Today houses with several storeys of the 17th to 19th c. are the last remaining group of the architecture of Old Hamburg. Preservation of the historic Deichstrasse, now a protected area, is due to private initiative. Some of the houses are now inns typical of the period (see Practical Information – Restaurants).

Cremon Bridge

In front of the huge new building of the Landeszentralbank (1981; decorative metalwork by G. Engst) at the beginning of the Deichstrasse, the Cremon Bridge, an angled pedestrian bridge, leads across the broad traffic corridor of the Ost-West-Strasse to the Hopfenmark which extends as far as the ruins of the Nilolaikirche (see Nikolai Church Tower).

Deichstrasse Nos. 19–23

The forerunner of these houses were destroyed in the Great Fire of 1842 which broke out in No. 42; the replacements on the original foundations date from the same year. Their façades have simple plaster divisions.

Deichstrasse No. 25

When it took hold of this house the Great Fire of 1842 reached the east side of the Deichstrasse. The house was built in 1659 and in 1728 a porch was added which was damaged by the fire and walled up during rebuilding; in 1974 it was uncovered. On the side facing the Fleet the old half-timbered façade has survived. Inside there can still be seen a 17th c. painted wooden ceiling.

Deichstrasse No. 27

This house was built in 1780 as a warehouse and is the oldest of its kind remaining in Hamburg. For many years it was used

The historic houses of the Deichstrasse by the Nikolaifleet

by vegetable traders from Bardowick (6 km (4 miles)) north of Lüneburg as a store and is, therefore, also called the Bardowick Warehouse. The massive brick façade with its central doors on the upper storey of the street and waterfront reveal its former use. The interior is constructed of wood with a central row of supports.

Deichstrasse No. 39

This townsman's house dates from 1700 and still has its simple Baroque façade with a stepped gable over which garlands of fruit and flowers are carved in sandstone.

Deichstrasse No. 42

An inscription on a tablet at the entrance to this house records: "At the rear of these premises there broke out the Great Fire of 1842 which destroyed almost the whole of the centre of the city." The fire spread from the Deichstrasse to the north-east and enveloped the whole of the Old Town of Hamburg.

Deichstrasse No. 43

This town house was originally erected in 1697. The Baroque scrolled gable was restored in 1974; the old half-timbered façade facing the Fleet had been renewed in 1738.

Fleetgänge

The narrow alleys between several of the houses (e.g. Nos. 21 and 23; 35 and 37; and 39 and 41) are called Fleetgänge. They provided access to the waterfront for the houses on the opposite side of the street. The visitor should not fail to walk through one of these passages to the Nikolaifleet (see entry) in order to see the fronts of the houses facing the water.

Hohe Brücke

Where the Nikolaifleet (see entry) empties into the Inner Harbour at the end of the Deichstrasse, stands the Hohe Brücke (High Bridge) which has been known since 1260. From here there is a picturesque view of both sides of the Fleet with its old houses and stores. In the background rise the towers of the Inner City. In the Haus der Seefahrt (Hohe Brücke 1) the Greenpeace environmental organisation maintains its German office.

Deutsches Schauspielhaus

N5

Address
Kirchenallee 39–41
HH 1

S-Bahn station
(S 1, S 2, S 3, S 4, S 11, S 21, S 31)

U-Bahn stations
Hauptbahnhof-Nord (U 2)
Hauptbahnhof-Süd (U 1, U 3)

Buses
31, 34, 35, 36, 37, 38, 102, 108, 109, 112, 120, 122, 123, 124, 125

Built at the end of the 19th c. and opened in 1900 the Deutsches Schauspielhaus stands not far north-east of the Main Station in the district of St Georg (see entry). Between 1955 and 1963 when Gustaf Gründgens (1899–1963) was General Manager, the Hamburg Schauspielhaus was one of the leading legitimate theatres in German-speaking countries. Even if afterwards a frequent change of managers was not in the best interests of continuity, the Schauspielhaus, as the most important State theatre of the City of Hamburg still offers a prestigious programme.
After rebuilding and restoration work the 1400-seat theatre in Kirchenallee was reopened at the end of September 1984. Until further notice the former Kampnagel factory in Barmbek (Jarrestrasse 20–26) is used as a subsidiary theatre.

Dom

See Heiligengeistfeld

Breckland in the Duvenstedter Brook

Duvenstedter Brook

Location
about 23 km (14 miles) NE from the centre of Hamburg

U-Bahn station
Ohlstedt (U 1)
(4–5 km distant)

Bus
276

The Duvenstedter Brook nature reserve extending over some 600 ha (1483 acres) is situated in the extreme northern point of Hamburg. In this extensive natural area, which is barred to motor vehicles, stretches of wood and heath are interspersed with fen and breckland (Low German *Brook*). Footpaths and tracks for cycling and riding open up this area for the visitor, in which rare plants thrive and herds of deer live, together with endangered species such as otters.

* Elbchaussee and Elbe Footpath E–H4

Elbchaussee
(Express bus 36)

The 9 km (6 mile) long Elbchaussee, well known even outside Hamburg, joins the districts of Altona and Blankenese (see entries). Mostly at some distance from the steep bank of the Elbe it leads through the river suburbs with their extensive parks and gardens, including the Jenischpark (see entry) and the Hirschpark. Beautiful villas and manor houses, some of which have the appearance of castles (dating in part from the 18th and 19th c. together with many modern houses fringe the Chaussee from which there are from time to time views of the river.

Elbe Footpath

Parallel to the Elbchaussee and right on the bank of the river between Palmaille (see Altona) and the Blankanese River Path (see Blankenese) runs the charming Elbe Footpath (a walk of about 2–3 hours). It passes by the idyllic Lotsenviertel (pilots'

The Jenischpark bordering the Elbchaussee

quarter – see Oevelgönne), the Teulfelsbrücke Ferry House by the Teufelsbrück landing-stage and the Mühlenberg Jollenhafen (*Jolle* = little boat). In several places steps lead up the steep bank of the river to the Elbchaussee.

Elbe shore

Parts of the Elbe shore are sandy, but bathing is prohibited because of the high degree of pollution.

Elbe

River Elbe

From the earliest times the River Elbe has always been of prime importance to Hamburg. On the one had it provides a lifeline between the port and the open sea and on the other it is an important waterway for Central European trade.

Upper Elbe

The total length of the river is about 1160 km (720 miles); its name is of Germanic origin, rendered in Latin as "Albis" and in Czech as "Labe". One of the principal rivers of Central Europe, the Elbe rises in Czechoslovakia on the crest of the Riesengebirge (Giant Mountains) in the Elbbrunnen (Elbe spring) at a height of 1384 m (4542 feet). It crosses the Bohemian Basin in a broad curve, it receives to the north of Prague the waters of the Moldau (Vitava), breaks through the mountains of Central Bohemia and in the Elbsandsteingebirge, the sandstone hills of "Saxon Switzerland", enters the territory of the German Democratic Republic through which it passes for a distance of 556 km (345 miles), finally leaving East Germany near Lauenburg (see entry). The largest tributaries of the Elbe in East Germany are the Black Elster, the Mulde, the

North Elbe, South Elbe

Lower Elbe

Saale and the Havel; important towns on the river are Dresden, Meissen, Torgau, Wittenberg (the town of Luther), Dessau, Magdeburg and Tangermünde. After entering the territory of Hamburg the river divides into the North Elbe and South Elbe (with the Köhlbrand) which enclose the island of Wilhelmsburg (see entry). Two tributaries, the Bille and the Alster join the North Elbe. The road and rail bridges over the North Elbe and the South Elbe as well as both Elbe tunnels (see entry) are of great importance for communications. Below the port of Hamburg begins the 110 km (68 miles) long estuarine stretch of the Lower Elbe which, about 500 m (550 yd) wide in Hamburg, broadens at Cuxhaven to 15 km (9 miles) and joins the North Sea (German Bight). Into the Lower Elbe there flow on the right bank the Pinnau, the Krückau and the Stör and on the left the Este, Lühe, Schwinge and Oste.

The ecological situation and the geographical importance of the Elbe for communications are explained in "Facts and Figures" at the beginning of this book.

*Elbe Tunnels

Two tunnels run under the Elbe (see entry) in Hamburg. If the Old Elbe Tunnel at the time of its construction was a technical sensation, then the New Elbe Tunnel is a successful enterprise of modern technical road construction. A third Elbe tunnel is planned.

Old Elbe Tunnel (St Pauli-Elbtunnel) K3/4

S-Bahn station
Landungsbrücken (S 1, S 2, S 3)

U-Bahn station
Landungsbrücken (U 3)

Bus
112

Harbour ships
Landungsbrücken (Services 61, 62, 66, 75, 77)

From the outside the Old Elbe Tunnel can be recognised by the striking square domed building near St Pauli-Landungsbrücken (see Landungsbrücken). It was bored beneath the Lower Elbe between 1907 and 1911 to relieve the ferries from St Pauli to the island of Steinwerder in the Free Port. Recently the tunnel has been strengthened with a reinforced-concrete mat on the bed of the river.

At night and on Sundays the tunnel is closed; at other times everybody, whether on foot or in a vehicle, can use the tunnel without charge; there is, however, a toll for vehicles. Both people and vehicles are carried up and down in great lift-cages. The twin tunnels are lined with tiles and are each 448·5 m (490 yd) long and lie 23·5 m (77 ft) below street level; in each tunnel the carriageway is only 1·92 m (6 ft) wide.

New Elbe Tunnel (Motorway Elbtunnel) F–H3/4

The New Elbe Tunnel was constructed between 1968 and 1974 about 3 km (2 miles) west of the Old Elbe Tunnel. This triple-road tunnel has a total length of 3325 m (3638 yd), of which 2653 m (2902 yd) form the actual tunnel. It takes the motorway A 7 underneath the Elbe for a distance of 1056 m (1155 yd) at a depth of up to 28 m (92 ft) below the average high-water level; the diagonal course is between Othmarschen and the port area of Waltershof (container terminal) and is one of the longest underwater road tunnels. It enables long-distance traffic to circumvent without problems the centre of Hamburg.

Old Elbe Tunnel

New Elbe Tunnel (south entrance)

Eppendorf

The district of Eppendorf, bordered by the canalised River Alster, has noticeably increased in popularity in recent years. Not only have its residential parts been renovated, but there are many excellent shopping facilities and restaurants which attract younger people in particular.

Shopping is especially good on the Eppendorfer Baum, Eppendorf Market Place, Eppendorfer Weg, Eppendorfer Landstrasse and Lehmweg; nor is there any lack of restaurants, inns and bars. The Ise Market below the tracks of the Hochbahn (U-Bahn line 3) along the Isestrasse, which extends into the district of Harvestehude, has developed into Hamburg's favourite weekly market.

In Eppendorf mention should also be made of St John's Church, the former village church (originally 13th c.) by the River Alster; also Hamburg's oldest remaining manor house (17th–18th c.; Ludolfstrasse No. 19) as well as the well-known University Hospital of Eppendorf (about 2000 beds) to the north-west.

Location
4–6 km (2–4 miles) N from the centre of Hamburg

U-Bahn stations
Eppendorfer Baum (U 3)
Kellinhusenstrasse (U 1, U 3)

Klosterstern (U 1)

Buses
38, 39, 106, 113, 114, 118, 190, 214

Exhibition Grounds (Messegelände) L5

The Hamburg Exhibition Grounds (Messegelände) below the "Tele-Michel" television tower (see entry) adjoin the south-west of Planten un Blomen recreation park (see Wallringpark) and are enclosed by Jungiusstrasse (north entrance; two

Location
1 km (0·62 mile) NW from centre of Hamburg

U-Bahn station
Messehallen (U 2)

Buses
34, 35

pedestrian bridges from Planten un Blomen), Karolinenstrasse (west and south entrances) and the streets of Holstenglacis and Bei den Kirchhöfen. On the area which covers altogether 55,000 sq. m (65,780 sq. yd) stand 13 exhibition halls, some with two floors, in which a great variety of fairs and exhibitions take place throughout the year (see Practical Information – Fairs).

Together with the nearby Congress Centre (see entry), Hamburg provides in the middle of the city, but nevertheless in park-like surroundings, an extensive modern forum for congresses, fairs and specialist exhibitions. The Hamburg Messe und Congress Company, is responsible for the general administration and organisation.

*Fabrik H5

Address
Barnerstrasse 36
HH 50 (Ottensen)

S-Bahn station
Altona (S 1, S 2, S 5, S 11, S 31)

Buses
36, 37, 112, 113, 115, 150, 187, 188, 250

Opening times
Tues.–Sun. midday–6 p.m. During evening events from about 7.30 p.m.–1 a.m. Every Sunday Jazz-Frühschoppen (jazz with drinks)

In a disused engineering and munitions factory of the first half of the 19th c. in Ottensen ("Mottenburg") the almost legendary Communication Centre Fabrik (factory) came into existence in 1971. After a fire in 1977 had destroyed this "cultural workshop" for young people, it was able to be revived in 1979 thanks to a great number of bookings and many donations.

The main room, with its wooden pillars, encircling gallery and dimmed overhead lighting, is used for a wide variety of theatrical, literary and musical events (in the last case especially for jazz, rock and folk music). There are also film shows, a photographic laboratory, a multi-media room and a section for painting and pottery.

Special attention is paid to creative work with children and young people.

The bodily needs of visitors are also catered for; there are inns, a bar and a tea-room, etc.

The free monthly magazine "Fabrik" gives information about all the activities.

Fernsehturm

See Television Tower

Finkenwerder E/F1–3

Location
8–12 km (5–8 miles) SW from the centre of Hamburg

Harbour ships
Service 62 (from St Pauli-Landungsbrüken in about 25 min.) Ferry service 64 (from Teufelsbrück/Elbchaussee in about 10 min.)

The former fishing and farming village of Finkenwerder, now largely a residential district on the edge of the port, was an island until dikes were built along the Southern Elbe after the catastrophic floods of 1962. From the 17th to the 19th c. the Finkenwerder fishermen maintained a considerable fleet, and still today a number of fishing smacks from Finkenwerder are engaged in fishing in the North Sea and the Baltic. The heart of the old village still has idyllic features; in the inns typical fish dishes of good quality can be enjoyed.

Finkenwerder is widely known through the works of the poet Johann Kinau, alias Gorch Fock (1880–1916) who wrote in the local Low German dialect; his birthplace at Nessdeich No. 65 has more recently come to notice again through the folk group Finkwarder Speeldeel.

The firm of Messerschmitt-Bölkow-Blohm (MBB; partners in the airbus project) are one of the largest industrial concerns in Hamburg. Their works, with a private landing-strip, are situated in the extreme north-west of Finkenwerder.

*Fish Market (St Pauli Fischmarkt) J4

Location
about 1 km (0·62 mile) W of St Pauli-Landungsbrücken

S-Bahn station
Landungsbrücken
Reeperbahn, Königstrasse
(all S 1, S 2, S 3)

U-Bahn station
Landungsbrücken
(U 3)

Bus
112

Market
Sunday 6–9.30 a.m.

The traditional fish market is perhaps the oldest attraction of Hamburg. It is held every Sunday from 6 to 9.30 a.m. and always attracts large numbers of visitors both from Hamburg itself and from all around. The tourist ought not to miss this colourful market spectacle, perhaps after an exploration of the night life of St Pauli (see entry).

Whereas originally (in the 18th c.) fishermen used to offer their perishable wares (mainly herring) for sale before the church services began, today anybody can try to sell every conceivable article to the public. The goods which are sent to market here range from fish and other marine creatures (sometimes sold directly from the fishing-boats), through fruit, vegetables, flowers and plants to antiques, *objets d'art*, bric-à-brac and junk of every kind. The cheapjacks are a particular source of amusement; they offer their wares, which are quite often exceptionally good value, with a witty line of patter and coarse innuendos.

The restaurants, inns and harbour bars around the fish market are open during the strictly enforced market hours and naturally do not lack customers.

Former fish auction hall

Bric-à-Brac

Owing to the construction of a new through road the market area has become restricted; however a broad tree-lined brick promenade has been laid among the new flood-protection wall on the bank of the Elbe, and the old fish-auction building of 1895 was completely restored in 1983.

Fleets

Origin

The fleets (Fleete) are a curiosity of the townscape of Old Hamburg. They are canal-like connecting waterways, which either originated as part of the original winding course of the River Alster, or they were artificially made for drainage purposes, later being also used for the transport of goods by water. Of the once considerable network of fleets there remain today in the Old Town, apart from the meandering Nikolaifleet (see entry), only the Alsterfleet, the Bleichenfleet and, in its extension, the Herrengrabenfleet (all three having practically straight courses). There are other fleets in the area of the Speicherstadt (see entry) in the Free Port; one which is particularly picturesque is the Wandrahmsfleet

Fleet-watchers

The expression "Fleetenkieker" – the name is also that of a well-known lively bar in the premises of the Patriotic Society (see entry) – is Low German for "fleet-watcher", and originates from the time when people used to watch for flotsam in the mud of the fleets at ebb tide.

Flughafen

See Airport

Gänsemarkt

L5

U-Bahn station
Gänsemarkt (U 2)

Buses
31, 34, 36, 38, 102, 109

The Gänsemarkt (goose market) is situated not far west of the Inner Alster in the prolongation of the Jungfernstieg (see entry), and is the central and very busy square of Hamburg New Town; from it the shopping arcades Gänsemarkt-Passage and Neuer Gänsemarkt (for both see Passages) lead off.

Until 1984 there stood in the triangular area of the Gänsemarkt a monument to Lessing, created by Friedrich Schaper in 1881. It is possible that this seated statue of the poet and philosopher, Gotthold Ephraim Lessing (1729–81), will be brought back here. Lessing was dramatic advisor at the theatre in the Gänsemarkt which replaced the Deutsches Opernhaus (German Opera House), erected in 1678. The new theatre, the Comödienhaus opened in 1765 but lasted only two years.

The north-west corner of the Gänsemarkt is taken up by a huge building which was constructed between 1918 and 1926 to the plans of Fritz Schumacher for the Finance Deputation of that time. The building is of reinforced concrete with a facing of clinker-brick. Opposite on the north side is the Deutschlandhaus (dating originally from 1929) which once housed the legendary Ufa Palast cinema; in 1979–82 it was renovated for the Dresden Bank. Adjoining, in Valentinskamp, stands the modern Berolina Haus (1980–83).

Görtz-Palais (old town house) L4

The former Görtz Palais was built (1710–11) by Johann Nikolaus Kuhn for the Holstein-Gottorf Ambassador, Georg Heinrich Freiherr von Schlitz, called von Görtz (1675–1719). Görtz, the most influential adviser to the Swedish King Karl XII, was accused after the death of the King of embezzlement and high treason. Found guilty he was sentenced to death and beheaded in Stockholm.
From 1722 to 1806 the building served as the residence of the Imperial Ambassador in Saxony; from 1814 it was the headquarters of the police. In the Second World War the palais was destroyed, leaving only the façade. In 1953–54 it was restored and linked to an office building.

Address
Neuer Wall 86
HH 36

S-Bahn station
Stadthausbrücke (S 1, S 2, S 3)

U-Bahn station
Rödingsmarkt (U 3)

Buses
36, 37

Petersen Monument

In the little square opposite the Görtz Palais stands a bronze monument (1897 by Victor Tilgner) commemorating the respected Hamburg Bürgermeister Karl Friedrich Petersen (died 1982).

Grosse Freiheit

See Reeperbahn

Grossneumarkt L4

The Grossneumarkt, the historic main square of the 17th c. New Town, has in recent years become a favourite meeting-place for the Hamburg scene. Around the tree-lined square (partly a pedestrian zone) and in the streets radiating from it (Wexstrasse, Alter Steinweg, Erste Brunnenstrasse, Neuer Steinweg, Marcusstrasse, Thielbek) a great many pleasant cellar bars, wine vaults, music taverns, small theatres, inns and small shops can be found. In Alter Steinweg No. 32 is the old-established Cotton Club jazz cellar.

Location
about 800 m (875 yd) SW of the Jungfernstieg

Bus 37

S-Bahn station
Stadthausbrückew (S 1, S 2, S 3)

U-Bahn station
Rödingsmarkt (U 3)

Hummel Fountain

Not far north-east of the Grossneumarkt at the junction of Breiter Gang and Rademachergang the Hamburg eccentric Hummel has been immortalised. Here in 1938 the Society of Native-born Hamburgers put up a memorial to Hummel in the form of a fountain. It represents the water-carrier Johann Wilhelm Bentz (1787–1854), known as Hummel; it is said that the battle-cry of the Hamburgers "Hummel, Hummel – Moors, Moors!" originated with him. When the children of the New Town mocked him by calling after him "Hummel, Hummel!" the water-carrier is said to have replied in a Low German corruption of a quotation from Goethe's "Götz von Berlichingen" with "Moors, Moors!".

Hummelfest see Heiligengeistfeld

Hafen

See Port

Hagenbecks Tierpark

See Zoological Garden

Hammaburg M4

Location
Domplatz in the angle of Speersort, Domstrasse, Schopenstehl and Curienstrasse
HH 1

U-Bahn station
Rathaus (U 3)

Buses
31, 34, 35, 36, 37, 38, 102, 105, 108, 109

The heart of Hamburg, the Hammaburg, was founded in the first quarter of the 9th c. by the Franks as a military base and mission station. It consisted of a square mound of earth and wood provided with a ditch and palisade, each side being 130 m (142 ft) in length. In it were the Bishop's quarters and the Cathedral of St Mary which had replaced the wooden hall-church of St Ansgar and which was pulled down about 1806. In 1837 a building was erected on the Domplatz for the Humanistic School called the Johanneum which had been founded in 1529 and which later housed the State Library (see University Quarter); it was destroyed in 1943 in the Second World War. During the post-war years the site remained undeveloped; since 1980 archeological excavations have been taking place which should lead to a better understanding of the fate of the old Hammaburg. In 1983 some remains pre-dating the Hammaburg were discovered; these probably date from the 5th or 6th c.

Bischofsburg

Immediately north of the Domplatz in the cellar of the house on the corner of Speersort and Kreuslerstrasse can be found the viewing room for the Bischofsburg (see entry).

Hansa-Theater

See St Georg

Hanse-Viertel

See Passages

Harburg

Location
about 15 km (9 miles) S from the centre of Hamburg

S-Bahn stations
Harburg (S 3)
Harburg Rathaus (S 3, S 31)

Access
Motorways
A 1 (E 4) or A 7 (E 3)
Main roads
B 4/B 75 (Wilhelmsburger Reichsstrasse); from Hamburg Inner City follow the signs Elbbrücken

Harburg, until 1937 an independent town, lies on the southern shore of the South Elbe which is here fringed by a sandy ridge and the wooded Harburger (Black) Hills. This part of Hamburg is characterised by extensive industrial development (refineries, oil-presses, rubber and synthetic material factories, engineering works, etc.) and has at its disposal an important industrial port (Inner Harbour and four harbour basins).

Originally named Horeburg (= castle in the marsh), first mentioned in 1140/42, Harburg protected the Elbe crossing and belonged until 1236 to the archbishopric of Bremen when it passed to the Duke of Brunswick-Lüneburg. The settlement by the Horeburg received a charter in 1297; in 1527 Harburg was the residence of a branch of the ducal house. On the site of

History

the castle an imposing Renaissance mansion was built, the last remains of which were pulled down in 1972 (the star-shaped foundation can still be recognised in the area of the Inner Harbour). In 1642 Harburg was acquired by the Dukes of Lüneburg-Celle and passed through this line came to the principality of Hanover (Prussian from 1866). Not until 1872 were the bridges over the Elbe to Hamburg built when, thanks to its favourable situation on important rail and road routes, industrialisation made rapid progress. Hamburg, together with the Elbe island of Wilhelmsburg (see entry) was created a major town in 1927 and incorporated within Greater Hamburg by the Decree of 1937. Bombing attacks in the Second World War destroyed almost two-thirds of Hamburg. After a difficult period of reconstruction in post-war years an attempt was made to re-create the old heart of the town by taking measures to reduce traffic. Since the beginning of 1979 the Technical University of Hamburg-Harburg has been under construction (students were admitted in 1982; to the south-east lies a modern redevelopment area, with shops, houses and a leisure centre.

Lüneburger Strasse

The ring road (Harburger Ring) runs round the centre of Harburg. The principal shopping street is Lüneburger Strasse, now a pedestrian zone, and the adjoining Lüneburger Tor area to the east.

Town Hall

Not far west of Lüneburger Strasse lies the Harburger Rathausplatz on which stands Harburg's Town Hall, originally dating from 1892, but which was rebuilt in a simpler style after destruction in the Second World War. Near by are the indoor swimming-baths, the central bus station and the public library; on the far side of Knoopstrasse in the Museumplatz the interesting Helms Museum (see entry) – also the home of the Harburg Theatre – and the Roman Catholic St Mary's Church (originally dating from 1885).

Sand

North of the Harburger Ring (S-Bahn station Rathaus Harburg) lies the Sand, an open space on which on all working days a market has always been held; in the northern corner stand the offices of the newspaper "Harburger Anzeigen and Nachrichten".

Lämmertwiete

Also north of the Sand beteen Neue Strasse and Schlossmühlendamm a pedestrian zone has been created. Here stand the ruins of Holy Trinity Church, built in 1650 and destroyed in the Second World War, as well as several 17th and 18th c. half-timbered houses faithfully restored to their original appearance. The Milieu-Insel Lämmertwiete is protected as an ancient monument.

Schwarzenberg

North-west of the Sand rises the Schwarzenberg; on its broad plateau the traditional Harburg Vogelschiessen (Low German Vagelscheeten = bird shoot) takes place annually in June. This event originated in 1528 and is now combined with a fair. In the park on the slope lies a small Jewish cemetery, laid out at the end of the 17th c. The campus of the new Technical University extends to the south as far as Eissendorfer Strasse. It began to operate in 1982. Farther west in Heimfeld can be found the stately Friedrich-Ebert-Halle (a hall for entertainments).

Aussenmühlenteich

The Aussenmühlenteich (literally "mill-pond outside the town") lies about 1 km (0·62 mile) south of the centre of Harburg. On the west bank of this picturesquely situated lake extends the charming Stadtpark which includes a school garden, where botanical instruction is given, and an open-air stage. On the opposite bank of the lake is a heated swimming-pool, open in summer.

Sinstorf Church

In rural Sinstorf, the most southerly suburb of Hamburg, stands a stone church with a separate wooden tower, originally 12th c. and possibly a foundation of Bishop Ansgar's. This is probably the oldest sacred building in Hamburg.

*Schwarze Berge (Harburger Berge)

The Schwarze Berge (Black Hills) or Harburger Berge in the west of Harburg rise to a height of 150 m (490 ft). The wooded stretches with their pleasant footpaths attract many people; these stretches include Haake, which has a seismic station and which is ideal for skiing and tobogganing, Emme, Sunder and Stuck, as well as the heaths of Fischbek and Neugraben.
In the territory of Lower Saxony lie the Schwarze Berge Big Game Reserve, the Kiekeberg Open-air Museum (see entry) near Ehestorf and the extensive Rosengarten State Forest.

Hauptbahnhof

See Main Station

Heiligengeistfeld

K4/5

U-Bahn stations
Feldstrasse, St Pauli (U 3)

Buses
36, 37, 111, 112

The Heiligengeistfeld (Field of the Holy Ghost) lies in the north-east of the Grosse Wallanlagen (see Wallringpark) on the far side of the Glacischaussee. This extensive open space of nearly 30 ha (74 acres) once belonged to the Hospital of the Holy Ghost and was at one time used as a military parade ground.

Dom (Volkfest)

Every year in November/December the traditional Hamburger Dom, one of the largest German popular festivals, takes place on the Heiligengeistfeld. The unusual designation "Dom" is a relic of earlier times in the Old Town when a Christmas market was held in a hall at the side of St Mary's Cathedral (see Hammaburg) which was pulled down in 1806. Other fairs in the Heiligengeistfeld amusement park are the Frühlingsdom (April) and the Hummelfest (July/August).

Creative Bunker

On the northern edge of the Heiligengeistfeld near Feldstrasse there is a souvenir of the Second World War, in the shape of a former air-raid shelter which also served as an anti-aircraft tower. In this massive concrete block, which is now called the Creative Bunker is a service centre for photographic work as well as a number of studios for photographers and other creative artists.

F.C. St Pauli

South-west of the bunker lies the ground of St Pauli Football Club and an indoor swimming-bath (in Budapester Strasse).

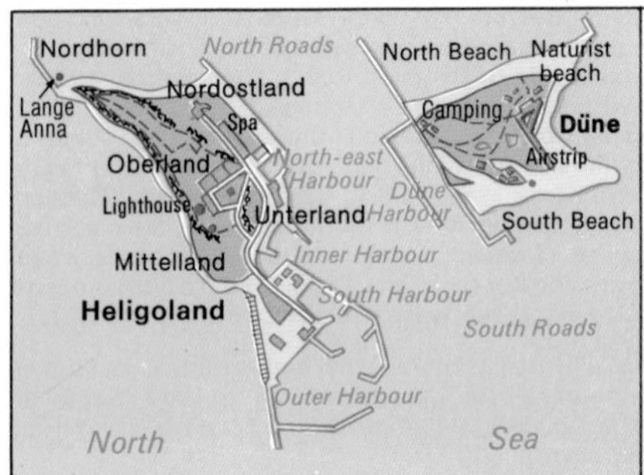

Heligoland

The rocky island of Heligoland (Helgoland in German) together with the island of Dune has an area of about 2 sq. km (0·77 sq. mile). It lies in the North Sea about 65 km (40 miles) north-west of Cuxhaven. Until 1807 it was Danish, then British and in 1890 was acquired by Germany in exchange for Zanzibar. It is now in Schleswig-Holstein. The inhabitants ("Halluner") get their living from tourism (North Sea spa) and lobster fishing – ornithological station.

1 km (0·6 mile)

*Heligoland

The red sandstone cliffs of the Island of Heligoland (in German Helgoland) tower up like a huge natural fortress out of the wide expanse of Heligoland Bay. The island (area 0·9 sq. km (0·35 sq. mile)) lying 70 km (43 miles) off the mouth of the Elbe, has belonged to Germany only since 1890 when it was exchanged by Britain for the protectorate of Zanzibar. It was developed as a naval base and served a strategic function during the Second World War. On 18 April 1945 it was severely damaged by air attack. After the end of the war the remaining inhabitants were evacuated, and in April 1947 the fortifications were blown up, leading to the collapse of huge masses of rock. Thereafter it was used as a bombing target by the RAF. After its restoration to Germany in March 1952 reconstruction began.

Heligoland is now again a popular holiday resort, not least because it is a duty-free area. With its mild climate, its pure sea air and its excellent facilities for "taking the cure", it is also a much-favoured health resort. The only lobster-fishing grounds in Germany, off Heligoland, are the preserve of the local fishermen who also enjoy the long-established privilege of bringing visitors ashore and taking them back to the ships which anchor just offshore.

Location
about 160 km (85 nautical miles) NW of Hamburg in the North Sea (Heligoland Bight)

Province (*Land*)
Schleswig-Holstein

Information
Kurverwaltung Nordseebad
Helgoland Südstrand
Box 720 D-2192 Helgoland
tel. (0 47 25) 7 01

By air Heligoland can be reached from Hamburg in 40–60 minutes (several times daily in summer), or by ship from Cuxhaven (about 130 km (81 miles) from Hamburg); special trips and reduced fares by German Railways daily in about 2 hours. The ships anchor off the south of the island and visitors are landed and brought back according to old custom in open motor-boats (Bortebooten). Protective clothing is advised! A day trip allows a stay of about 6 hours on the island.

Access
Ship/aircraft HADAG

Since Heligoland is a customs free area, it is much visited for duty-free shopping, i.e. for such items as alcoholic drinks, tobacco goods, confectionery, photographic apparatus, textiles, cosmetics, perfume, etc. It should be noted, however, that when returning to the mainland, dutiable articles must be declared and duty paid if the concessionary allowances are exceeded. The allowances are less than those granted in EEC countries. Full details are available on a leaflet.

Customs

Unterland

Heligoland consists of three parts – Unterland, Mittelland and Oberland, and the separate little island of Düne. Unterland, on the south-east side of the main island, has been completely redeveloped since 1952, with a Kurhaus, a Town Hall (1961), hotels and pensions. At the head of the landing-stage stands a larger than life-size bust of the poet August Heinrich Hoffmann von Fallersleben (1789–1847), who wrote the German National Anthem while in exile on the island. To the north are the Biological Research Establishment, with a sea-water aquarium, and the Kur (spa) installations, with a heated open-air swimming-pool (sea-water; temperature 23 °C (73 °F)).

Mittelland

South-west of Unterland is the rather higher Mittelland, formed when the fortifications were blown up in 1947. South of Mittelland is the artificial harbour (trips round the island from the landing-stage).

Oberland

Oberland, linked with Unterland by a lift and a flight of 181 steps, is a triangle of rock some 1500 m (4923 ft) long and up to 500 m (1641 ft) across, largely flat and grass covered, rising to a height of 59 m (194 ft) above the sea. On the east side is the village (rebuilt), with St Nicholas's Church (1959; tower 33 m (108 ft)) and the recently built bird observatory. The former anti-aircraft tower to the west of the village is now a lighthouse. At the northern tip (Nathurn = north horn) are an isolated crag known as the Hengst (stallion) or Lange Anna and the Lummenfelsen (guillemots' rock), the highest point on the island. There is a very attractive walk round the whole island on the cliff-top path (a good hour).

Düne

About 1·5 km (1 mile) east of Unterland and separated from it by a channel 10 m (33 ft) deep (ferry) lies the island of Düne. Here there are bathing facilities on the south beach, as well as on the north beach (camping site; naturist area). In the eastern part of the island is an airstrip for regional traffic (including flights to and from Hamburg).

Helms Museum (Hamburg Museum for Pre- and Early History)

Address
Museumsplatz 2
(Knoopstrasse)
HH 90 (Harburg)

S-Bahn station
Rathaus Harburg (S 3, S 31)

Opening times
Tues.–Sun. 10 a.m.–5 p.m.
Closed Mondays

Entrance fee

The Helms Museum was founded in 1898 by the mill-owner and Senator August Helms as a local museum for the town and region of Harburg. Since 1930 the emphasis of the collections and research activities of the museum has been in pre- and early history.

Many finds from all periods provide a good survey of the lifestyle of prehistoric man in the Hamburg region. There are also many relics from Lower Saxony. A diorama (Panorama of the Centuries) 22 m (72 ft) long in 17 sections traces the development of the region from the Last Temperate Age but one to the present day together with the cultural history of the people. In addition the history of Saxony is traced.

In the pedestrian tunnel outside the museum the geological development of the Hamburg region is portrayed.

In the Fischbeker Heide (near Neugraben) an archaeological footpath with restored prehistoric funerary monuments has been laid out.

Branch Museum

The Kiekeberg Museum (see entry) is a branch of the Helms Museum.

Inner Alster

See Alster

*Jacobikirche (St James's Church) M4

Location
in Steinstrasse in city centre
HH 1

U-Bahn station
Mönckebergstrasse (U 3)

Buses
31, 34, 35, 36, 37, 38, 102, 108, 109

A church dedicated to St James in Hamburg is first mentioned in 1255. The history of the present Evangelical church begins about 100 years later and every century since is represented in its present appearance.

The nucleus of the building, a three-aisled Gothic brick hall-church, dates from the 14th to 15th c. The sacristy was erected between 1434 and 1438 on the north side of the choir, presumably from the beginning in its present two-storeyed form; the upper storey, the present Herransaal (with paintings and coats of arms), served as a library until 1543.

Between 1493 and 1508 the church was enlarged by the addition of an asymmetrical second south aisle; between 1582 and 1588 the tower acquired its first conical cap – this was removed in 1810 and in 1826–27 replaced by the "pencil" (spire) by H. Fersenfeldt. The elongated addition on the north side was built (1707–08) as a church school; today it is the parish hall. The west front gained its present form between 1738 and 1742; the neo-Gothic porch on the south dates from 1869.

In the Second World War the church was destroyed in 1944 apart from the sacristy, the base of the tower, the pillars and arches and the exterior walls; almost all the interior furnishings, however, could be saved. By 1962 the church had been rebuilt; the top of the 125 m (410 ft) high tower is a modern creation by the architects Bernhard Hopp and Rudolf Jäger.

The Jacobikirche

Interior
Mon.–Fri. 10 a.m.–4 p.m.;
Sun. 10 a.m.–1 p.m.

The most valuable treasures in the church are the Arp-Schnitger organ (built 1689–91) of which the greater part survived and which is the largest Baroque organ in North Germany (J. S. Bach played on it in 1720), the St Luke Altar of the Guild of Painters (end of 15th c.) from the former Cathedral of St Mary, the Altar of St Peter of the Guild of Fishermen (about 1508) and the St Trinitatis Altar of the Coopers (1518) as well as the marble pulpit with alabaster reliefs by Georg Baumann (1610–11).

Jacobikirche (St James's Church)

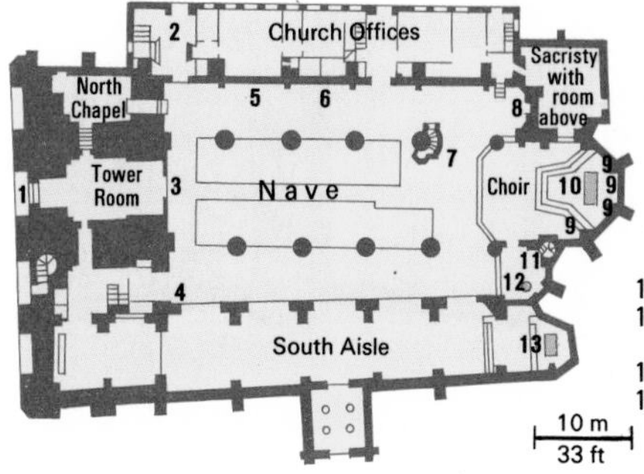

1 Doorway (bronze doors, 1966)
2 Baroque staircase
3 Arp-Schnitger organ (1689–91)
4 Kemper organ (1960/70)
5 "Death and the Rich Man" Oil-painting by David Kindt (1622)
6 View of Hamburg from Grasbrook (1681)
7 Pulpit (marble and alabaster; 1610–11)
8 Statue of St James (oak; 17th c.)
9 East Window (stained glass, 1959)
10 St Trinitatis's Altar of the Coopers (1518)
11 St Peter's Altar of the Guild of Fishermen (*c.* 1508)
12 Font (marble, 1814)
13 St Luke's Altar of the Guild of Painters (end of 15th c.; from the former Cathedral)

Jenisch Park E4/5

Location
about 9 km (6 miles) W from the centre of Hamburg
HH 52

S-Bahn station
Klein Flottbek (S 1, S 11)

Buses
36, 39, 184, 286

In Klein Flottbek, approximately on the level of the Teufelsbrücke Ferry House, the beautiful Jenisch Park (picture p. 65) rises to the north of the Elbchaussee (see entry). From north to south through the 43 ha (106 acres) of this English-style park flows the little Flottbek stream. The park was laid out at the end of the 18th c. with exotic trees and in 1828 was acquired by the Hamburg Senator, Martin Johann Jenisch.
In the north-west part of the Jenisch Park stands the Jenisch-Haus, built from sketches by Karl Friedrich Schinkel and plans by Franz Gustav Joachim Forsmann (1829–32); it is now a branch of the Altona Museum (see entry) and displays examples of the lifestyle of well-to-do citizens.

Jenisch-Haus
Tues.–Sat. 2–5 p.m. Sun. 11 a.m.–5 p.m. Closed Mon.
Entrance fee

The ground-floor rooms are of the period when the house was built, i.e. Louis XIV to Biedermeier (the simple style of 1800–50); the rooms of the upper floor cover the period from Baroque to Jugendstil (Art Nouveau).

Ernest-Barlach-Haus
Tues.–Sun. 11 a.m.–5 p.m.
Closed Mon.
Entrance fee

Not far north-east of the Jenisch-Haus stands the Ernst-Barlach-Haus (1960–62) which was donated by the Hamburg cigarette-manufacturer, Hermann Reemtsma, for his Barlach Collection. On view are originals and copies of works by the sculptor, graphic artist and poet Ernst Barlach (1870–1938) who was outlawed by the Nazis. There are numerous carvings (e.g. the series of wooden figures "Frieze of the Listeners") as well as several hundred drawings and Barlach's collection of prints. In addition there are works by contemporaries of Barlach for comparison.

The Jenisch-Haus

Barlach Sculpture

Landing-stage of the Alster boats at the Jungfernstieg

*Jungfernstieg M4/5–L5

The Jungfernstieg is Hamburg's most popular street. Laid out in 1665 as a promenade, the boulevard borders the south-west side of the Inner Alster between Reesendamm and Gänsemarkt (see entry). The carriageways are separated by a central strip. On the south-east side of the street, from which the Alster Arcades (see Passages) and the busy shopping streets Neuer Wall and Grosse Bleichen lead off, are a number of exclusive shops, the big Alsterhaus department store and the Hamburger Hof with the Jungfernstieg Passage (see Passages).

Location
by the Inner Alster
HH 1/HH 36

S-Bahn station
Jungfernstieg (S 1, S 2, S 3)

U-Bahn station
Jungfernstieg (U 1, U 2)

Buses
31, 34, 36, 38, 102, 109

Alster Boats

On the waterside of the Jungfernstieg broad terraces and steps lead down to the landing-stages of the Alster Boats. From here the whole of the Inner Alster can be seen, bounded by Ballindamm, Lombardsbrücke (see entry) and Neuer Jungfernstieg. In the south-west corner stands the well-known Alster Pavilion (see entry).

Neuer Jungfernstieg

The tree-lined Neuer Jungfernstieg connects the Jungfernstieg and the Esplanade; it begins at the junction of the Colonnaden (see Passages). Noticeable here are the elegant city hotel Vier Jahreszeiten (Four Seasons) and the premises of the Overseas Club (No. 18), a Late Classical building of 1833.

Katherinenkirche (St Catherine's Church) M4

St Catherine was a Princess of Alexandria who suffered martyrdom at the beginning of the 4th c.; the first mention of a church in Hamburg dedicated to her is in 1256, that is a few years after the Grimm Island was first surrounded by a moat and

Location
on southern edge of the Inner City (Zollkanal)
HH 11

U-Bahn station
Messberg (U 1)

Bus
111

walls. The nave of the present church, a long pseudo-basilica without transepts (55 m (184 ft) long, 28 m (92 ft) wide and up to 26 m (170 ft) high) built of brick, dates only from the 14th/15th c. The west front of the tower was given a Renaissance façade in 1566–68. At the end of the 16th c. the tower received a spire surmounted by a golden crown, which, however, fell down in 1648 during a hurricane. In 1656–57 Peter Marquardt, a carpenter from Plauen in Vogtland, created the Baroque roof of the tower with the so-called Störtebeker Crown on the spire which, until it was destroyed in the Second World War, gave the church its unmistakable appearance. In place of the Renaissance façade which had meanwhile become dilapidated, Johann Nikolaus Kuhn created in 1732–38 the existing Baroque façade to support the tower.
Spared by the Great Fire of 1842, the Evangelical Church of St Catherine was severely damaged in 1943 and 1944 by fire and bombs, the ancient interior being almost completely destroyed. Reconstruction was finished in 1956; the 115 m (377 ft) high tower was restored according to the old plans of the Baroque era.

The Katherinenkirche

Interior
Daily 9 a.m.–6 p.m.; winter until 4 p.m.

The plain white walls, pillars and vaulting are enlivened by stained-glass windows, the work of G. H. von Stockhausen in 1955–57. Of the former interior furnishings there remain only two 17th c. epitaphs (to Moller and von der Fechte); a third one (to Wetken) came from the destroyed Nikolaikirche (see Nikolai Church Tower). Everything else has been acquired or is modern post-war work.

In the Kiekeberg Open-air Museum

Katherinenkirche
(St Catherine's Church)

10 m
33 ft

5 6 8 9 7 Small organ NAVE 4 1 2 3 13 12 11 10 17 13 15 18 16 14 19 Church Offices

1 Tower entrance hall (in the style of an old Hamburg merchant's hallway); on the upper floor Gothic arches
2 Pamir memorial tablet (21.9.1957)
3 Former winter church (above the gallery)
4 Great Organ
5 Baptistery window
6 "David Playing the Harp" (bronze; 1972)
7 Epitaph to Georg von der Fechte (d. 1630)
8 Christmas Window
9 Wetken Epitaph (sandstone; 1566)
10 East Window (Christ in Glory)
11 Altar (limestone and bronze-gilt; 1960)
12 Font (bronze; 1963)
13 Choir-stalls (oak; 1960)
14 Epitaph to Caspar Moller (d. 1610)
15 Crucifix (wood; *c.* 1300)
16 South Doorway (bronze door; 1963)
17 Pulpit (oak; 1956)
18 St Catherine (South German woodcarving; first half 15th c.)
19 Meeting Hall (1st storey)

Kiekeberg Open-Air Museum

The Kiekeberg is 126 m (414 ft) high in the Black Hills (Harburg Hills; see Harburg) and belongs to the parish of Rosengarten (Ehestorf) in Lower Saxony south-west of Harburg and not far from the A 7 motorway and the boundary of Hamburg and Lower Saxony.

As a branch of the Hamburg Museum for Pre- and Early History (see Helms Museum) various farm buildings of the 17th–19th c. from the northern part of the Lüneberg Heath were re-erected from 1953 onwards on the Kiekeberg museum site. Their present layout represents a large farm about 100 ha (247 acres) in extent, which was formerly typical of this district. Storehouses (including a honey store of 1688), barns, a sheep-pen, a wagon store, a bakehouse, a row of beehives made of plaited straw and a draw-well (Wübbsood) are grouped round the Meybohm House, a typical example of a Lower Saxon farmhouse (with living quarters and accommodation for animals under the same roof). The Meybohm House was originally built in Kakensdorf in 1797. Also of interest are the Corbelin Hof and the Silberhof.

The completely furnished building with a vegetable and herb garden, and various domestic animals, provides a graphic picture of rural life in former times. In the bakehouse bread is sometimes baked and sold.

Address
D-2107 Rosengarten (Ehestorf)

Province
Lower Saxony

S-Bahn station
Harburg (S 3) then HVV bus 144 to Appelbüttel and then 3 km (2 miles) on foot – or Postbus to Vahrendorf and then 1 km (0·62 mile) on foot – or private bus from Harburg Rathaus to Ehestorf

Opening times
Mar.–Oct., Tues.–Fri. 9 a.m.–5 p.m.; Sat., Sun. & pub. hols. 10 a.m.–6 p.m.; Nov.–Feb., Tues.–Sun. 10 a.m.–4 p.m. Closed Mons.

Gasthaus zum Kiekeberg (inn) in the Open-Air Museum

*Köhlbrand Bridge H–K1/2

The Köhlbrand Bridge (picture, p. 118), altogether almost 4 km (2·5 miles) long, sweeps boldly across the Köhlbrand, a northern section of the South Elbe, at this point about 300 m (330 yd) wide. The original course of this arm of the river was cut off by a dam between Finkenwerder (see entry) and Neuenfelde (see Altes Land) after the disastrous floods of 1962.

This high-road bridge has, since 1974, linked the port areas of Waltershof (container terminal) and Neuhof (in the Free Port

Location
about 6 km (4 miles) SW from the centre of Hamburg HH 93

Access
Waltershof motorway junction on A 7

Bus 151

Harbour ships
Service 61

area) and has become a new landmark of Hamburg, visible from far away. Visitors should note that there may be customs control in the vicinity of the bridge.
The four-lane carriageway (maximum gradient 4 per cent) is borne on pillars on both sides of the actual suspension bridge, which is at a height of 54 m (177 ft) above low-water mark and which is supported by two imposing pylons, each 130 m (427 ft) high. The bridge is exclusively restricted to motor vehicles. Cyclists and pedestrians are barred.

Kattwyk Bridge

About 3 km (2 miles) to the south the Elbe is spanned by the Kattwyk Lift Bridge, built in 1973. This rail and road bridge connects the districts of Moorburg and Hohe Schaar.

Rethe Bridge

Not far to the north is the Rethe Lift Bridge (lift of 42 m (138 ft)) which was built between 1932 and 1934.

*Kontorhaus Quarter M4

Location
in the eastern part of the Inner City
HH 1

S-Bahn station
Hauptbahnhof (S 1, S 2, S 3 S 4, S 11, S 21, S 31)

U-Bahn stations
Steinstrasse, Messberg (U 1)
Mönckebergstrasse (U 3)

Buses
31, 34, 35, 36, 37, 38, 102, 108, 109, 111, 112

The imposing groups of buildings of the Hamburg Kontorhaus (business house) Quarter, between Steinstrasse and Messberg, provide one of the most impressive townscapes of the 1920s in Germany. They are the work of the architect and town-planner Fritz Schumacher, who created a compact block of buildings with clinker-brick façades in the expressive architectural forms of the New Objectivity style.
Of particular interest are the unique Chilehaus (see entry), the Sprinkenhof (1927–31; between Burchardstrasse and Altstädter Strasse with vehicle access through the inner courtyard), the Messberghof (1923–25; corner of Messberg and Pumpen), the Mohlenhof (1928; in the Burchardplatz) and the Montanhof (1924–26; corner of Niedernstrasse and Kattrepel).

Schopenstehl

The road called Schopenstehl, a continuation of Niedernstrasse leads westwards to the Old Fish Market. In Schopenstehl is an interesting three-storeyed 18th c. patrician house (Nos. 32–33). This gabled house of 1760 has a fine Rococo façade and a richly ornamented double doorway.

*Krameramtswohnungen L4

Address
Krayenkamp 10–11
HH 11

S-Bahn station
Stadthausbrücke (S 1, S 2)

U-Bahn station
Rödingsmarkt (U 3)

Bus
37

The so-called Krameramtswohnungen (the name may be approximately rendered in English as "shopkeepers' guild dwellings") are situated close to the Michaeliskirche (see entry), and in them is preserved an idyllic corner of Old Hamburg. These dwellings were the last to be built with a courtyard in the 17th c. About 1620 there was in Krayenkamp a pleasure-garden with a country house and a summer-house. In 1676 the Krameramt (= Shopkeepers' Guild) acquired the land and installed two ranges of half-timbered houses, each of two storeys, with dwellings for the widows of former colleagues. After the introduction of freedom to practise a trade (1866) the buildings came into the possession of the city and were used as homes for old people. From 1971 to 1974 a thorough reconditioning was carried out. The twisted chimneys are an original detail.

The historic Krameramt Dwellings are protected buildings ▶

Widows' dwelling

The House 'C' contains a branch of the Museum of Hamburg History (see entry) in the form of an historically furnished widows' dwelling which can be visited (Tues.–Sun. 10 a.m.–5 p.m.).
In this picturesque courtyard group of buildings there are also an art gallery, antique and souvenir shops and a charming restaurant in Old Hamburg style.

**Kunsthalle (Art Gallery) M5

Address
Glockengiesserwall
HH 1

S-Bahn station
Hauptbahnhof (S 1, S 2, S 3, S 4, S 11, S 21, S 31)

U-Bahn station
Hauptbahnhof-Nord (U 2)

Bus
112

Opening times
Tues.–Sun. 10 a.m.–5 p.m.;
Closed Mons.

Entrance fee

The Hamburg Kunsthalle consists of two buildings, the old building of 1863–68 in a style reminiscent of the Renaissance and the new building which was added on the east side in 1911–17; the entrance is now situated on the south-eastern corner of the new building. On the other side of the old building stands the modern Kunsthaus.
The gallery houses one of the most important art collections in the Federal Republic. Its great fame is due above all to the initiative of Alfred Lichtwark, who was Director of the Kunsthalle from 1886 to 1914 and was able to bring into the collection a number of first-rate works of art. The best-known example of his success was the acquisition of the altar-paintings of Meister Bertram and Meister Francke which are internationally famous. The excellent collection of German Romantic works is also largely the result of his efforts.

*Hamburg Painters
Medal Collection

On the ground floor is the exceptionally comprehensive collection of works by Hamburg painters of the 16th to 20th c., also the collection of coins and medals comprising more than 3000 items. An additional series of rooms is provided for special and periodic exhibitions.

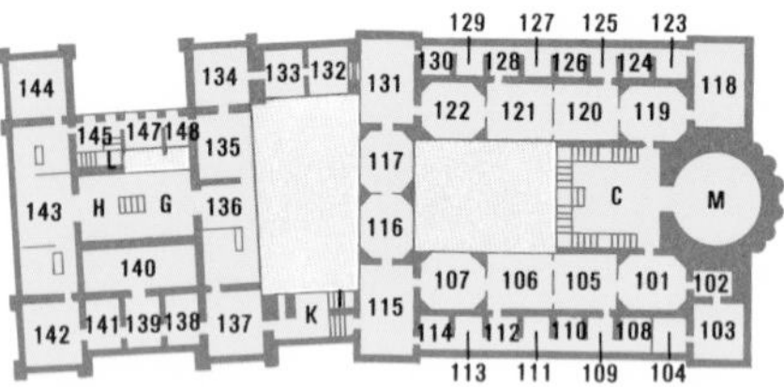

UPPER FLOOR
C Main staircase to ground floor
G Old Building staircase to ground floor
H Schwabe Bequest
I Stairs to ground floor
K Café
L Stairs to Department of Hans Arp and Surrealists
M Dome: temporary exhibitions
101–117 Old Masters from Late Gothic to 18th c.
118–134 19th c. painting
135–144 20th c. art

Hamburg Kunsthalle

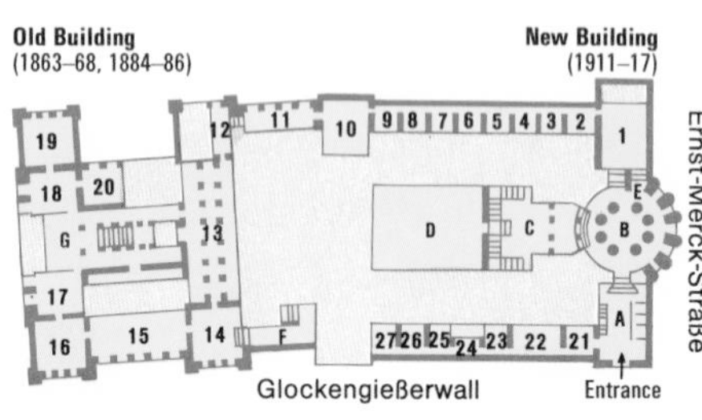

GROUND FLOOR
A Ticket office, cloakroom, toilets
B Sales counter
C Main staircase to upper floor
D Etchings, library
E Stairs down to Department of Contemporary Art
F Stairs to upper floor and café
G Old Building staircase to upper floor
1 Lecture room
2–20 Painting in Hamburg from 15th to 20th c.
13 Coins, medals and sculpture
21–27 Temporary exhibitions

Metal Sculpture in the forecourt of the Kunsthalle

Etching Collection

The graphical collection exhibits etchings from Italy and Germany, drawings from Italy, Germany and the Netherlands and prints of the 17th to 19th c., principally from France.

**Meister Bertram
*Meister Francke

The collection of European painting and sculpture on the first floor includes two especially noteworthy exhibits; the High Altar (Grabower Altar) from the Petrikirche (see entry), a work of Meister Bertram (1379), and the Thomas Altar (1424) by Meister Francke.

Mention should also be made of the paintings by Holbein, Lucas Cranach (father and son), Tischbein and Zick. The Dutch school is represented chiefly by Rembrandt, Van Dyck, Jordaens, Terborch and Ruysdael, the Italians by Tiepolo and Canaletto.

**German Romantics

The collection of works from the different schools of German Romantic painting is outstanding. Probably nowhere else does there exist such a comprehensive collection of paintings of this movement, which include works by Runge, C. D. Friedrich, Schwind and Spitzweg.

From the late 19th c. (especially Impressionism) mention must be made of Leibl, Menzel, Liebermann, Corinth and Slevogt, as well as Manet, Monet and Renoir. Represented in the Modern Section are many well-known German Expressionists, Constructivists, Surrealists, etc., and the sculptors, Kolbe, Lehmbruck and Barlach.

Kunsthaus

The Kunsthaus contains the exhibition rooms of the Kunstverein (Society of Art), in which special exhibitions (mostly of contemporary work) are mounted. On the upper floor is a restaurant with a panoramic view of the Inner and Outer Alster.

*Landungsbrücken (St Pauli Landing-Stages) K4

Location
in the Harbour about 2 km (1 mile) SW from the centre of Hamburg

S-Bahn station
Landungsbrücken (S 1, S 2, S 3)

U-Bahn station
Landungsbrücken (U 3)

Bus
112

Harbour ships
Services 61, 62, 66, 75, 77

The Landungsbrücken are situated in the district of St Pauli (see entry) on the north bank of the North Elbe, between the Lower Harbour and the Fish Market (see entry). They are used chiefly for local passenger vessels in the port (see entry), both for river services and ferries, and on the Lower Elbe (see Elbe) as well as for the ferry to England. In addition they are the points of embarkation for the popular round trips of the port (several different trips; see Practical Information – Sightseeing). There is usually a fresh breeze down by the harbour.
On the quayside stands the large booking hall 200 m (660 ft) long which was erected between 1907 and 1909 according to a joint plan for services to the North Sea and resorts. The architecture is in the monumental style of the turn of the century with limestone facing; there are two towers at the corners and two cupolas. The architects were L. Raabe and O. Wöhlecke, the stone-carving by A. Bock.

Harbour View

From the eastern tower (with a clock and a tide indicator) there is a very fine view of the port, as there is from the first floor (Hafenterrasse) of the adjoining Landungsbrücken Restaurant.

Pontoons

Six arched passages in the booking hall lead to the covered bridges which, because of the changing tidal conditions, provide a movable connection to the floating landing-stages. The ships tie up at this row of pontoons, almost 700 m (766 yd) long, which were rebuilt between 1953 and 1955; in the

The Landungsbrücken with the Bismarck Monument and the Youth Hostel

buildings on the pontoons there are several fish restaurants and shops (especially souvenir shops); on the roof is a promenade with a fine view of the activity in the harbour.

Brückenhaus

Between 1975 and 1976 the buildings between the entrances to landing-stages 4 and 5 were converted into a modern Brückenhaus. Here is located the port information office (Hamburg – Information am Hafen – see Practical Information) where every kind of information about the port and the city can be obtained.

Old Elbe Tunnel

Not far west of the landing-stages stands the domed entrance to the Old Elbe Tunnel (see Elbe Tunnels).

Überseebrücke

To the east of the landing-stages the Überseebrücke leads from Vorsetzen, the quayside of the Lower Harbour, to a line of floating pontoons at which cruising liners tie up, as well as vessels coming to Hamburg on the occasion of naval visits. On the flood-protection wall promenade is the Überseebrücke café-restaurant.

Geestrand

The shore to the north of the Landungsbrücken slopes steeply up. A pedestrian bridge crosses the broad busy Uferstrasse and leads to the joint S- and U-Bahn station Landungsbrücken half-way up the slope. Steps go on up to the Stintfang and the Bismarck Monument (see entry). To the west, above Helgoländer Allee, which descends to the river from the north in a cutting, stand the Hafen Hamburg Hotel with a panoramic restaurant, the German Hydrographical Institute, the Marine Weather Station of the German Meteorological Service and the well-known Bernhard-Nocht Institute of Marine and Tropical Diseases. The original building of the last named, by Fritz Schumacher, dating from 1910 to 1914 were destroyed in the Second World War, and have been rebuilt in a simpler style. Farther north still on the far side of Seewartenstrasse is the Port Hospital.

Lauenburg

Location
about 40 km (25 miles) SE from the centre of Hamburg

Province
Schleswig-Holstein

Access
Bundesstrasse B 5

Lauenburg (pop. 11,000) which dates from 1260, is the most southerly town in Schleswig-Holstein (district of the Duchy of Lauenburg) and was once an important station on the Old Salt Road between Lüneburg and Lübeck. It has a charming situation on the high northern bank of the Elbe which is crossed by road and rail bridges and from which the Elbe-Lübeck Canal branches off to the north. The Palm Lock (about 1725) on the old Stecknitz–Delvenau Canal is the oldest remaining chamber-lock in Europe. Not far east runs the border with the German Democratic Republic (crossing at Lauenburg/Horst for traffic on Federal road/DDR long-distance road No. 5).

Elbe Shipping Museum

There are still fine 16th and 17th c. half-timbered houses to be seen in the old Lower Town. No. 59 houses the interesting Elbe Shipping Museum (with a collection of regional art; Mon.–Fri. 10 a.m.–1 p.m. and 2–5 p.m.; Sat. and Sun. 10 a.m.–5 p.m). At summer week-ends trips on the Elbe in paddle-steamers are arranged. Originally built in 1227, the Church of St Mary Magdalene was considerably altered in later times; the south doorway (1598) with a pillory is notable.

The tower on the Schlossberg (50 m (164 ft)) is the oldest remaining part of the former castle of the Dukes of Lauenburg; from the terrace there is a pleasant view over the marshes bordering the Elbe as far as Lüneburg

Elbe Lateral Canal

About 5 km (3 miles) downstream is the confluence on the south of the Elbe Lateral Canal which enables inland shipping to reach the Mittelland Canal; 9 km (6 miles) south stands the interesting Scharnebeck Ship Lift (twin basins; maximum 1350 tonnes; 38 m (125 ft) lift in about 3 minutes). Excursion ships from Lauenburg in summer.

*Lombardsbrücke M5

Location
Between the Inner and Outer Alster

S-Bahn stations
Hauptbahnhof, Dammtor (S 11, S 21, S 31)
Jungfernstieg (S 1, S 2, S 3)

U-Bahn station
Jungfernstieg (U 1, U 2)

Bus 112

The well-known Lombardsbrücke spans the channel connecting the Inner and Outer Alster, on the line of the former 17th c. fortifications. It owes its name to a pawnshop called Lombard, which was built on the west bank of the Alster in 1651 and existed there until 1827.

The triple-arched road bridge was built in 1865–68 by Johann Hermann Maack to replace a previous wooden bridge in the middle of the old enclosing dam. It was widened on the northern side in 1900 and again, for the railway, in 1908. Barely 50 m (55 yd) wide, the bridge caters for heavy road and rail traffic (4 tracks for long-distance and local trains).

Celebrated view of the Inner City

One of the classic views of Hamburg with its many towers and the Inner Alster in the foreground, is to be enjoyed from the

View of the Inner Alster from the Lombardsbrücke

Lombardsbrücke. This picture-postcard view includes also the 8 fine wrought-iron lamp-standards with sculpted decoration by C. Börner (1868).

Kennedybrücke

To relieve pressure on the old Lombardsbrücke for road traffic the New Lombardsbrücke was added between 1951 and 1953 on the side of the Outer Alster. After the assassination of the 35th President of the United States of America, John F. Kennedy (1917–63), the name of the bridge was changed to the Kennedybrücke. On the western part of the garden between the Lombardsbrücke and the Kennedybrücke stands a monument (1802) to the mathematician and economist Johann Georg Büsch (1728–1800), a founder-member of the Patriotic Society (see entry) of 1765.

*Lüneburg Heath

Location
30–50 km (19–31 miles) S from the Elbe

Province
Lower Saxony

Access
Motorway A 7 S to the exits for Garlstorf, Egestorf, Evendorf or Bispingen

Information
Fremdenverkehrsverband
Lüneburger Heide e.V.
Postfach 21 60
D-2120 Lüneburg
tel. (0 41 31) 4 20 06

The much-visited Lüneburg Heath, the largest area of moorland in the Federal Republic, extends between the Elbe in the north-east and the Aller and the Lower Weser in the south-west. In the moraine heights of the Black Hills (Harburg Hills; see Harburg) which were formed during the Ice Age, the area extends almost as far as Hamburg. The dry and infertile upland stretches, interspersed with marshy ground, are largely covered with heather which gives the melancholic landscape a cheerful atmosphere during the flowering season in August (in many places heather festivals are held). Strangely shaped elder bushes, footpaths framed with birch trees, upland farms hidden behind oaks complete the unusual scene. Many barrows called Hünengräber (giants' graves) are relics of prehistoric settlement. Bee-keeping, sheep-rearing (small moorland sheep) and agriculture are no longer of great importance; tourism, together with the output of mineral oil and the extraction of salt and kieselguhr, are significant.

Lüneburg Heath Nature Reserve

The Lüneburg Heath Nature Reserve, extending over 20,000 ha (49,420 acres) dates from 1909 and was the first to be established in Germany. In the middle of the park rises the Wilseder Berg (169 m (555 ft)) the highest point of the North German Plain and from which there is a magnificent view across the heath to Hamburg, Lüneburg, to the Brocken (summit in the Harz Mountains) and as far as Hanover. To the east near the moorland village of Wilsede, which cannot be reached by motor vehicles, lies the beautiful Totengrund, a forest-fringed depression covered with heather and elder bushes, through which those who had died in Wilsede used to be brought to Bispingen.

Other attractive moorland landscapes can be found at Hermann-Löns-Grab near Fallingbostel and in the triangle between Uelzen, Soltau and Celle.

The Südheide Nature Park lies considerably farther south-east near Hermannsburg.

Near Soltau (pop. 19,000; regional museum, toy museum, salt-water therapeutic bath) lies the Heide Park, a popular leisure park with many attractions.

The Ameisenbär (anteater), an historic railcar, runs every Sunday in summer between Soltau and Döhle, on the south-east edge of the Lüneburg Heath Nature Reserve.

Walsrode Bird Park

There is a fine bird park, with about 4000 birds from all over the world (tropical aviary, etc.) near Walsrode (pop. 22,000; monastery).

Serengeti Game Park

Near Hodenhagen (exit Westenholz from motorway A 7) lies the popular Serengeti Game Park, where lions, tigers, elephants, buffaloes, antelopes, rhinoceroses, giraffes, llamas, etc. roam freely in the reserve; visitors view the animals from motor vehicles.

Main Station (Hauptbahnhof) M/N4/5

Location
on the northern edge of the city between Glockengiesserwall and Kirchenallee
HH 1

S-Bahn station
Hauptbahnhof
(S 1, S 2, S 3, S 4)

U-Bahn stations
Hauptbahnhof-Nord (U 2)
Haputbahnhof-Süd (U 1, U 3)

Buses
31, 34, 35, 36, 37, 38, 102, 103, 109, 112, 119, 120, 122, 123, 124, 125

The Main Station of Hamburg was built at the beginning of the century on the site of the old town ramparts and opened in 1906. It replaced a series of stations scattered about the town which could no longer cope with the increasing rail traffic. In addition to the Main Station, the considerable volume of national and international rail traffic as well as the S-Bahn suburban traffic of Greater Hamburg is catered for by the Dammtor Station (see entry) and Hamburg-Altona Station (see Altona).
Bombing attacks in the Second World War caused considerable damage to the imposing station buildings.

The tracks of this through station, which run below the level of the street, are spanned by a station building of steel and glass supported only at each end and measuring 140 × 120 m (460 × 394 ft) with a height of 35 m (115 ft). The booking hall (with two square flanking towers, the one on the west contains a clock) is situated at an angle in front of the main building.

Hamburg Main Station

Beneath the station at both north and south ends is a U-Bahn station and on the east side a modern addition for the new S-Bahn line to the district of Harburg, south of the Elbe, the platforms for which are under ground.

ZOB (Central Bus Station)

A short way south-east of the Main Station the Central Bus Station (Zentralomnibusbahnhof – ZOB for short) was constructed in 1951 for both regional and long-distance buses. At the entrance (corner of Steintorplatz/Adenauerallee) a round watch-tower of 1819 serves as a restaurant.

Tourist Information

In the Bieberhaus, in Hachmannplatz, north-east of the station can be found the information bureau of the Hamburg Tourist Board (Fremdenverkehrszentrale Hamburg).

**Michaeliskirche (St Michael's Church; "Michel") L4

Location
in the S of the New Town, between Ost-West-Strasse, Krayenkamp and Englische Planke
HH 11

S-Bahn stations
Stadthausbrücke
Landungsbrücken)
(both S 1, S 2, S 3)

U-Bahn stations
Rödingsmarkt
Landungsbrücken
St Pauli (all U 3)

Bus
37

The "Michel", as the Hamburgers call the Evangelical Church of St Michael, the old landmark of the city, is the "youngest" of Hamburg's old churches and has had an eventful history.

Ships entering or leaving the port of Hamburg are greeted by the green patina-covered tower of the church on the ridge above the harbour in the southern part of the historic New Town; not far to the north runs the broad traffic artery of the Ost-West-Strasse.

Among the Nordic Baroque churches St Michael's is the finest, even though the building we see today has been renewed several times. The first Great St Michael's Church was built between 1647 and 1661 as a three-aisled brick hall-church by Christoph Corbinus and Peter Marquardt, the tower being completed in 1669. Near by the Little St Michael's Church of 1606 remained standing.

History

On the 10 March 1750 lightning struck St Michael's Church and it fell in ruins; in 1747 Little St Michael's had been pulled down as it was dilapidated. And so St Michael's parish no longer had a church.
Two master builders were chosen for the construction of the second Great St Michael's Church, Leonhard Prey and Ernst Georg Sonnin; Prey lived only long enough to see a beginning made. Sonnin built the new church between 1750 and 1762 and the tower followed between 1776 and 1786. Cruciform in design and borne only on 4 mighty pillars, so that from every place in the church there was an uninterrupted view of the chalice-shaped pulpit, the Baroque building became the model for Evangelical preaching churches.
On 3 July 1906, an intensely hot summer's day, fire destroyed church and tower apart from the external walls. With the help of the Senate, Parliament and donations from many sources, the church was rebuilt between 1907 and 1912 in exact confirmity with Sonnin's original plans. The external measurements are 71 × 51 m (233 × 167 ft). In the Second World War the third St Michael's Church was severely damaged in 1944 and 1945, but by 1952 it had been restored. For renovation work, which has again become necessary in the meantime, a Hamburger living abroad has recently donated millions of marks to the church authorities.

Interior
In summer daily 9 a.m.–5.30 p.m.
In winter Mon.–Sat. 10 a.m.–5.30 p.m.; Sun. 11.30 a.m.–5.30 p.m.

The nave, decorated in white and gold, corresponds in its proportions to Sonnin's building, since the external walls and the pillars survived the fire of 1906. The interior, which is 27 m (89 ft) high and which holds 3000 people, is impressive because of the cantilivered roof, the bold shape of the galleries and the 20 m (66 ft) high marble altar. Also of marble are the pulpit and the old font. The largest of the three organs has over 85 stops and a total of 6665 pipes.
Concerts are given in the church by St Michael's Boys' Choir.

Tower
(Ascent/Lift; charge)
In summer Mon.–Sat. 9 a.m.–5.30 p.m.; Sun. 11.30 a.m.–5.30 p.m.
In winter Mon., Tues., Thurs., Fri., Sat. 10 a.m.–4 p.m.; Sun. 11.30 a.m.–4 p.m. Closed Weds.
The spiral staircase in the cupola is not open to the public.

The height of St Michael's Church tower (i.e. the actual "Michel") is 132 m (434 ft); that is 155 m (507 ft) above the level of Hamburg itself. The base of the tower remains from Sonnin's building; the upper part is of iron. The viewing-platform, at a height of 83 m (271 ft) is reached from Doorway 2 by climbing 449 steps or in a lift. The magnificent panoramic view embraces the whole of Hamburg, including the Elbe, the port and the Alster Basins.
On the 8th level of the tower (about 75 m (246 ft) above street level) is the largest tower clock in Germany. The dial has a circumference of 24 m (79 ft) and a diameter of 8 m (26 ft). The large hands are each 4·91 m (16 ft) long, the small one 3·65 m (26 ft), the figures 1·35 m (4 ft) high.
There are 5 bells in the tower with weights between 4900 kg (96 cwt) and 1103 kg (22 cwt).

Tower musicians

For over 250 years a chorale has been sounded in all directions from the tower below the clock every day at 10 a.m. and 9 p.m.; on festivals a wind band performs on the platform.

Krameramtswohnungen

Visitors are urged to have a look at the historic courtyard buildings in Krayenkamp 10 and 11 (see Krameramtswohnungen) close to St Michael's Church; at No. 5 is the Ecumenical Chapel of the German Seamen's Mission.

Foreign churches

Attention is drawn to the various foreign churches in the immediate vicinity of the "Michel"; to the south in Schaarmarkt Danish, Norwegian and Finnish seamen's churches stand close to one another; farther south-west at the end of Ditmar-Koel-Strasse is the Swedish sailors' church.
West of St Michael's on the south side of the Zeughausmarkt stands the Anglican Church of St Thomas à Becket, which is under the jurisdiction of the Bishop of London.

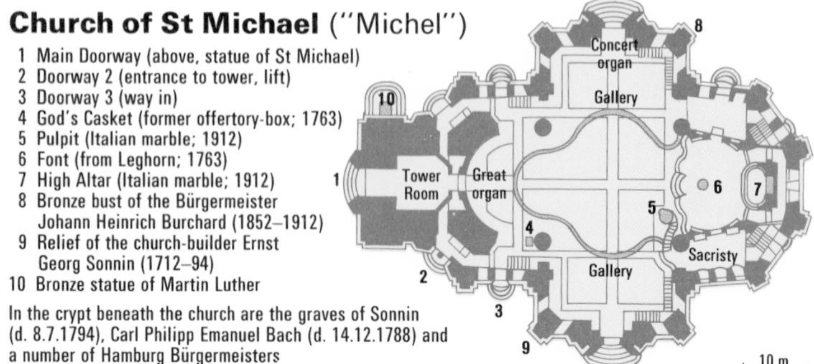

The "Michel", the best-known landmark in Hamburg ▶

Mönckebergstrasse M4

Location
between the Main Station and the Rathausmarkt
HH 1

S-Bahn station
Haputbahnhof
(S 1, S 2, S 3, S 4, S 11, S 21, S 31)

U-Bahn station
Mönckebergstrasse
(U 3)

Buses
31, 34, 35, 36, 37, 38, 102, 108, 109

The Mönckebergstrasse, named after the respected Hamburg Bürgermeister Johann Georg Mönckeberg (1839–1908), links the Main Station (see entry) with the Rathausmarkt (see entry). This gently curving street was laid out in 1908 in the course of a comprehensive reconstruction of the numerous alleys and passages in this part of the Old Town and from 1911 to 1913 business houses were built along the street to a homogeneous plan. As has always been the case the Mönckebergstrasse, below which runs line 3 of the U-Bahn, is a popular shopping street in the Inner City of Hamburg, with several department stores and a great number of shops. However, the range of goods is less exclusive than those offered by the shops in the area of Jungfernstieg (see entry), Neuer Wall and Grosse Bleichen and more especially by the arcade shops in that area (see Passages), but as a consequence of the recent successful restriction of through traffic and the associated enlargement of pedestrian zones, the Mönckebergstrasse has become somewhat more attractive.

Spitalerstrasse

Just to the north of Mönckebergstrasse and parallel to it is Spitalerstrasse which has been laid out as a pedestrian street, with shops on both sides. A café (Mövenpick im Café Vernimb) is situated in the bridge which links the Semperhaus on the north side with the large twin commercial buildings of the Barkhof on the opposite side.

Art Nouveau furnishings in the Hamburg Museum of Art and Industry

Spitalerstrasse and Mönckebergstrasse converge as an open space where, in a pedestrian area popular as a meeting-place, stand the Mönckeberg Fountain by Georg Wrba (1926) and the Lichtplastik (light sculpture), a steel column 16 m (53 feet) high by G. Göpfert (1969).

Mönckeberg Fountain

About half-way between the Main Station and the Rathausmarkt Mönckebergstrasse crosses the former Horse Market, which since 1946 has been called Gerhart-Hauptmann-Platz and which, apart from the line of roads on the south-east has been free from vehicular traffic since 1974. Not far from here stand the Jacobikirche (see entry) and the Petrikirche (see entry).

Gerhart-Hauptmann-Platz

On the north of the square stands the glass pavilion of the information centre – Hamburg Information in the City (see Practical Information – Information). Behind it is the entrance to the two-storey Landesbank Gallery (including shops) and the Hamburg Landesbank building (1972–74).

Hamburg Information in the City

Landesbank Gallery

At the extreme north end of the square stands the Thalia Theatre, founded in 1843 and especially popular with the people of Hamburg.

Thalia Theatre

In the southern part of Gerhart-Hauptmann-Platz can be seen a metal stele by H. J. Frielinghaus (1975). The building at the corner of Steinstrasse is occupied by the Hamburg Hochbahn Aktiengesellschaft (HHA) and Gerhart-Hauptmann-Platz 4 by the passenger booking and information office of the HHA.

HHA-Haus

** Museum of Art and Industry (Museum für Kunst und Gewerbe) N4

The Museum of Art and Industry was founded with the aim of counteracting a threatened decline in taste through industrial mass-production, and to illustrate alternatives of an artistic nature by presenting old and new examples – that is to be active educationally.

Address
Steintorplatz 1
HH 1

S-Bahn station
Hauptbahnhof
(S 1, S 2, S 3, S 4, S 11, S 21, S 31)

U-Bahn stations
Hauptbahnhof-Süd (U 1, U 3)
Hauptbahnhof-Nord (U 2)

Opening times
Tues.–Sun. 10 a.m.–5 p.m.
Closed Mon.

Entrance fee

The large three-storeyed building of the time of the foundation was constructed by the Hamburg master builder Karl Johann Christian Zimmermann in 1876 as a school and museum building. The façade of the Renaissance town house Kaiserhof of 1873 was incorporated into the walls of the northern glass-roofed court.

The founder and for many years Director of the Museum was the scientist, art historian and enthusiastic collector, Justus Brinckmann (1843–1915) who was especially interested in collecting ceramics all over the world. This serves to explain the emphasis in the collections.

On the ground floor are the medieval, Renaissance, Baroque and 19th c. collections. Of particular merit are a Madonna (in limewood) by Tilman Riemenschneider, faience from Italy, the collection of scientific instruments of the 15th to 18th c., silver articles and Baroque porcelain.

Ground Floor

On the first floor can be found the departments of Far Eastern and Islamic art, the Collection of Antiquities as well as Art Nouveau and modern art. Of considerable interest are the coloured woodcuts of the Japanese Hokusai, Hiroshige, etc., Attic painted vases and, finally, the exceptional collection of

First Floor

Museum of Art and Industry

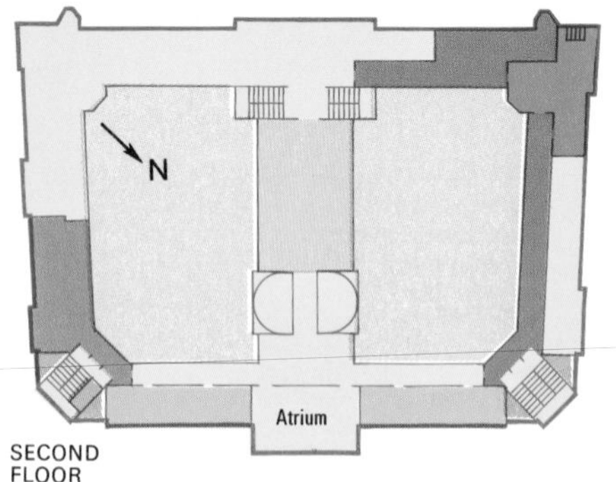

SECOND FLOOR
- Textiles
- History of Photography
- Modern Art
- Education
- Print Dept.

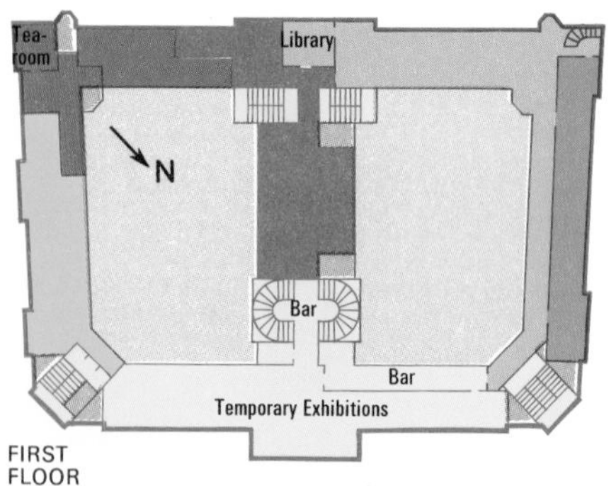

FIRST FLOOR
- Antiquity
- China
- Japan
- Islam
- Art Nouveau
- Modern Art

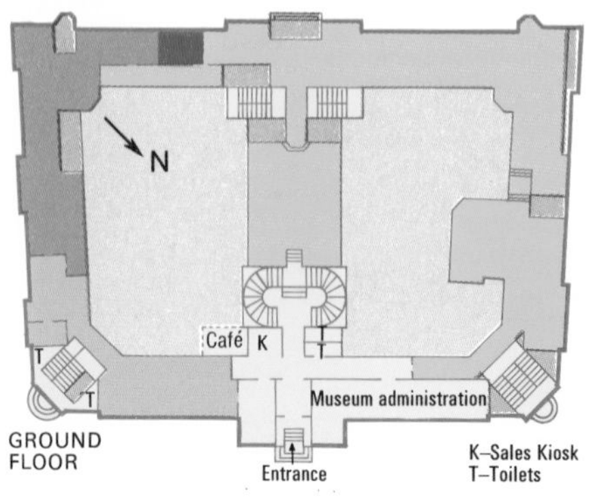

GROUND FLOOR
- Middle Ages
- Renaissance
- Scientific Instruments
- Baroque
- 19th c.

Jugenstil (Art Nouveau furniture, etc.). Also on the first floor is the museum restaurant Destille (closed on Sundays) which provides a convenient place for a rest.

Second Floor

The second floor houses the textile collection, the print department and the exhibition of the history of photography as well as part of the modern art collection.

The educational department serves a purpose which the founder of the museum had envisaged, to free art from the sterile museum-like atmosphere and to place it in the context of its production, use and cultural significance. For this purpose individual creative activity and exploration of the possibilities of materials play a part.

* Museum of Ethnology (Museum für Völkerkunde) L6

Address
Rothenbaumchaussee 64
HH 13

S-Bahn station
Dammtor (S 11, S 21)

U-Bahn station
Hallerstrasse (U 1)

The Hamburg Museum of Ethnology was founded in 1879 and transferred to its present building in 1915. Extensions followed in 1928–29. The fact that Hamburg was in close contact with many other countries favoured the beginning and setting up of the collections; expeditions, especially in 1908–10 to Melanesia and Micronesia, and to Africa (Upper Volta, North Ghana) in 1954–56, produced new exhibits for the collection and broadened specialist knowledge. Today the museum is one of the largest of its kind in the Federal Republic.
Opening times are Tuesday–Sunday 10 a.m.–5 p.m. Closed Mondays. There is an entrance fee.

Golden Jaguar from Peru in the Museum of Ethnology

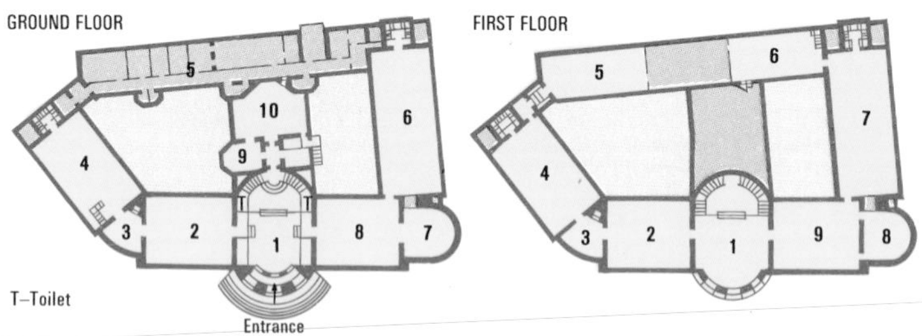

Hamburg Museum of Ethnology

GROUND FLOOR
1 Entrance hall
2 Africa
3 Gold room and Ancient Egypt
4 Africa
5 Administration, Library
6 Europe, Near East
7 Soviet Union
8 Soviet Union
9 Small lecture theatre
10 Large lecture theatre

FIRST FLOOR
1 Pacific (boats, large exhibits)
2 South and East Asia
3 America
4 America
5 Special exhibitions
6 Pacific (Polynesia, Maori house)
7 Pacific (Melanesia, Micronesia)
8 Pacific masks
9 Indonesia, Australia

Exhibits

The exhibits, are, within their territories (Eurasia, South and East Asia, Ancient Egypt, Africa, America), frequently arranged neither chronologically nor geographically but according to affinities, parallels or analogies and thus draw the attention to facts and principles which are universally valid. Even present-day problems and phenomena are presented, especially topical is the example of the Turkish national group in Hamburg. The showpieces of the extremely comprehensive collections are, among others, the bronze castings of the Benin tribe (Africa), the gold room (Indian culture), the assembly house of the Maoris (New Zealand) and the Pacific masks.

Educational Department

Since 1979 the Museum has had an educational department which endeavours to interpret ethnological themes, not only to individual pupils and school classes but also to other interested groups, to clarify interrelationships and to stimulate personal creativity.

Temporary Exhibitions

Special exhibitions are housed in a separate room on the first floor.

*Museum of Hamburg History — K4

Address
Holstenwall 24
HH 36

S-Bahn station
Landungsbrücken (S 1, S 2)

U-Bahn station
St Pauli (U 3)

Buses
36, 37, 112

The Museum of Hamburg History has its origins in a collection of Hamburg antiquities which the Verein für Hamburgische Geschichte (Hamburg Historical Society) had been building up since 1839, and which had been increased by architectural items saved from the Great Fire of 1842. The remains of a formerly even more important collection of weapons from the old armories were added in 1875. When in 1883 the effects of Bismarck's fiscal policies led to the destruction of a number of street blocks to make way for the Free Port, the collection acquired additional material so that the erection of a new museum building became necessary.

Museum of Hamburg History

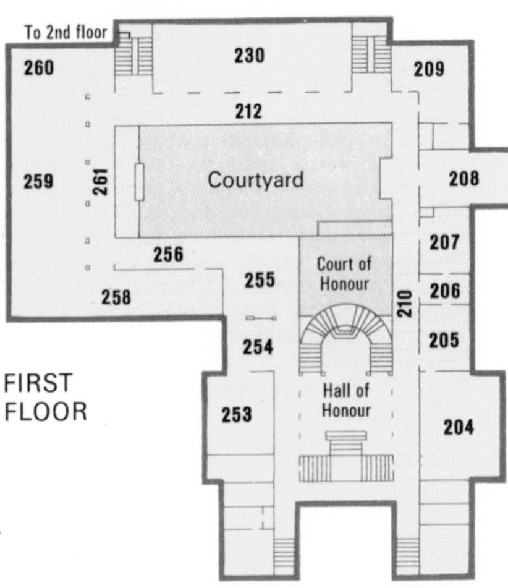

FIRST FLOOR

N.B.: The Museum of Hamburg History is undertaking a lengthy rearrangement of all its collections. Consequently some rooms are closed; also in the course of time there will be alterations to the rooms at present open.

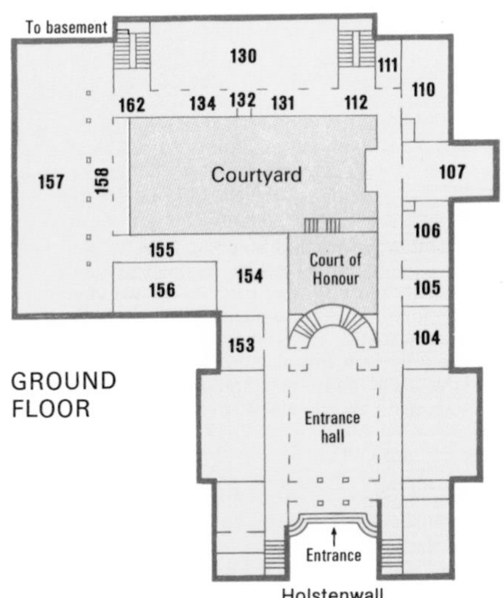

GROUND FLOOR

SECOND FLOOR
(no plan)
Domestic living style in town and country;
Model railway layout

FIRST FLOOR
Hall of Honour:
"Hamburg in the Hansa Age"
(13th–16th c.)
Rooms 204–210 at present closed

212 Social history of the 17th & 18th c.; Hamburg's consular representation abroad up to 1867
230 Hamburg's shipping from 1650–1860
253 Bridge of the steamship "Werner"

Bureau of historic emigration

254 Aircraft industry and air travel; Marine technology and research
255 Port and shipping after the Second World War
256 The Elbe Waterway
258 Large model of the port of 1928; Maritime trade up to 1945; Iron ship construction, maritime motive power
259 Large model of the port of 1900; Local maritime traffic
260 Wooden ship construction, ships' equipment
261 Pictures of ships; Emigration to America HAPAG steamers

GROUND FLOOR
Entrance hall: temporary exhibition "Hammaburg, Viking settlement and Neue Burg"
(9th–12th c.)
Rooms 104–112 at present closed

130 Military system
131 Period of French occupation
132 Pewter figures
134 Civic guard
153 "Historant" inn
154 Historicism in Hamburg
155 Reconstruction after the Great Fire of 1842
156 Great Fire of 1842
157 at present closed
158 at present closed
162 Local public transport

Museum of Hamburg History

Opening times
Tue.–Sun. 10 a.m.–5 p.m.
Closed Mons.

Entrance fee

Otto Lauffer's ideas for a museum were realised on the former bastion Henricus of the defences built between 1616 and 1625 on the Holstenwall. Here in the great ramparts at the Millerntor, the first Hamburg observatory (now in Bergedorf, see entry) had been standing since 1825.

Museum buildings

From plans by the eminent architect, Fritz Schumacher, an imaginatively articulated brick building was erected. The heavy sloping hip roof, crowned by a turret reminiscent of a lighthouse, is both a protective covering and also a suitable setting for the exhibits. The exterior façades with modest carved stone decoration form a modern frame, within which old sandstone doorways, precious window-frames, busts, statues, palm branches and many more architectural decorations have a functional significance but which can also be classed as exhibits. In addition the architecture is intended to show the euphoric conception of history of the time before the First World War, by drawing the attention of the visitor to lavish staircases from the entrance hall up to the Hall of Honour with coats of arms and inscriptions of notable citizens on the first floor.

Inside the Museum of Hamburg History

The museum was made a protected building in 1976. The work already completed on the exterior and the measures now being undertaken to rearrange the exhibits have provided an opportunity to restore the building, in collaboration with the Department for the Protection of Historic Buildings, in an appropriate manner. As a result of the rearrangement of the exhibits, which it is anticipated will take a number of years, alterations in the placing and layout of the collections must be expected in the future.

Notice

Provisional Exhibition Entrance Hall on the ground floor and in the Hall of Honour on the first floor

The section Hamburg in the Middle Ages tells the story of the beginnings in the 9th c. with Hammaburg and a Viking settlement and shows models of Hamburg in the 11th and 12th c., with examples of relics and the illustrated manuscript of the civic charter of 1497 which throw light on medieval everyday life; in addition Hamburg's role during the Hansa Age is portrayed (architecture, shipbuilding, the construction of the port, military defensive measures and the history of coins and money).

In the section Hamburg in Modern Times are included such themes as the military (weapons, uniforms, flags; 1619–1868), Hamburg under French occupation, local public transport, historicism in Hamburg, the Great Fire of 1842, retail trade and craft and also a collection of pewter figures.

First Floor Information Service; Historic Immigration Office (Information and Documents in 1 hour for a fee)

The section Hamburg's Port and Shipping from 1650 to 1860 is presented in a new form. By means of numerous models the development of the port, the construction of wooden ships, various occupations connected with the fitting out of ships and with water-borne trade are portrayed, together with the creation of the Admiralty and of shipping convoys to counter piracy and the slave trade. In addition the flourishing of maritime trade up to the threshold of the Industrial Age is illustrated.

The Historic Emigration Office, in the former officers' mess of the steamship "Werner", has at its disposal almost 5 million names on 274 microfilms of all those who emigrated to America from the Port of Hamburg between 1850 and 1914.

Other pictures and models, including large models of the port of Hamburg in 1920 and 1928, deal not only with connecting traffic and the supply of Hamburg via the Upper Elbe, the Lower

Elbe, the Alster and the Bille, but also with the importance to both river and port of the continuing technical development of ships, vehicles and equipment. Further exhibits deal with the maintenance of the navigable channel on the Elbe, with the wharves and docks, with reconstruction after the Second World War, with new port industries and techniques for the handling of cargoes (container traffic) and not least with ecological problems right up to the present day.
The rooms in the north wing (temporarily closed) are devoted to various subjects; wooden housing components (doors, thresholds, etc.) from middle-class houses of Old Hamburg, dwelling-houses, middle- and upper-class clothing, Renaissance and Baroque craft, a general store and a tobacconist's of about 1830, the hallway of a merchant's house from the Deichstrasse (about 1860), old musical instruments, together with a large model reconstruction (dating from about 1680) of Solomon's Temple in Jerusalem.

Second Floor

On the second floor are examples of the domestic culture of town and country (sitting-rooms, living-rooms, furnishing, domestic equipment, toys) and a glimpse of life in a market of past times (costumes, customs, etc.).

Displays of the Model Railway (about 25 minutes; additional fee)
Tues.–Fri. 10.30 a.m., midday, 2 and 3.15 p.m.; Sat. 10.30 a.m. and midday; Sun. 10.30 and 11.15 a.m. midday, 1, 2.10 and 3.20 p.m.

The railway section of the museum rightly occupies a considerable space, since the introduction of the railway network and the connection with road and waterways played a not inconsiderable part in the development of Hamburg as an important traffic junction. The principal attraction is a model railway layout (scale 1:32) of the line between Hamburg Main Station and Harburg Station, including the bridges over the North Elbe.

Branches

Branches of the Museum of Hamburg History are the Krameramtswohnungen (see entry) in Krayenkamp, the Museum of Bergedorf and the Vierlande (see Bergedorf), the Museum of Work (under construction), the Document House of the Neuengamme concentration camp memorial (see Vierlande and Marschlande) and the steam launch and fire-fighting tender in the Museum Harbour of Oevelgönne (see entry).

Musikhalle L5

Location
Karl-Muck-Platz/
Holstenwall
HH 36

U-Bahn station
Messehallen, Gänsemarkt (both U 2)

Buses
35, 36, 111, 112

The building of the Musikhalle (picture, p. 19) was made possible by a bequest in the will of the Hamburg shipowner Carl Heinrich Laeisz. Following the Baroque brich architecture of the city there arose in the years 1904–08 a sumptuous example of Hamburg Neo-Baroque to the plans of Haller and Meerwein. Since then Hamburg has had at its disposal a representative venue for musical event of all kinds. The Great Hall (with organ) has about 2000 seats, the Small Hall about 640; two monuments in the Musikhalle honour the composers Johannes Brahms and Peter Ilich-Tchaikovsky.
The Musikhalle survived the Second World War undamaged, and on the occasion of its 75th anniversary (1983) underwent a thorough external renovation. Restoration of the two auditoriums and technical equipment is pending.

Surroundings of the Musikhalle – Karl-Muck-Platz

The Musikhalle, originally known as the Laeiszhalle, stands on the north-east side of Karl-Muck-Platz, which was earlier called Holstenplatz; the square bears the name of the well-known conductor who worked here from 1922 to 1933.

Brahms Memorial

The space in front of the Musikhalle which is reserved for pedestrians, has recently been provided with two sculptures as a memorial to Brahms. A large bronze sculpture is intended to represent Brahms's music, a red granite cube bears portraits of the composer.

Dragonerstall and Bäckerbreitergang

Leaving the Musikhalle and following the short street known as the Dragonerstall (Dragoons' stable) one comes to a turning on the right, the Bäckerbreitergang. A short distance north-east rises the striking 78 m (256 ft) high Unileverhaus.

Unileverhaus

In the northern part of the Bäckerbreitergang which was a part of the Gängerviertels (quarter of narrow streets) in the New Town, is a compact row of simple half-timbered houses, Nos. 49–58 dating from the 18th and 19th c, faithfully restored to their original appearance.

Neuwerk (Island)

Location
about 130 km (70 sea miles) NW of Hamburg

The island of Neuwerk situated in the North Sea near the mouth of the Elbe, is barely 3 sq. km (just over 1 sq. mile) in area; from 1299 to 1937 it belonged to Hamburg and from 1970 it has once more reverted to the city. About a third of the island consists of arable land protected by dikes, the terrain outside the dikes is used as pasture for cattle.

Neuwerk is reached from Cuxhaven in Lower Saxony. At ebb tide carts with high wheels are pulled by horses along the 10 km (6 mile) long stretch to the island. There is also a footpath through the shallows but it is imperative to watch the tide!

The 35 m (115 ft) high lighthouse ws converted from an existing defence tower in the 14th c. and from it there is a magnificent view over the expanse of the Watt (shallows). Near the lighthouse lies the Friedhof der Namenlosen (Cemetery of the Unknown) with crosses made of driftwood. The territory beyond the dikes and the little island of Kleine Vogelsand to the north are bird sanctuaries.

Scharhörn Island

The lonely sandy island of Scharhörn lies 5 km (3 miles) north-west of Neuwerk (walk through the shallows about 1 hour 30 minutes; watch the tides). On the north-west beach stands a 28 m (92 ft) high beacon; the east part of the island is a bird reserve.

The plan of building a new deep-water harbour for Hamburg near Scharhörn is at present not being pursued.

Nikolai Church Tower (Monument) M4

Location
On the Ost-West-Strasse between Hopfenmarkt and Neue Burg
HH 11

Near Hopfenmarkt ("Tempelstein" by U. Rückriem, 1984) on the north side of the busy Ost-West-Strasse rises the 145 m (476 ft) high Nikolai Church Tower, the highest church tower in Germany apart from the towers of Ulm Minster (161 m

The tower of St Nikolai, the sole relic of the church

(528 ft)) and Cologne Cathedral (157 m (515 ft)). Together with the adjoining remains of the former Evangelical Church of St Nicholas (the replacement post-war church is in Harvestehuder Weg), the slender Neo-Gothic tower, dating from 1882, has been kept as a memorial ruin; originally yellowish in appearance, the clinker-brick has become blackened with age.

U-Bahn station
Rödingsmarkt (U 3)

Bus
111

History of St Nicholas's Church

In 1195 a chapel for the New Town, founded by Count Adolf III von Schauenburg, was erected in this area. In the 13th and 14th c. this original building was enlarged into a brick hall-church which was destroyed by the Great Fire of 1842. In a competition for the rebuilding Gottfried Semper won the first prize with a design for a domed church; however, the realisation was carried out not far from the old site between 1845 and 1875 to the plans of the Englishman, George Gilbert Scott. His design was for an aisled basilica with a high west tower in pure Neo-Gothic style. This early example of Protestant Church architecture of the 19th c. was destroyed in 1943 and 1944 except for the tower and the outside walls.

Memorial of the Ruins

It was decided not to rebuild the church and the ruins were declared a memorial to the victims of persecution and war during the years 1933 to 1945. The mosaic of the Crucifixion in the passage beneath the tower was carried out by S. Cicognani after a drawing by O. Kokoschka.

Wine Cellar under the Church

In the cross-ribbed vault under the former church (entry from the Ost-West-Strasse) can be found Hamburgs weltoffener Weinkeller unter St Nikolai (Hamburg's wine cellar under St Nicholas's Church which is open to the world). It is managed by the firm of C. C. H. Fischer and has a small wine museum (Mon.–Fri. 1–6 pm; Sat. 9 a.m.–1 p.m.). Wine can be tasted and bottles purchased in the former charnel-house.

*Nikolaifleet L/M4

Course
Through the Old Town
HH 11

U-Bahn station
Rödingsmarkt (U 3)

Bus
111

Apart from the Bleichenfleet, the Herrengrabenfleet and the Alsterfleet, the Nikolaifleet is the last of these old canals (see Fleets) in the Inner City of Hamburg. It is the remains of a former course of the Alster on which lay Hamburg's first port, and it meanders from the Mühlenbrücke (Grosser Burstah) not far south of the Stock Exchange (see entry), first southwards as far as the Nikolaibrücke (Ost-West-Strasse), then turns to the west and becomes wider and finally runs south-west between Deichstrasse (see entry) and Cremon (see entry) before it flows into the Inner Harbour at the Nikolai Barrier short of the Hohe Brücke.
In the area of the Nikolaifleet, which is included in a tour of the fleets (see Practical Information – Sightseeing), a number of old Hamburg houses and warehouses have been restored so that, to some degree, a certain impression of the former appearance of the old merchants' town can still be obtained.

Trostbrücke

In the northern section the Trostbrücke, completed 1882, crosses the Nikolaifleet. On the parapets are statues of St Ansgar (first Bishop of Hamburg from 832) and Count Adolf III of Schauenburg (1164–1203)

The Nikolaifleet

Statue of Bishop Ansgar on the Trostbrücke

Zollenbrücke

The Zollenbrücke on the east of the Nikolaifleet actually crosses the Gröningerstrassenfleet, of which only a small part remains. It counts as Hamburg's oldest bridge, having been built in 1633 and restored in its original form in 1955; it owes its name to a customs house which was once situated here. A bridge in this location is first mentioned in the 13th c.; it joined the area of St Catherine's Church to the New Town on the Ness.

Holzbrücke

The so-called Holzbrücke (= wooden bridge) crosses the Nikolaifleet in its southern part, and from it there is an excellent view of the fronts of the warehouses in Deichstrasse (see entry) and Cremon (see entry) which face the fleet.

Theatre-Ship

Just above the Holzbrücke is moored "Das Schiff", a seaworthy theatre-shop with excellent cabaret entertainment.

Hohe Brücke

See Deichstrasse entry

North German Radio (Norddeutscher Rundfunk/NDR) L/M7

Address
Funkhaus
Rothenbaumchaussee 132
HH 13 (Harvestehude)

U-Bahn station
Hallerstrasse (U 1)

Bus
31

The North German Radio Company (NORAG) began to send out programmes from the Funkhaus in Rothenbaumchaussee on 2 May 1924. Today this building is the headquarters as well as the radio studios and editorial offices of the Norddeutscher Rundfunk (NDR), the second largest radio and television company in the Federal Republic. In the course of time the Funkhaus complex has extended eastwards as far as Mittelweg.

Origin

After the Second World War the Nordwestdeutscher Rundfunk (NWDR) was first set up for the British Occupation Zone of Germany with radio stations in Hamburg, Hanover and Cologne; this existed from 1948 to 1955 and played a decisive part in the development of television in Germany. Following an agreement between the provinces of Hamburg, Schleswig-Holstein and Lower Saxony the Norddeutscher Rundfunk (NDR) came into existence in Hamburg in 1955. At the end of the 1970s this triple agreement threatened to break into a legal wrangle, as Lower Saxony and Schleswig-Holstein wanted to exert more influence. Finally the affair was resolved by a new agreement commencing in 1981 which compromised by granted Schleswig-Holstein and Lower Saxony more time for regional news.

Radio

The NDR radio broadcasts three programmes; the general First Programme in co-operation with the Westdeutscher Rundfunk (WDR) in Cologne on medium and short wave, the Second Programme (NDR 2) with light music, talks, magazine programmes and traffic news, and the Third Programme (NDR 3) with more serious talks and music on short wave.

Television

The NDR Television Service produces its programmes for the First and Third Programme of ARD with its studios at Gazellenkamp 57, in the district of Lokstedt (near the Zoological Garden; see entry). Within the framework of the national news "ARD aktuell" the main news and current affairs programmes "Tagesschau" and "Tagesthemen" are broadcast from Hamburg. The week-end magazine programme "Die aktuelle Schaubude" (= topical showcase) is very popular in North Germany; tickets for these programmes are always difficult to obtain.

Studio visits

Both radio and TV studios of the Norddeutscher Rundfunk can be visited by prior arrangement with the Press office of the NDR (tel. 4 13 – 1).

*Oevelgönne F/G3/4

Location
on the N bank of the Elbe, about 6 km (4 miles) W from the centre of Hamburg

Buses
36, 183

Boat service
Neumühlen landing-stage (line 66)

Oevelgönne is the name of a stretch of shore of the Lower Elbe about 1 km (0·6 mile) long, which starts from Neumühlen landing-stage and runs parallel to the Elbchaussee (see entry) at the foot of a rugged gap. The name, which is found elsewhere in North Germany, indicates "unfavourable" and is applied to land which is unsuitable for cultivation.
For a very long time the Elbe pilots have been based in Neumühlen and Oevelgönne; the first pilots' association came into being in 1745. Pilots, skippers, shipping merchants and craftsmen built their little houses on the slopes above the path along the bank of the Elbe. With pretty bay-windows, balconies, glass verandas and decorative lattice-work the huddle of little houses with their tiny well-tended gardens on the river-side of the path, create an idyllic atmosphere.
Along the roadway, which is impassable for motor vehicles, are old street lamps as far as the west end of Oevelgönne where the actual Elbe Footpath begins and where the steep flight of steps called Himmelsleiter (=Jacob's Ladder) provides a connection with the Elbchaussee.

Oevelgönner Seekiste

In many places there are cosy little inns. A curiosity is the Oevelgönner Seekiste (sea-chest), at Oevelgönne 63, gener-

Pilots' houses at Oevelgönne . .

. . and the Harbour Museum

ally open on Saturday and Sunday afternoons; this is the private maritime museum of Kapt'n Lührs who loves to spin sailor's yarns.

View

From Oevelgönne one can look across the river which is here about 500 m (450 yds) wide to Finkenwerder (see entry), towards the former BP refinery at the oil port, to Waltershof (container terminal) and to the soaring Köhlbrandbrücke (see entry).

Oevelgönne Museum Harbour

At the beginning of the Oevelgönne river path there has been in existence since 1977 the Museum Harbour. It is situated in the little harbour basin to the west of the Neumühlen landing-stage, at the place where the New Elbe Tunnel (see entry) runs under the river. The Museum Harbour is run by the Vereinigung zur Erhaltung segelnder Berufsfahrzeuge, a purely private association for the maintenance of working ships, which has as its aim the restoration of ships of the North German coastal region to their original condition, to make them seaworthy and to show them to the public. Meanwhile there are a number of ships here, including two-masted cargo- and fishing-boats, cutters, galleases, etc. which have been restored by the members of the association to their original condition and made seaworthy. To the registered company Museumshafen Oevelgönne itself belong the former lightship "Elbe 3" (built 1888) and the two steam-tugs "Tiger" (built 1910; coal-fired) and "Claus D" (built 1913; oil-fired), together with the wooden sea-going cutter "Präsident Freiherr von Maltzan" (Built 1928; under sail). The steam-launch "Otto Lauffer", built in the Stülckenwerft in Hamburg and which was formerly a police launch and the fire-fighting tender "Walter Havernick" (built 1832) are the property of the Museum of Hamburg History (see entry). All the restored "old-timers" are ready and able to sail and are occasionally in use, especially in summer. Entry to the area of the Museum Harbour is unrestricted.

**Ohlsdorf Cemetery

Location
in the Alster Valley about 10 km (6 miles) NW from centre of Hamburg

Address
Fuhlsbüttler Strasse 756 HH 63 (Ohlsdorf)

S-Bahn station
Ohlsdorf (S 1, S 11)

U-Bahn station
Ohlsdorf (U 1)

Buses
39, 170, 172, 270

Because of its size and layout as well as for the historic and artistic merit of its gravestones, the Ohlsdorf Cemetery is known far beyond the borders of Germany. It was opened on 1 July 1877 and is about 402 ha (993 acres) in extent. Without doubt the Ohlsdorf Cemetery is the largest in Europe, probably in the whole world. Some 17 km (over 10 miles) of roadway traversed by two bus routes open up the extensive area of this, probably the most attractive, park in Hamburg. Opening Times are daily during the summer 8 a.m.–9 p.m., and in winter 8 a.m.–7 p.m.
The western section of the cemetery, designed by Wilhelm Cordes (1840–1912), with curving roads and paths, was the first cemetery-park in Germany and served as a model for countless others. From 1920 the eastern section was laid out according to the strictly architectural plans of Otto Linné (1896–1937). Today the Ohlsdorf Cemetery is ringed by cultivated land, so that further extension is no longer possible. Up to the present time more than 1,280,000 interments have taken place.

Ohlsdorf Cemetery

Cemetery-Park

In addition to its primary function as a place of burial (a crematorium and 12 chapels), the Ohlsdorf Cemetery, as the largest open space in Hamburg, also provides a "green lung" for the million plus inhabitants of the city. Large numbers of people from far and near make use of the cemetery as a recreational zone. As well as the fine old trees, it is particularly the extensive rhododendron plantations and the numerous ponds which determine the character of the place, and at blossom time (beginning of June) it is a very popular rendezvous for pleasant strolling.

Orientation

The cemetery has 5 entrances; the main entrance is situated on the narrower western side, where are also the principal buildings. North of this entrance stands the crematorium, built by Fritz Schumacher in 1932. The entire cemetery is laid out on a grid plan, which makes it easier to locate graves; there are orientation plans at many places.

Old Hamburg Memorial Cemetery

Among the graves in the Old Hamburg Memorial Cemetery not far from the main entrance are those of the painter Philipp Otto Runge, the architect Alexis de Chateauneuf, the art historian Alfred Lichtwark and the master builder Fritz Schumacher. In 1949 a memorial was erected opposite the crematorium to the victims of National Socialism (urns with ashes and earth from more than 100 concentration camps).

Museum of Monuments

In two open-air museums, in the hedgerow garden and on the Kapellenstrasse monuments from former cemeteries situated outside the city are displayed.

Individual graves

In the older western part of the cemetery the following individual graves are notable; Paul Abraham (composer; O 11, 123), Hans Albers (actor; Y 23, 245–254), Peter Anders (singer; P 7, 11–12), Albert Ballin (shipowner; Q 10, 420–429), Hermann Blohm (shipbuilder; Q 25 28–38), Wolfgang Borchert (writer; AC 5, 6), Hans von Bülow (musician; V 22, 1–8), Julius Campe (publisher; Y 13, 266–270), Willi Fritsch (actor; AC 16, 151), Gustav Gründgens (actor; Q 6, 5), Carl Hagenbeck (founder of Hagenbeck's Zoo; AE 15, 43–58), Heinrich Hertz (physicist; Q 25, 1–6), Martin Johann Jenisch (merchant; AH 16–17, mausoleum), Alfred Kerr (critic; Z 21, 217), Felix Graf Luckner (naval captain; AB 13, 89–90).
Around the North Pond lie the graves of well-known Senators and Bürgermeisters of Hamburg.
Near the centre of the cemetery are various commemorative burial-plots for the dead of both world wars.

Mass grave and memorial for the Victims of Air-raids

In the north, near Chapel 13, a tall building by Fritz Schumacher (1931), is the cruciform mass grave of the 37,000 victims of the catastrophic aerial bombardment during the Second World War (1943), and a monument with sculptures by Gerhard Marcks, erected in 1952.

Jewish cemetery

In the south-west corner of the Ohlsdorf Cemetery lies a Jewish cemetery; of special interest is the monument to the pioneer of Jewish emancipation, Gabriel Riesser (first member from Hamburg of the Frankfurt Parliament of 1848), and the monument to the Jews deported from Hamburg during the tyranny of Nazi rule.

Ohnsorg Theatre L4

The Hamburg librarian and actor Richard Ohnsorg (1876–1947) founded in 1902 an amateur theatre group from which the Hamburg Low German Theatre came into being in 1920. This tradition was continued after the Second World War by the Richard Ohnsorg Theatre.
The Ohnsorg Theatre has become widely known in Germany through the television transmissions of popular plays from its repertoire. Although the TV versions are given in generally comprehensible language, with a Hamburg accent; pure Low German (Plattdeutsch) is spoken on the stage in live theatrical performances.

Address
Grosse Bleichen 25
HH 36

S-Bahn stations
Jungfernstieg, Stadthausbrücke (both S 1, S 2, S 3)

U-Bahn station
Jungfernstieg (U 1, U 2)

Buses
34, 35, 36, 38, 102, 109, 111

Öjendorf Park

The former Öjendorfer Kuhle (Öjendorf Pit) was formed between 1925 and 1929 when about 8 million cubic metres (10·5 million cubic yards) of sand were excavated in order to raise the Horn Marsh for the purposes of civic building. Following clearance work in the districts of Rothenburgsort, Hammerbrook and Barmbek which were devastated by bombing during the Second World War, it was resolved to deposit rubble here between 1950 and 1953, and after preparatory work until 1966, this was used as building material.

Location
In the triangle between the A 1 and A 24 motorways
HH 74 (Billstedt)

U-Bahn station
Merkenstrasse (U 3)

Buses
133, 161, 167, 233, 263, 333

Öjendorf Lake

By means of a connection to the Schleem Stream the newly created depression was filled with water and has since become the Öjendorf Lake, the 60 ha (140 acres) stretch of water which forms the centre-piece of the Öjendorf Park with a total area of 137 ha (338 acres).
In addition, since 1958 while excavation was in progress, a large-scale plan was put into effect, whereby landscaping was carried out from the point of view of plant sociology. As a result many leisure facilities were created, such as rest and play areas, beaches and footpaths.

Bird Sanctuary Island

Special mention should be made of the bird sanctuary on the island in the lake where, among other species, the rare kingfisher nests.

Öjendorf Cemetery

The Öjendorf Park adjoins in the west the Öjendorf Cemetery (see entry) – with a museum of gravestones.

Outer Alster

See Alster

**Passages (Passagen) L/M4/5

Already in the 19th c. covered arcades – the Alster Arcades and the Colonnades – had been built, in which people were and are able to stroll, protected from the inclement weather. In addition there were and are in several business houses throughways and passages such as exist in other European cities, e.g. Milan, Brussels and London.

Location
In the city, SW of the Inner Alster
HH 36

S-Bahn station
Jungfernstieg (S 1, S 2, S 3)

U-Bahn stations
Jungfernstieg (U 1, U 2)
Gänsemarkt (U 2)

Buses
34, 36, 38, 102, 109

Alster boats
(only in summer)
Jungfernstieg landing-stage

In more recent times, when measures were increasingly being undertaken to control the noise of traffic and when many pedestrian zones were being established, not only have the existing passages taken on a new lease of life but also a whole series of new arcades has been established. Today in the city of Hamburg an almost labyrinth-like network of passages exists, with a combined length of several hundred metres.

Although several hundred shops, restaurants and cafés offer a wide range of goods and services of a somewhat exclusive nature, the arcades are predominantly visited for window-shopping. On a small number of the many thousand people who stream through the arcades every day come with the intention of buying something or of having a meal. Primarily the passages serve as a leisure area where people meet, chat or stroll. "To see and be seen" is the motto in the cafés, wine bars, fashion houses, boutiques, art galleries and antique and speciality shops, where everything under the sun can be found. It is mainly the younger generation who enjoy visiting the passages, presumably because it is "the thing to do", and not only by day but also in the evenings and at week-ends, which has led to an astonishing revitalisation of the city centre, previously deserted outside business hours.

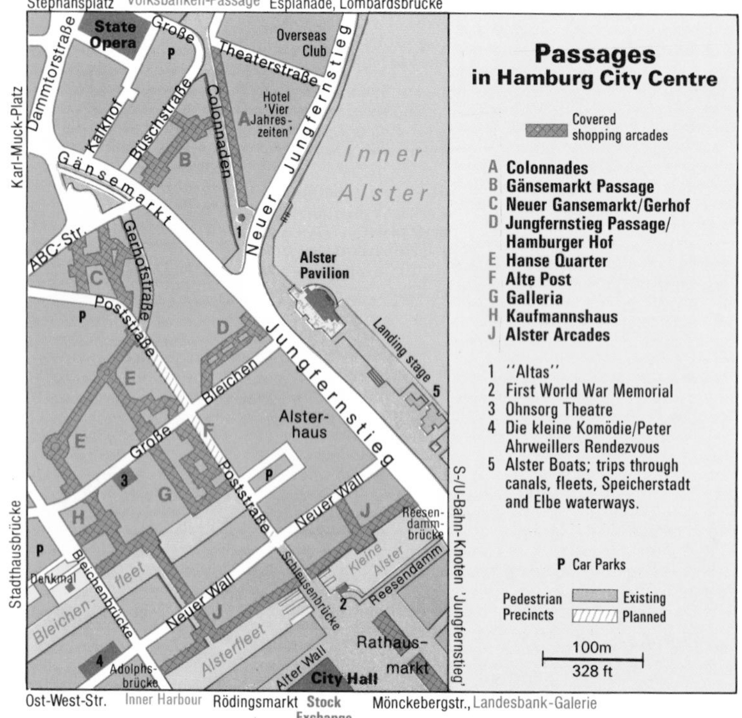

Alster Arcades

Hanse Quarter

Kaufmannshaus

Galleria

In the following section the passages between Dammtor and Rathausmarkt are described; the plan on page 110 shows their location.

Colonnades

The line of streets now laid out as the pedestrian zone of the Colonnades led in 1877 diagonally from Stephansplatz to the south-west point of the Inner Alster. The former pavement on the east side runs beneath protective arcades. On both sides are shops, restaurants and offices. On the small square at the south end stands the metal sculpture "Atlas" by Jörn Pfab.

Volksbanken-Passage

From the north end of the Colonnades a footbridge leads across the esplanade into the so-called Volksbanken-Passage, a small gallery of shops on the first floor of the Phrix-Haus on the Stephansplatz.

Gänsemarkt-Passage

The Gänsemarkt-Passage, opened in 1979, extends between the Colonnades (one entrance), Büschstrasse (two entrances) and the Gänsemarkt (one entrance). Here there are about 50 shops selling fashions and sports goods, jewellery, arts and crafts and food as well as several restaurants.

New Gänsemarkt/Gerhof

In the complex of buildings bordered by the Gänsemakrt, ABC-Strasse, Poststrasse and Gernhofstrasse are several intercommunicating shopping arcades. Entrances in the Gänsemarkt lead into two units of the Neuer Gänsemarkt Passage, Gucken & Kaufen (look and buy) and Essen & Trinken (eat and drink), where there are several self-service restaurants specialising in foreign dishes. The Gerhof, with passages on three levels, and entrances from Gerhofstrasse and Poststrasse forms a connection on the south.

Hamburger Hof/
Jungfernstieg-Passage

In the large sandstone building of the former luxury Hotel Hamburger Hof (1881–83) in Jungfernstieg there are at least 40 shops and snack-bars on three levels. Full of corners, they form the heart of the Jungfernstieg Passage which has an entrance on both the Jungfernstieg and the Grosse Bleichen.

Hanse Quarter

A highlight in the labyrinth of passages is the Hanse Quarter, built 1979–81 between Heuberg, Grosse Bleichen (two entrances) and Poststrasse (two entrances). These walkways, altogether 200 m (220 yds) long with about 60 shops and restaurants of high quality, are covered by a glass barrel roof with two glass cupolas at the corners, so that daylight can penetrate. In the reddish-brown clinker-brick floor metal plates with inscriptions have been let in, and these give details of the history of the Hanse. Included in the Hanse Quarter is the clinker-bridge building of the former Broschekhaus, built by Fritz Höger in 1926 and into which the luxury hotel Ramada Renaissance has been incorporated.

Alte Post

In Poststrasse, between Grosse Bleichen and Bleichenfleet, stands the Alte Post (see entry). The ground floor of this historic building was converted during its last renovation into a shopping arcade with several walkways.

Galleria

Hamburg's latest passage, the Galleria, completed in 1983, starts from Grosse Bleichen 21 and runs 80 m (88 yds) long straight through the entire complex of buildings as far as the Bleichenfleet (pedestrian balconyto Poststrasse). Pilastersand floor are patterned in black and white and radiate a certain coolness. There are some 25 shops and restaurants of a high standard. Parallel (Grosse Bleichen 19), is the large Thalia bookshop.

Kaufmannshaus

In the Kaufmannshaus (a merchant's house built between 1907 and 1909) by the Bleichen Bridge, between Grosse Bleichen and Bleichenfleet, an arcade with three branches was put in when the office building was being reconstructed. From the crossing by the Bleichenfleet a footbridge leads over the fleet to Neuer Wall and from there a narrow passage goes on to the Alster Arcades.

Alster Arcades

The Alster Arcades line the north side of the Little Alster (see Alster) between Jungfernstieg (see entry) and Schleusenbrücke. They were built in 1843 according to plans of the master builder Alexis de Chateauneuf within the framework of the reconstruction of the Rathausmarkt. After alteration in the late 19th c. and damage in the Second World War, they were restored to their original form.

Under the arcaded walkway with its fine cast-iron balustrade, from which there is a charming view of the City Hall (see entry), one walks past the windows of high-class shops.

On the far side of the Schleusenbrücke the Alster Arcades, here newly designed as a shopping passage, continue along the Alsterfleet. Not far from Adolphsbrücke a passageway leads to the Neuer Wall and from there to the Kaufmannshaus (see above).

Rathausmarkt Galleries

See Rathausmarkt

Landesbank Gallery

See Mönckebergstrasse, Gerhart Hauptmann Platz

Patriotic Society (Patriotische Gesellschaft) M4

Location
Trostbrücke/Börsenbrücke
HH 11

U-Bahn station
Rathaus (U 3)

Buses
35, 37, 111

One of the most traditional institutions of Hamburg is the Patriotic Society, founded on 11 April 1765 "to foster arts and useful crafts". This public-spirited organisation has in the course of its existence proposed and carried through many noteworthy achievements in the sphere of cultural and business life, and in the truest sense of the words one could define this as an early example of "citizens' initiative".

The Patriotic Society Building

The building of the Patriotic Society at the Trostbrücke (see Nikolaifleet), stands on the site of the former Hamburg City Hall of 1290 which was destroyed in the Great Fire of 1842. It was constructed between 1844 and 1847 by Theodor Bülau and from 1859 to 1897 served as the council chamber of the Hamburg Parliament (Bürgerschaft). The Neo-Gothic brick building had another storey added in 1923–24 and after severe damage in the Second World War was restored and partially simplified.

Restaurant and Bar

In the premises of the Patriotic Society can be found the old-established restaurant Zum Alten Rathaus and a lively bar (music) the Fleetenkieker, both at Börsenbrücke 10.

*Peterstrasse L4

U-Bahn station
St Pauli (U 3)

Buses
36, 37, 112

After the very recent successful renovation work Peterstrasse, between Holstenwall and Neanderstrasse, now provides a decorative architectural group of old Hamburg buildings. The brick and half-timbered houses are typical of this part of Hamburg, the former Gängeviertel (quarter of narrow streets) of the New Town. On the north side of Peterstrasse and of the nearby Neanderstrasse several Baroque houses of the 17th and 18th c. have been restored, as well as some of the former soldiers' houses in the street known as Hütten.

Beyling Foundation

Of particular interest is the former Beyling Foundation (Nos. 35, 37 and 39). The half-timbered buildings, grouped round a picturesque inner courtyard, were erected between 1751 and 1770 as dwellings and in 1824 were acquired by Johann Beyling who incorporated them into a foundation as old people's homes. From 1965 the Beyling Foundation was restored in its historic form and still provides housing for elderly citizens.

Johannes Brahms Commemorative Rooms (Tues. and Fri. midday–1 p.m.; Thurs. 4–6 p.m.)

On the first floor of No. 39 can be found a memorial to the composer Johannes Brahms (1833–97) who was born in this part of Hamburg; his birthplace at Speckstrasse 6 was destroyed in 1943 during the Second World War.
In the memorial rooms, furnished by the Brahms Society, can be seen documents concerning the life and works of the composer, including several musical manuscripts in his own hand.

*Petrikirche (St Peter's Church) M4

Location
in the city centre between Mönckebergstrasse, Bergstrasse, Speersort and Kreuslerstrasse
HH 1

U-Bahn station
Rathaus (U 3)

A market church on the "Hill" is first mentioned in Hamburg in 1195; the name St Petri (St Peter's) does not appear until 1220. Thus St Peter's is considered the oldest of Hamburg's city churches.
A new three-aisled brick hall-church was erected in the first half of the 14th c. and about 1418 a second side aisle was added on the south. This medieval church was a victim of the Great Fire of 1842. In the same year the planned rebuilding was entrusted to the architects Alexis de Chateauneuf and Hermann

Petrikirche (St Peter's Church)

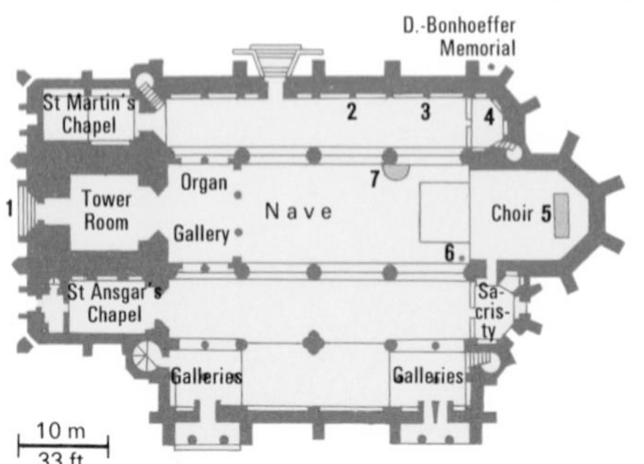

1 Main Doorway (tower doorway); on the left-hand door a lion-head handle (post-1342), on the right-hand door a replica (1849)
2 Panel of St Ansgar (probably by Hans Bornemann, *c.* 1460)
3 "Standing Madonna with Child" (Lübeck sandstone work, *c.* 1470)
4 St Barbara's Chapel (Altar *c.* 1490/1500)
5 Altar; Crucifixion Group (Hamburg woodcarving, *c.* 1490); the wings of this altar are on the wall of the Choir (painting 15th/16th c.)
6 Wooden statue of St Ansgar (probably by Bernt Notke, *c.* 1480/83
7 Pulpit (1849; canopy, *c.* 1400)

Fersenfeldt. Between 1844 and 1849 they built the Evangelical Church of St Peter in Neo-Gothic style on the old foundations, and basically this is the church which we see today. The reconstruction of the tower was undertaken in 1866; in 1878 the copper-covered iron spire was completed (total height of the tower 132·5 m (435 feet)).
Only comparatively slight damage was caused to the church during the Second World War and repairs were finished in 1959.

Buses
31, 34, 35, 36, 37, 38, 102, 108, 109

One of the oldest works of art in Hamburg is the bronze handle on the left-hand side of the main door. The encircling inscription refers to the laying of the foundation-stone of the church tower in 1342. The counterpart on the right-hand side is a copy dating from 1849.

Lion's-head Door-handle

Interior
Mon.–Fri. 8 a.m.–6 p.m.; Sat. 9 a.m.–5 p.m.; Sun. 9 a.m.–7 p.m.; every Wed. an hour of church music 5.15 p.m.; first Sat. in every month 6 p.m. motets

Many works of art saved from the Great Fire of 1842 are to be found in the new church. Two granite pillars from the so-called Schappendom, an annex of the Cathedral of St Mary which was pulled down in 1806, were built in under each of the two south galleries. All the new furnishings have been deliberately designed to accord with the style of the Neo-Gothic architecture.

Petrikirche

The artistic furnishing of the interior of the church, which including the tower chamber is 58 m (190 ft) long, 34 m (112 ft) wide and up to 20 m (66 ft) high, to a great extent survived the last war unscathed. The oldest items are the Gothic pulpit canopy (about 1400), a sandstone figure of St Paul (about 1440/50), a votive panel of St Ansgar (probably by the Hamburg painter Hans Bornemann, about 1460) from the former Cathedral of St Mary, a sandstone Madonna and Child (about 1470) from the reliquary of the lost Altar of St Theobald, a wooden statue of St Ansgar (about 1480/83; attributed to Bernt Notke or his workshop), the Crucifixion Group on the altar (about 1490; Hamburg work), and the triptych in St Barbara's Chapel (about 1490/1500), purchased in 1962. In the second south aisle stands a model of St Peter's Church as it was before the Great Fire of 1842.
The most important work of art of the medieval Petrikirche, the High Altar created by Meister Bertram in 1379, had been taken to Grabow in Mecklenburg in 1734 (therefore also known as the Grabow Altar). In 1903 it was repurchased by Alfred Lichtwark for the Hamburg Kunsthalle (see entry).

Bischofsburg

Below the Parish Rooms of St Peter's, on the corner of Speersort and Kreuslerstrasse the foundations of the Bishop's Castle (see Bischofsburg) can be seen in a cellar.

*Planetarium M8

In 1930 the Hamburg Planetarium was installed under the dome of the 60 m (197 ft) high water-tower, built of brick by Fritz Schumacher in 1912–14, in the Stadtpark. In the centre of the dome space stands a Zeiss projector Mark VI (the most modern planetarium instrument of its day) which projects an accurate picture of the stars in the sky on the inner surface of the

Address
Hindenburgstrasse Öl
HH 60 (Winterhude)

U-Bahn stations
Borgweg (U 3)
Hudtwalckerstrasse (U 1)

Buses
108, 109, 118, 179

dome. It is able to demonstrate the stars in all sectors of the sky and at all periods, the movements of the heavenly bodies as the day and year run their course, and also the impressive effects of space travel. Hundreds of additional pieces of apparatus add to the interest of the demonstrations with representations of planets, galaxies, pulsars, panoramas, Northern Lights and cloud formations. There is seating for 270 in the lecture-room where programmes are changed monthly and special events take place. Attractions include observation by telescope, lectures, exhibitions, shows and concerts.
Opening times for exhibition and tower: Sunday–Friday 10 a.m.–3.30 p.m., closed Saturday. Demonstrations (1 hour): Wednesday and Friday at 4 and 6 p.m.; Sunday 11 a.m. 2.30 and 4 p.m. Introductory talks Friday 4 p.m. There is an entrance fee.

Astronomical Exhibition

In adjoining rooms is a permanent astronomical exhibition which had its origin in a bequest by the Hamburg historian Aby Warburg (1866–1929). It gives information about the history of astronomy, modern astronomy, space travel and the history of the planetarium. Also on view as a show-piece of planetarium apparatus are the huge globe of the moon, about 80 model spacecraft and a few rarities from antiquity and the Middle Ages.

Astro Shop

In the Astro Shop of the Society for Popular Astronomy books, manuscripts, slides, posters, etc. are on sale and technical information is available.

Planetarium in the former Water-tower

The observation platform in the water-tower can be reached by lift. From it there is an extensive view over northern Hamburg.

Observation Platform

Planten un Blomen

See Wallringpark

** Port of Hamburg (Hafen)

E–Q1–4

Location
on the Elbe to the S of the centre of Hamburg

In spite of the development of Hamburg into the greatest industrial town of the Federal Republic of Germany, the heart of the Hansa city remains the port, which is probably the chief attraction for the visitor. Nobody should leave "Germany's Gateway to the World" without taking one of the almost obligatory trips round the port and see for himself the confusing variety and size of the port of Hamburg.

Development

The first port in Hamburg came into being at the time of the Schauenburg Duke Adolph III (1164–1203) and was situated where the Alster meets the Elbe (see Nikolaifleet). In the middle of the 13th c. a channel, the present Zollkanal, was made to the mouth of the Bille, and not until the 16th c. was the North Elbe included in the port area. In the 17th c. the Niederhafen (lower port) was established at the mouth of the Alster, and during the following 200 years the area of the port extended farther and farther to the south.
When, about the middle of the 19th c., commercial shipping was rapidly expanding and the first steamers were taking the place of sailing-ships, a methodical extension of the port layout was begun. In only a few years it stretched across the terrain between the two arms of the Elbe (island – see Wilhelmsburg) and meanwhile the port has been extended and improved again and again. Today Hamburg is among the leading group of commercial seaports in Europe and the most important container port in the world.
The geographical importance of the Port of Hamburg from the point of view of communications is dealt with at the beginning of this book (see Facts and Figures – Transport).

Port Industry

On a total area of about 100 sq. km (39 sq. miles) there has arisen an impressive port complex of technology and communications, the like of which can be found in few other places. Around a considerable number of small and large docks are grouped workplaces for more than 100,000 people: terminals for the handling of cargoes, warehouses, railway goods yards and a whole host of industrial concerns, including a number of shipyards (e.g. Blohm+Voss and the Howaldswerke Deutsche Werft/HDW), oil-refineries, the largest copper plant on the Continent, as well as steel and aluminium plants. Industry profits from the fact that ocean-going ships bring raw materials to their very doors. For future extension of the port to the south and west of its present limits, land which up to now has been used for agriculture is earmarked for new docks, quays and factories. It must be said, however, that these plans are meeting strong resistance from the residents of this area.

Modern Port

The port is in a constant process of adaptation to the demands of industrialisation and rationalisation. The rejection of the traditional image of the layout of a port can best be seen where container ships load and unload. The extensive Walterhof Container Centre (3 sq. km (1·1 sq. miles)) scarcely corresponds to the old idea of a seaport. Here the industrialisation of waterborne traffic becomes obvious. With its modern layout the Port of Hamburg (see the table Port of Hamburg in Figures opposite) is a great and "rapid" universal port in which the expensive turn-round time of ships is kept to a minimum.

Freihafen (Free Port)

The heart of the port is the Freihafen, one of the very oldest and largest institutions of its kind. Within the customs-free area cargoes and goods can be dealt with free from customs formalities. Here merchandise of all descriptions from any country can be kept, handled, inspected, traded in and processed for as long as necessary.

Speicherstadt

Particularly worth seeing in the Freihafen is the historic Speicherstadt (see entry).

Port Services

The service requirements in the Port of Hamburg demand well-adjusted organisation (partly controlled by computer) and trouble-free co-operation of many institutions and firms. The specialist know-how and experience of the port concerns are complemented by the activities of shipping companies, brokers, shipping agents, business houses, banks, insurance companies, consulates, research institutions, various specialist undertakings for repair and packing and many other firms.

Movement of ships

The arrival and departure of vessels (see Willkommhöft – Ship Greeting Point) is accomplished in a traditional manner: in the port itself a harbour pilot, on the Lower Elbe an Elbe pilot, takes over control. The harbour tugs help (*verholen* = haul) to manœuvre ships. At the quays vessels are moored by Festmacher (moorers); loading and unloading (Löschen) is carried out by Schauerleute (dockers).

Harbour Trips

Throughout the year tours around the port take place several times a day with different itineraries. The boats can be found at the pontoons of the Landungsbrücken (see entry) from where most of the ferries and local river services also depart.

Hamburg Information in the Port

In the booking hall of the Landungsbrücken (see entry), between the gangways to landing-stages 4 and 5, can be found the Hamburg Information in the Port bureau, where information on all matters concerning the Port of Hamburg can be obtained.

Birthday of the Port

Every year on the seventh of May the Port Birthday (also called the Overseas' Day) is celebrated. It commemorates the signing of the charter by the Emperor Friedrich Barbarossa in 1189 which granted the people of Hamburg freedom from duty and taxes on the Lower Elbe. This is made an occasion for events of a popular nature in the port (parades of vessels, dedication of new installations, etc.).

◀ *The Kohlbrand Bridge, a new landmark of the Port of Hamburg*

The Port of Hamburg in figures

More than 15,000 ocean-going ships from over 90 countries in the world use the Port of Hamburg every year; every second ship is engaged on a regular service.

TURNOVER OF GOODS
50 million tonnes total annual turnover, of which 19 million is in individual consignments (45% of this in containers), 14 million tonnes liquid cargo, 9 million tonnes of cargo unloaded by grab and 8 millions by suction.

AREA
100 sq. km/39 sq. miles (=13% of the total area of the State of Hamburg)
69 sq. m/27 sq. miles useable space (38 sq. km/17 sq. miles on land, 31 sq. km/12 sq. miles of water)
19 sq. km/7 sq. miles area available for expansion
16 sq. km/6 sq. miles free port territory

FACILITIES
33 harbour basins for ocean-going ships, 27 for inland vessels
500 berths for ocean-going ships at quays and groups of mooring posts (Dalben)
39 km/24 miles of quaysides for ocean-going ships; 235 km/146 miles of river banks
19 floating docks, 2 dry docks (up to 320,000 tonnes dead weight)
3300 "Dalben" (groups of mooring posts)
667 quayside cranes (on quays, in buildings, mobile and floating; up to 1000 tonnes capacity)
31 container bridges, 10 container cranes
73 straddle lifters (Van/Straddle-Carrier)
19 roll-on/roll-off berths; 45 suction unloaders
19 stacking and loading bridges (Constacker, Transtainer)
680 km/423 miles of port railway track; 185 km/115 miles of roadways
179 road and rail bridges

STORAGE CAPACITIES
1·3 million sq. m/14 million sq. ft of space in stores (for tobacco, tea, coffee, cocoa, spices, carpets, etc.), warehouses and sheds of the free port
5·4 million cu. m/7 million cu. yds of tank depots for oil, chemicals, etc.
1 million tonnes bulk cargo (cereals, oil seed, feedstuffs, etc.) in silos and sheds
320,000 cu. m/419,000 cu. yds cold storage (of which 50,000 cu. m/65,000 cu. yds is frozen storage)
84,000 sq. m/904,000 sq. ft for fruit storage (partly air-conditioned)
422,000 sq. m/4,542,000 sq. ft open space for bulk cargo (ore and potash, etc.)

SHIPPING IN THE PORT
144 tugs, 234 launches, over 1000 lighters
37 auxiliary tugs for sea-going vessels
82 port pilots; radar chain with 10 stations
3 m/10 ft average tidal difference
13·5 m/44 ft – 16·5 m/54 ft average channel depth

DISTANCE FROM THE SEA
56 sea miles (104 km) on the Lower Elbe between Hamburg and Cuxhaven (Alte Liebe); radar chain with 12 stations

Important Flag Signals

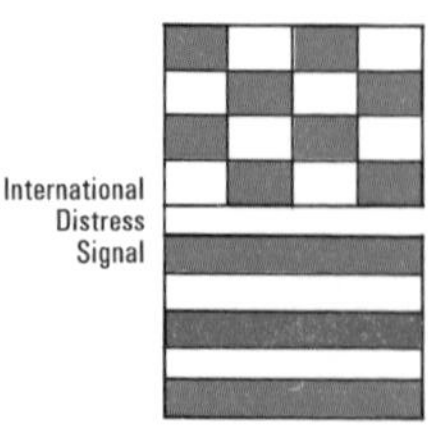
International Distress Signal

Help!

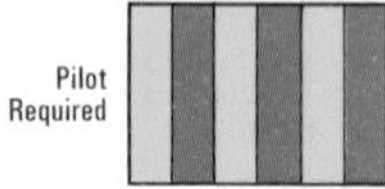
Pilot Required

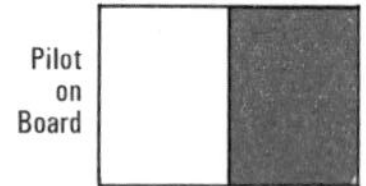
Pilot on Board

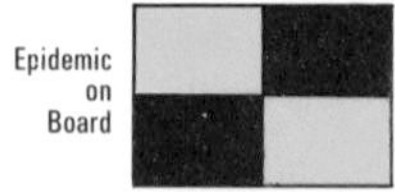
Epidemic on Board

Customs

Inflammable Cargo

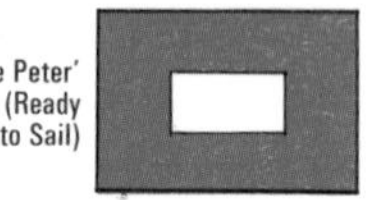
'Blue Peter' (Ready to Sail)

Pöseldorf

M6/7

In spite of all the prophecies of doom Pöseldorf is still "in"! The name arose in the early 19th c. and was presumably derived from "pöseln" (dialect for "potter about"). It is an unofficial description of an area in the east of the fashionable district of Harvestehude, bounded approximately by Harvestehude Weg and its fine villas and the beautiful Alster Park in the east, by busy Mittelweg in the west, by Klosterstieg and Pöseldorfer Weg in the north and by Badestrasse in the south, with Milchstrasse forming a diagonal axis.
Originally only working-class people lived here, many of whom were employed on the upper-class estates by the Alster; today, however, Pöseldorf is a stylish and expensive residential district appealing especially to younger people. In addition exclusive boutiques are to be found here (notably the Hamburg fashion house of Jil Sander, Milchstrasse 8), as well as antique-dealers, art galleries, speciality and delicatessen shops (e.g. J. W. M. Broders, Mittelweg 172), restaurants, discothèques and bars where there is always something going on.
For its informal atmosphere Pöseldorf is chiefly indebted to the initiative of the Hamburg architect and art-dealer, Eduard Brikama, who also laid out the nostalgic Pöseldorf market by making use of old half-timbered buildings which were previously stables and outhouses.
Mention should also be made of the little Theater im Zimmer (theatre in a room) in a Neo-Classical mansion at Alsterchaussee 30, where the auditorium accommodates only about 100 people. On the southern edge of Pöseldorf stands the Inter-Continental Hotel (Fontenay 10) with the Hamburg Casino in the penthouse (entrance from Badestrasse).

Location
in the district of Harvestehude, 2/3 km (1/2 miles) N from the centre of Hamburg

U-Bahn station
Hallerstrasse (U 1)

Buses
109, 115

Alster boats
(only in summer) landing-stages Rabenstrasse and Fährdamm

Rade Museum in Castle Reinbek

The Rade Museum, opened in 1970, is a creation of the much travelled author and ethnologist, Rolf Italiaander (born 1913) and H. L. Spegg. Until 1984 it was housed in an old farmhouse in the Upper Alster Nature Park (Tangstedt-Rade), and after the founders had presented it to the German nation, the museum acquired a new home in the Castle of Reinbek in Holstein.
The collection consists of pictures and other articles which Rolf Italiaander has brought back from his journeys all over the world. The exhibits portray native and primitive art from Europe, Africa, Asia, Australia and Oceania.
Opening times are Wednesday, Saturday, Sunday and public holidays. There is an entrance fee.

Location
in Reinbek about 20 km (12 miles) S from the centre of Hamburg

Address
Schloss Strasse 4
D-2057 Reinbek

S-Bahn Station
Reinbek (S21)

Rathaus

See City Hall

*Rathausmarkt

M4

The Rathausmarkt, the square in front of the City Hall (see entry) forms the central point of the Inner City. In the north-west this prestigious square opens on to the Little Alster (see Alster); on the other sides it is surrounded by large business premises.

Location
In city centre between Mönckebergstrasse and the Little Alster
HH 1

S-Bahn station
Jungfernstieg (S 1, S 2, S 3)

U-Bahn stations
Rathaus (U 3)
Jungfernstieg (U 1, U 2)

Buses
31, 34, 36, 37, 38, 102, 108, 109

Alster boats
(only in summer)
Jungfernstieg landing-stage

The Rathausmarkt was laid out after the Great Fire of 1842 on the area of the medieval Church of St Johannis Kloster which had been previously pulled down. Before the present City Hall was built, the square consisted of a spacious green area extending as far as the buildings of the Stock Exchange. The master builder Alexis de Chateauneuf wanted to create a kind of Hanseatic Markusplatz (St Mark's Square) modelled on Venetian lines. In the presence of the Kaiser Wilhelm II a monumental bronze equestrian statue of the Kaiser Wilhelm I (by J. Schilling) was unveiled on the Rathausmarkt in 1903; when the square was altered in 1929 this was removed to the Holstenwall (see Wallringpark, Grosse Wallanlagen).

In June 1919 the Rathausmarkt was the scene of a bloody revolt when Spartacists attempted a *putsch* which was put down by Government troops under General Lettow-Vorbeck. It was a miracle that the City Hall and the Rathausmarkt remained almost unscathed from the severe bombing of the Second World War which caused tremendous damage to the centre of Hamburg. At the end of the war the square was used by British occupying forces as a collection point for military vehicles.

In the early hours of 17 February 1962 the great flood reached its highest level in the Rathausmarkt.

Rathausmarkt

Following controversial remodelling of the Rathausmarkt, the allegorical figures from the old Kaiser-Wilhelm Monument were temporarily installed here in 1977. The newly laid out Rathausmarkt, conceived by the firm of architects Timm Ohrt & Partner as a "turntable for pedestrian traffic in the Inner City", was opened to the public on 11 May 1982. A prominent feature now enlivening the extensive square is a glass arcade bordered by trees; on the side facing the City Hall stand two tall flagpoles surmounted by gilded ships.

Heine Memorial

After considerable discussion a new Heinrich Heine Memorial has been erected on the narrower south-east side of the Rathausmarkt. Designed by Waldemar Otto, it was modelled on Hugo Lederer's memorial to Heine.

War Memorial

Where the broad steps of the Reesendamm, leading down to the Little Alster with its colony of swans, approach the Schleusenbrücke, there stands at the foot of a curved flight of steps (1846), on the north-west side of the Rathausmarkt, a stone-clad pillar (12·5 m (41 ft) high), the memorial to the fallen of the First World War. It was put up here in 1932 to the design of Claus Hoffmann. On one side it bears a relief ("Weeping Woman with Child"); this was originally the work of Ernst Barlach but it was destroyed by the Nazis and was refashioned by F. Bursch in 1949. On the other side is the inscription "Vierzigtausend Söhne der Stadt liessen ihr Leben für euch 1914–1918" (forty thousand sons of the city laid down their lives for you).

*Reeperbahn — J/K4

Situation
in the district of St Pauli
HH 4

S-Bahn station
Reeperbahn (S 1, S 2, S 3)

Diagonally through the world-famous pleasure quarter of St Pauli (see entry) runs the no less renowned Reeperbahn between Millerntor in the east and Nobister in the west. It is a 600 m (656 yd) long through road, where ropemakers used to wind ships' ropes (Low German *reep* = rope). Here in St Pauli, where once popular shows had been given on the "Hamburg

Neon advertising signs in the Reeperbahn

Davidswache Police Station

U-Bahn station
St Pauli (U 3)

Buses
36, 37, 112

Hill", an amusement quarter developed from the early 19th c., the like of which can probably not be found elsewhere in the world.

At the beginning of the Reeperbahn, in front of the Millerntor multi-storey building which houses the Verwaltungsgerichte (administrative court), stands the "Hamburg Baum," a great oak sculpture by W. Gerthagen and F. Vollert, erected in 1980.

Spielbudenplatz

Up to its junction with Davistrasse the Reeperbahn is known as the Spielbudenplatz. Here can be found the large Brunswick Bowling, the former Operettenhaus (Theater am Spielbudenplatz; now utilised for various purposes), the waxworks Panoptikum, the rock discothèque After Shave, the popular rendezvous Herz von St Pauli, the dance-halls Allotria and Kaiserhof, the beer-palace Zillertal and the St Pauli Theatre, founded in 1841 (popular plays in Hamburg dialect; pleasant theatre restaurant).

Among the establishments on the north side of the Reeperbahn are the well-known Cafe Keese, where the ladies invite you to the Paradox Ball and the Top Ten Club, the last remaining beat and rock temple of the 1960s.

Davidswache

The legendary Davidswache, often featured in films and television, is the police station responsible for St Pauli (duty room and criminal department at No. 15). Its efficiency is unquestioned; it has St Pauli "firmly in its grip" and will help anybody who gets into difficulties.

The Davidswache occupies a noteworthy clinker-brick building (Spielbudenplatz 31, corner of Davidstrasse) which Fritz Schumacher created in 1913–14 with the original articulated eaves on the façade.

Bernhard Nocht Strasse

Davidstrasse begins at the Davidswache and leads south to the Bernhard Nocht Strasse near the Elbe, where stands the large Bavaria St Pauli Brewery (No. 99; Bavaria-Blick Restaurant with a magnificent view of the port) and at No. 63 Harry's Hamburger Hafenbazar with curiosities from many countries.

Herbertstrasse

Half-way along Davidstrasse the short narrow Herbertstrasse branches off to the west. This, the last brothel street in West Germany and to which only adult males are admitted, is screened at both ends.

Hans Albers Platz

The heart of old St Pauli is known to habitués as Kleiner Kiez (little red-light district). Its centre is Hans Albers Platz and the streets in the vicinity, where there are innumerable dives and appropriate establishments.

Grosse Freiheit

Just before the Nobistor at the west end of the Reeperbahn, the well-known Grosse Freiheit branches off to the north. This street, which was in Altona until 1937, was featured in Hans Albers's film "Grosse Freihert No. 7" (1944). The name refers to the freedom of religion and trade once enjoyed in Altona in contrast to Hamburg. Here one sex show venue follows another (picture, p. 126). The once-renowned Star Club, where the Beatles and others began their international careers, no longer exists.

St Joseph's Church

In the midst of the "babel of sin" of the Grosse Freiheit one comes unexpectedly upon a church (No. 5). It is the Catholic Church of St Joseph, originally built 1718–23, which was almost completely destroyed in the Second World War; the beautiful Baroque façade, set back from the street, however, has survived.

Sachsenwald

Location
about 25 km (16 miles) E from the centre of Hamburg

Access
B 5 to Bergerdorf then B 207

S-Bahn stations
Aumühle, Friedrichsruh (both S 21)

The Sachsenwald, the largest enclosed area of forest in Schleswig-Holstein with an area of almost 70 sq. km (27 sq. miles), is situated outside the boundaries of Hamburg. The trees are mostly beech, spruce and fir, and there are many attractive footpaths.
On 24 June 1871, the year of the foundation of the German Reich, Count Bismarck (1815–98) received the Sachsenwald from the Emperor Wilhelm I in recognition of his services, and the extensive estate is still the property of his family.

Friedrichsruh Castle

The mansion of this huge estate was the home of the venerable Chancellor in his retirement. It was destroyed in 1945 during the final days of the Second World War but was rebuilt in the following year and is now the residence of Bismarck's descendants. A half-timbered building of 1889, opposite, houses the Bismarck Museum (memorabilia). Close by in a park lies the Bismarck Mausoleum containing the sarcophagi of the Chancellor and his wife. The museum and the funerary chapel are open daily in summer (closed on Mon. in winter; entrance fee).

Bismarck Museum
Bismarck Mausoleum

St Catherine's Church

See Katherinenkirche

St Georg

M/N4/5

Location
NE of Hamburg Main Station

S-Bahn station
Hauptbahnhof (S 1, S 2, S 3, S 4, S 11, S 21)

U-Bahn stations
Hauptbahnhof-Nord (U 2)
Hauptbahnhof-Süd (U 1, U 3)
Lohmühlenstrasse (U 1)

Buses
31, 34, 35, 36, 37, 38, 102, 108, 109, 120, 122, 123, 124, 125

The scintillating district of St Georg is almost square in shape and extends between the Outer Alster in the north-west and Hammerbrook in the south-east; it is separated from the city centre by the wide expanse of tracks of the main railway station which follow the lines of the 17th c. defensive works. It is the oldest part of Hamburg outside the ancient heart of the city and owes its name to an infirmary with a chapel dedicated to St George. On the churchyard there now stands the Church of the Holy Trinity (Kirche der Heiligen Dreieinigkeit); this was originally a Baroque building of 1743–47 which was destroyed in 1943. The nave was rebuilt in a modern style by H. Graf in 1957; the 67 m (220 ft) high tower was re-erected in 1959–61 in its original architectural form.

St Georg is a district of great contrasts. On the one hand there can be found here such prestigious cultural centres as the Kunsthalle, the Museum of Art and Industry and the Deutsches Schauspielhaus (see entries), situated close to the Main Station (see entry), and the Central Bus Station (ZOB), as well as a number of well-known hotels (including the elegant Atlantic by the Outer Alster) and not forgetting the police headquarters in a tower-block at Berliner Tor.

On the other hand, the area around the Steindamm is the scene of "pleasures by night" which are the equal of those in St Pauli (see entry) and in some respects even surpass the latter. It was in St Georg (Lange Reihe 71) and not in St Pauli, that the well-known actor Hans Albers (1891–1960) was born.

There are also residential streets with houses which have throughways into lively courtyards where artists have set up their studios. In many places can be found oriental taverns, because of the large number of foreign residents in this district.

Amusement Quarter

The world of pleasure in St Georg embraces a wide spectrum. In Kirchenallee behind the Main Station are a number of modest hotels, inns and bars; the Steindamm is known as the sündige Meile (mile of sin) with gambling houses, including the Kleine Casino, a subsidiary of the Hamburg Casino in Pöseldorf (see entry), with one-armed bandits and other mechanical games of chance, bars, striptease joints, homosexual bars and "hotels" with rooms rented by the hour. Notable among the many sex-show establishments is the Pulverfass (powder-barrel) with its well-known transvestite performances; in the Crazy Boys (same address) male strippers perform.

Hansa Theatre

Steindamm 17 is also the home of the famous Hansa Theatre, one of the last true variety theatres in Europe. Artistes from all over the world perform in this building which was opened in 1894 and which is still comfortably furnished in an old-fashioned style. The acts presented are basically those which are not seen on television. The members of the audience sit at small tables with a view of the stage and are served with drinks and snacks; smoking is permitted. Tickets should be ordered well in advance as the shows are invariably sold out.

Hansaplatz

The Hansaplatz, not far from the Steindamm is graced by the great Hansa Fountain with a figure of Hammonia, the patroness of Hamburg. (Visitors are advised that this square is a meeting-place for homosexuals.)

St James's Church

See Jacobikirche

St Michael's Church

See Michaeliskirche

*St Pauli J/K4/5

Location
Between the Inner City and Altona

S-Bahn stations
Landungsbrücken, Reeperbahn (both S 1, S 2)

U-Bahn stations
St Pauli, Landungsbrücken (both U 3)

It is ironic that Hamburg's notorious district of St Pauli – the epitome of "sinful pleasure" – should bear the name of the moralizing Apostle Paul, of all people. In 1682 a church was dedicated to St Paul on the "Hamburger Berg", as the district on the hilly land on the bank of the Elbe was originally called. This church existed until 1814 when the suburb was sacked by the French. It successor, the little Neo-Classical St Paul's Church (by C. L. Wimmel, 1820), after which the district was named in 1833, has been in the territory of Altona not far south of Hein Köllisch Platz since 1937.

"Entertainment" in the Grosse Freiheit, St Pauli

Buses
36, 37, 112

Harbour ships
Landungsbrücken (services 61, 62, 66, 75, 77)

When more and more steamships came to Hamburg at the beginning of the 19th c., a seamen's quarter developed near the Jonas Harbour (an additional haven outside the Jonas outer bastion). This seamen's quarter with hostels, sailors' homes, harbour bars, dance-halls and houses of ill repute, has spread into the extensive area in and around the world-famous Reeperbahn (see entry), and has become a "district of pleasure".

Development

As a result of the short time which most ships spend in the "rapid" Port of Hamburg, the seafaring element has become far less pronounced. Today St Pauli offers entertainment for everybody and since the Second World War has become a metropolis of the sex business.

Night Life

The range of entertainment on offer is remarkable: popular theatre, venues with music and dancing, extravagant sex shows and dives of every kind, right down to vulgar pornography and professional prostitution; a world of pleasure which the responsible authority is making increasing efforts to keep in check.

Not only can visitors from every country in the world be found in St Pauli, but a great many of the people who work here also come from abroad; the number of drop-outs cannot be ignored, the number of "life's failures" is considerable.

At night St Pauli with its harshly lit advertisements and the bustling activity of its establishments is, nevertheless, without any doubt something to be seen. It seems pointless to describe, even approximately, the multifarious facets of the place; the following list gives some indication of what goes on in St Pauli.

St Pauli A–Z

Accommodation addresses, amusement arcades, bars, bar vamps, beer-palaces, bowling centre, brothels, call girls, casinos, cinemas, clip joints, dance-halls, dealers, dives, drug addicts, fish market, folk music, gigolos, homosexual rendezvous, hookers, hotels, jazz, lesbian rendezvous, masseurs and masseuses, peep-shows, photo-models, pimps, pop music, pornographic cinemas and shops, porters, private booths, prostitution, red-light district, restaurants, rock music, rooms by the hour, sado-masochism clubs, saunas, seamen's bars, sex clubs, sex shops, sex shows, snack-bars, strip-tease, tarts, tattooists, theatres, tramps' shelters, transvestites, waxworks, etc . . ., etc. . . .

A selection of establishments, with tips on how to conduct oneself while strolling through St Pauli by night, can be found in the 'Practical Information Section – Night Life' of this book.

St Pauli Fishmarket

See Fish Market

St Pauli Landungsbrücken

See Landungsbrücken

St Pauli Theatre

See Reeperbahn

St Peter's Church

See Petrikirche

The Speicherstadt Warehouses, containing valuable merchandise

*Speicherstadt L/M3/4

Location
in the Free Port about 1 km (0·6 miles) S from the centre of Hamburg
HH 11

U-Bahn station
Messberg (U 1)

Bus
111

At the end of the 19th c. a new warehouse quarter was built on the site of the former residential and trading district which was intercepted by fleets. This new development on Brook Island, south of the Zollkanal, was associated with the Free Port which was opened in 1888. The long lines of warehouse blocks, facing both the fleets and the streets, are up to seven storeys high and exhibit an impressive unity of style. The severity of the reddish-brown façades is broken up by decorative elements including turrets, gables and ledges and in a Gothicised style.

Imports

These warehouses serve primarily for storing valuable imports. Some house tobacco, coffee, cocoa, tea, rum, dried fruit, nuts, spices, etc.; others contain canned food, electronic and optical apparatus, raw silk and Oriental carpets. In the largest carpet warehouse in the world are stored about 120,000 sq. m (143,500 sq. ft) of hand-woven carpets.
In the customs-free area of the Free Port goods cannot only be stored but also finished or further processed by the expert Quartierleute (quartermen) in the various storeys (Böden) of the warehouses.

Visit

The Speicherstadt is included in round trips of the fleets (see Practical Information – Sightseeing). Visitors who enter the Free Port on their own must be prepared for customs control as they leave the area.

Model Ship Pond in the Stadtpark

*Staatsoper

See State Opera

*Stadtpark

M/O8/9

With the acquisition in 1902 from the former owner of a forested area, 36 ha (89 acres) in extent, on the Winterhude Geest (moorland), the City of Hamburg was able to carry out its plans of 1890 and begin to lay out a park as a recreation centre for the people of this densely populated district. Subsequently Fritz Schumacher created from 1912 to 1914 a People's Park, of some 180 ha (445 acres), according to the ideas of Alfred Lichtwark and conforming to the requirements of the people of Hamburg. It reflects the socio-political and artistic problems of that time. Otto Linné so equipped the park, that from a central axis round the lake extend areas of woodland, meadow and gardens. In the park can be seen various sculptures, most of them by Hamburg artists.

The many opportunities for games, sport and amusement enhance the recreational value of this park. Among the facilities are an open-air pool, paddling-pools, sunbathing, sports and games areas, an open-air theatre, an ornithological station and restaurant.

Location
In the district of Winterhude about 5 km (3 miles) N from the centre of Hamburg
HH 60

S-Bahn station
Alte Wöhr (S 1, S 11)

U-Bahn station
Saarlandstrasse
Borgweg (both U 3)

Buses
E 17, 108, 118, 179

Leisure Park

The former water-tower on the end of the western axis of the park is now an observation tower; under the dome is the Planetarium (see entry). Its architectural complement at the eastern end of the axis of the park, the Stadthalle by the lake was completely destroyed, together with the Stadtcafé, in the Second World War.

City Nord

North of the Johnring, on the far side of the Stadtpark, lies the great new commercial town, Geschäftsstadt Nord (see City Nord).

*State Opera (Staatsoper) L5

Address
Dammtorstrasse 28
HH 36

S-Bahn station
Dammtor (S 11, S 21)

U-Bahn station
Stephansplatz (U 1)
Gänsemarkt (U 2)

Buses
34, 36, 38, 102, 109, 112

Hamburg Opera House has a rich tradition and is now counted among the most important opera houses in the world. It was in Hamburg that the Deutsches Opernhaus, the first permanent opera theatre in Europe, was opened in 1678 in the Gänsemarkt (see entry). In this theatre the operas of Handel were first performed and the composer himself played in the orchestra.
After the Second World War the Hamburg State Opera was able to gain a leading place in the international field, thanks largely to its Director, the Swiss composer Rolf Liebermann, with productions of all contemporary operatic works.

Ballet

The State Opera Ballet, directed by the American John Neumeier, is among the leading companies in the world. Until further notice ballet performances take place in the former Kampnagel factory building in Jarrestrasse 20, in the suburb of Barmbek.

The Building

The opera house in Dammtorstrasse was built in 1827 to the design of C. W. Wimmel and was remodelled in 1873–77 and again in 1925–26. The building, apart from the stage was burned out in 1943 but was rebuilt in 1953–55, when it received its glass façade. The modern auditorium has staggered balcony boxes, suspended on vertical concrete disks. It is planned to rebuild the opera house.

Opera Stabile

The Hamburg State Opera maintains a studio theatre with the designation of Opera Stabile in Büschstrasse, but its future is in doubt.

*Stock Exchange (Börse) M4

Location
Adolphsplatz
(rear of City Hall)
HH 11

U-Bahn station
Rathaus (U 3)

Buses
35, 37

The Hamburg Stock Exchange is considered to be the oldest institution of its kind in North Europe; it was founded in 1558. In 1841 the exchange was moved from the Trostbrücke (see Nikolaifleet) near the old Rathaus to its present site which was previously occupied by the Maria Magadalene Convent, founded in 1230. The original Late Classic building was designed by Carl Ludwig Wimmel and Franz Gustav Forsmann and was spared by the Great Fire of 1842. Various extensions followed later, among them the wing on the Alter Wall (1882–84), the wing with the clock-tower on the Grosse Johannisstrasse (1902–12); both wings were connected to the

City Hall (see entry). After destruction in the Second World War the whole group of buildings was restored in its old form between 1949 and 1957.

The Stock Exchange is controlled by the Chamber of Trade, founded in 1665, which also has its headquarters here, together with the commercial library, founded in 1735. Several exchange halls are at the disposal of the brokers of the Hanseatic Stock Exchange, the Hamburg Corn Exchange and the Hamburg Insurance Exchange (the only one of its kind); these halls are linked by arcades with commercial and banking offices. The Stock Exchange operates in the west hall (Picture, p. 24); on the façade is an electronic indicator for rates of exchange, below is the Devisenring (currency ring) for the currency brokers. In the central wing is the Commodity Exchange. In the east wing are the insurance, shipping and air-freight exchanges. Visitors can watch the operation of the exchanges from the galleries on the first floor (entrance free).

Explanation of the Stock Exchange with film
Mon.–Fri. 11.15 a.m to 12.15 p.m.

Süllberg

See Blankenese

*Television Tower

K6

Location
Rentzelstrasse/Lagerstrasse
HH 6

S-Bahn station
Sternschanze (S 11, S 21, S 31)

U-Bahn station
Sternschanze (U 3)

Opening Times
Observation Platform
daily 10 a.m.–11 p.m.
Revolving Restaurant
daily midday–11 p.m.

Charge for the lift

The Hamburg Television Tower (officially the Heinrich Hertz Tower) is by far the tallest tower in the city and, by association with the traditional landmark of Hamburg, the "Michel" (see Michaeliskirche), is popularly known as the "Tele-Michel". It was built between 1965 and 1968 as a telecommunications tower for the Federal Post Office. The total height is 271·5 m (890 ft), the conical concrete shaft being 204 m (670 ft) above ground-level. At a height of 128–132 m (420–430 ft) is the two-storeyed observation and restaurant "turret", above which, some 150 m (490 ft) higher can be seen the service "turret" of the Federal Post Office and higher still six smaller platforms.

Panorama

The tower, an elegant example of successful town-planning, at the extreme northern point of the Wallringpark (see entry), can be reached from the Planten un Blomen part of the park by one of the pedestrian bridges crossing Rentzelstrasse. Two express lifts take visitors in barely half a minute to the observation platform (with a self-service restaurant), from which there is a splendid panoramic view over Hamburg, with the Alster, the Elbe and the port, as well as farther afield into Lower Saxony and Schleswig-Holstein. The Skyline Tower Restaurant above the observation platform makes a complete revolution in about 1 hour.

Thalia Theatre

See Mönckerbergstrasse, Gerhart Hauptmann Platz

Auditorium Maximum of the University of Hamburg

Überseebrücke

See Landungsbrücken

University Quarter L/M6

The University Quarter – meeting-place not only of students but also of the "scene" – occupies a considerable part of the district of Rotherbaum and in the broadest sense extends over an area bounded in the south by the Moorweide, in the west by Bundesstrasse and the street known as Beim Schlump, in the north by Hallerstrasse and in the east by Heimhuder Strasse. Its centre is formed by Von Melle Park with the main roads of Rothenbaumchaussee, Grindelallee and Bundesstrasse as the principal axes.

Location
in the district of Rotherbaum
HH13

S-Bahn station
Dammtor (S 11, S 21, S 31)

U-Bahn station
Hallerstrasse (U 1)

Buses 35, 38, 102, 115

University of Hamburg

The University of Hamburg goes back to an academic secondary school (1613–1883), as well as the so-called Allgemeine Vorlesungswesen (general provision of lectures) and a Colonial Institute set up in 1908. The Hanseatic University was not founded until 1919 but has developed considerably, especially since the Second World War (teaching; see Facts and Figures – Culture).
The nucleus of the University of Hamburg is the old lecture building, a domed construction of 1909–11 in Edmund-

◀ *The "Tele-Michel", by far Hamburg's highest tower*

Siemers-Allee not far north of Dammtor Station (see entry). As well as lecture theatres it houses the university administration.

Carl von Ossietzky State and University Library

North-west on the far side of Moorweidenstrasse stands the building of the Carl von Ossietzky State and University Library which has a long tradition (see Facts and Figures – Culture).

Audimax

Adjoining lies Von Melle Park, round which are grouped several modern institutes as well as the Auditorium Maximum (Audimax) built 1957–60 with a curved roof and a total seating capacity of 1800.
A further group of individual institutes is concentrated between Grindelallee and Bundesstrasse.

Meeting-places

In the University Quarter of Hamburg a number of cultural and entertainment establishments are also located, including the well-known theatre of the Hamburg Kammerspiele (Hartungstrasse 9–11), the leading cinema Abaton (Von Melle Park 17), the celebrated rock music bar Logo (Grindelallee 5) and the interesting Museum of Ethnology in Rothenbaumchaussee (see entry).

*Vierlande and Marschlande

Location
10–15 km (6–9 miles) SE from the centre of Hamburg

S-Bahn stations
Billwerder-Moorfleet, Mittlerer Landweg, Nettelnburg and Bergedorf (all S 2, S 21)

Buses
120, 122, 123, 124, 125 (from ZOB Hamburg)

Like the Altes Land (see entry) the Vierlande and Marschlande form a fertile depression between the Elbe and the higher slopes of the Geest. Both the former arms of the Elbe, Dove Elbe and Gose Elbe, flow through the area which is protected by dikes, and are blocked off from the main river by Locks.
While the Altes Land is almost exclusively devoted to fruit-growing, the principal crops in the Vierlande and Marschlande, which together cover an area of 130 sq. km (50 sq. miles), are flowers and vegetables. For a time (until about 1930) the extraction of natural gas was an important factor in the economy; today imported natural gas is stored underground.
The Marschlande, in the west, consists of the former islands of Billwerder and Ochsenwerder, the names of which survive in two villages. The Vierlande gets its name from the four villages of Curslack, Altengamme, Neuengamme and Kirchwerder.

Boberg Dunes

North of Billwerder along the dike extends the rising ground of the Boberg Dunes. During quarrying of material for the dike many Stone Age relics came to light; today the dunes are popular for gliding. North-west lies the Achtermoor, a marshy area with characteristic plants and animals of this type of terrain and which serves as a breeding-ground for numerous species of birds.

Billwerder

At the Billwerder Billdeich (No. 138) stands the Church of St Nicholas, originally a baroque building (1737–39) by the Hamburg architect N. Kuhn. After a fire in 1911 the church and the tower, which had been added in 1885, were rebuilt according to the old plans. The Glockenhaus (Billwerder Billdeich 72; originally dating from about 1780) houses the German Museum of Painting and Lacquerwork.

Allermöhe

Holy Trinity Church in Allerhmöhe, south-east of Billwerder, is of 17th and 18th c. date and has a beautiful altar (1613/14) by Baxmann and a free-standing wooden belfry.

Rieck-Haus Vierlande Open Air Museum in Curslack

In Moorfleet farther to the west there is another church dedicated to St Nicholas. Originally built about 1330 it was reconstructed in 1680–81 in half timbering with external walls in brick. Of interest are the pulpit and the carved pews.

Moorfleet

The Dove Elbe which flows past Moorfleet on the south is closed off from the North Elbe by the Tatenberg Lock, thus at high tide the upstream current of the river is blocked; this and the lock (completed in 1951) is of assistance to shipping. Upstream lies the Dove Elbe Wasser und Friezeitpark (recreation area for water sports, bathing, etc.).

Tatenberg Lock

Ochsenwerder is situated south of the old waters of the Elbe. Of interest here is the Church of St Pancras, a brick building of 1673–74 which replaced a stone church. J. L. Prey, one of the architects of St Michael's, was involved in the design of the tower. In the church is a beautiful carved triptych.

Ochsenwerder

In Reitbrook (Vorderdeich 11), near the Dove Elbe, stands an old windmill of the Dutch-Gallery type. Alfred Lichtwark, who was subsequently an art teacher and Director of the Hamburg Kunsthalle, was born in Reitbrook in 1852 (memorial tablet).

Reitbrook

St John's Church, built about 1600 and extended in 1801, stands at Curslacker Deich (No. 142). Its wooden belfry (1761) reveals Late Baroque features.

Curslack

Farther along the Curslacker Deich (No. 284) we come to the very interesting Vierlande Open-air Museum Rieck Haus

Vierlande Open-air Museum
Rieck Haus

(April–Sept. Tues.–Fri. 8 a.m.–5 p.m., Sat. and Sun. 10 a.m.–6 p.m.; Oct.–Mar. Tues.–Sun. 10 a.m.–4 p.m.; entrance fee). The core of this stately farmhouse dates from the 16th c.; the gute Stube (best room) is decorated with coloured tiles, ceiling- and wall-paintings, intarsia work, etc. In the courtyard stands one of those bucket wells with the help of which the water-table was maintained at a low level.

Neuengamme

Neuengamme is situated between the Dove Elbe and the Gose Elbe. St John's Church (on the Neuengammer Hausdeich) was originally a stone building; in its walls there are remains of 14th, 17th and 19th c. work. The stone flood-marker shows the flood levels of 1741 and 1771. Following the Neuengammer Hausdeich we come to a row of solid farmsteads (e.g. Nos. 81, 245, 343 and 413).

The Neuengamme Concentration Camp Memorial

Away from the dike on the Neuengammer Heerweg there once stood a men's prison which was turned into a concentration camp in 1938. More than half the 100,000 prisoners who were held here and in camps outside during the time of the Third Reich lost their lives. The former concentration camp building, a memorial and a collection of documents are reminders of the horrors of Nazi persecution (Tues.–Sun. 10 a.m.–5 p.m.).

Kirchwerder

To the south, towards the Elbe, lies Kirchwerder. St Severin's Church dates from the late 18th c.; of particular interest are the Renaissance pews with intarsia decoration and a collection of grave-plates.

Hard by the river, at a former customs post, is the Zollenspieker ferry house, also an inn, dating from the 17th c.; near by is the landing-stage of the Elbe ferry and a marina.

Altengamme

Altengamme, situated upstream, has also many fine old farmhouses. The Church of St Nicholas is considered to be one of the most important examples of Vierlande popular art; in the painted interior can be seen pews with intarsia decoration and a font of 1380. The oldest of the three bells (1487) came from Hamburg Cathedral which was pulled down early in the 19th c. as it had become dilapidated.

Volksdorf Museum Village (De Spieker)

Address
im Alten Dorfe 46–48
HH 67 (Volksdorf)

U-Bahn station
Volksdorf (U 2)

Buses
174, 175

Opening times
Grounds:
Mon., Wed., Fri.–Sun.
9 a.m.–midday and 2 p.m. until dusk (latest 6 p.m.).
Closed Tues. and Thurs.
Tours of the buildings
Sat. 3 p.m., Sun. 10 a.m. and 3 p.m.

The Volksdorf Museum Village provides an insight into the rural domestic life of the past in the Geest of Hamburg and Holstein. It is situated on an old settlement and represents a traditional village.

In the museum village can be seen three houses of 18th c. Volksdorf. The Spiekerhus (= nail house), a restored former Vollhufnerhaus (*Vollhufner* = a yeoman owning a parcel of land), contains an old people's day centre and a meeting-hall. The restored Instenhaus (*Inste* = an agricultural worker living on the estate) has been furnished in rural style as an inn. Finally there is another Vollhufnerhaus, the Harderhof, which was reconstructed after being destroyed by arson. Here, forming one of the centre-pieces of the museum village, living-rooms and workrooms are on show with articles of rural economy of about 1800. Behind the house stands the bakehouse belonging to the farm. These buildings are

In the Volksdorf Museum Village

complemented by a reconstruction of the Hummelsbüttel grist-mill, the machinery of which is original and in working order. Incorporated in the village are barns with doors at both ends which were brought from Schnakenbek near Lauenburg and which have remarkable anchor-beam construction. In these buildings are housed at present old farm carts and implements. Also of interest is the reconstruction of the old smithy from the Duvenstedt Triftweg, which has been equipped with its original forge, and tools from the former Volksdorf smithy, all in working order.

The sponsor of the museum is De Spieker – Society for the preservation of and research into the villages of the Hamburg region – which has placed the site at the disposal of the City of Hamburg.

Entrance fee

Volkspark F/G7/8

Consciously renouncing the traditional conception of a park, the Parks and Gardens Director of Altona, F. Tutenberg, created in 1914–15 and 1918–20 a Schönheitswald (wood of beauty) from an existing forest in the hilly terminal moraine area of Bahrenfeld. With considerable scope for development areas for games, sport and recreation were created, together with an educational garden, model allotments and a dahlia garden. Also within the 160 ha (395 acres) of the Volkspark are a swimming-pool and a rustic inn; there are beautiful views from the highest points on the east of the park.

Location
in the district of Bahrenfeld, about 7 km (4 miles) NW from the centre of Hamburg HH 52

S-Bahn station
Stellingen (Volkspark-stadion; S 2, S 21)

Buses 111, 180, 188, 190

Volkspark Stadium

The Hamburg Volkspark Stadium was created in 1953 with rubble removed from the former Altona Stadium. With its huge

stands and four floodlighting pylons it is the home ground of the well-known Federal Football League Club Hamburger Sport Verein (HSV) and accommodates some 60,000 spectators.

DESY

Adjoining the Volkspark on the west is the principal cemetery of Altona; not far south-west lies the complex of the Deutscher Elektroner Synchrotron (DESY), with the Doris, Petra and – under construction – Hera reactors; to the south the Bahrenfeld trotting course; to the south-east of the park runs the federal motorway A 7 (E 3; exit HH Volkspark).

*Wallringpark K/L4–6

Location
Funnel between Rentzelstrase, Tiergartenstrasse, Dag-Hammarskjöld Platz, Stephansplatz, Gorch-Fock-Wall, Holstenwall, Millerntordamm, Glacischaussee (Heiligengeistfeld) and Karolinenstrasse

S-Bahn station
Dammtor (S 11, S 21, S 31)

U-Bahn stations
Stephansplatz (U 1)
Messehallen (U 2)
St Pauli (U 3)

Buses
31, 34, 35, 36, 38, 102, 109, 111, 112

For protection against the ravages of the Thirty Years War and to preserve its independence, Hamburg extended and strengthened the defences round the then city centre in the first half of the 17th c. Parts of these defences can still be recognised in the highways called Klosterwall, Steintorwall and Glockengiesserwall. To the west of the Alster the old defence ramparts and moats have been converted into parks and gardens with the titles of Planten un Blomen, Old Botanical Gardens, Kleine Wallanlagen and Grosse Wallanlagen. Although these four green zones are separated from one another by busy streets, they are united as the large Wallringpark leisure complex and connected by a light railway which at several points passes under the streets which divide the various sections.
The Wallringpark, which is broken up by a number of stretches of water (partly the remains of old defence moats), extends in a broad sweep between the huge Hamburg Congress Centre (see entry) near the Dammtor Station (see entry) and the Museum of Hamburg History (see entry) near the Millerntor. South-west of Planten un Blomen and to the north of the Kleine Wallanlagen – on the far side of the law courts in Sievekingplatz – are the Exhibition Grounds (see entry) which reach as far as the Television Tower (see entry).

*Planten un Blomen

Planten un Blomen (Low German for plants and flowers), an ornamental park known far beyond the boundaries of the city, is Hamburg's favourite green open space. It was on this land, between Rentzelstrasse, Tiergartenstrasse, Dammtor, Marseiller Strasse and Jungiusstrasse, that Hamburg's first zoological garden (originally under the direction of the famous zoologist Alfred Brehm) was located between 1863 and 1930. For the Horticultural Exhibition of Lower Germany in 1935 the area was converted into a great garden. International horticultural exhibitions (IGA) took place here in 1953, 1963 and 1973.
Among the attractions of the park, which is accessible from all sides, are many beautiful flower beds and borders, illuminated fountains in the lake which "dance" to music (Wasserlichtorgel; every evening in summer at 10 p.m.), several water-gardens and tropical gardens, as well as various leisure facilities for young and old and several cafés and restaurants. On the northern boundary of Planten un Blomen stands the Hamburg Congress Centre in Dag-Hammarskjöld Platz, with the

◀ *"Planten un Blomen" looking towards the Congress Centre*

Marseiller Strasse running under it in a tunnel; at the northernmost point of the park on the far side of Rentzelstrasse (pedestrian bridge) rises the Television Tower (see entry), and beyond Jungiusstrasse (two footbridges) extend the Exhibition Grounds (see entry) to the south-west.

Old Botanical Garden

Adjoining Planten un Blomen on the south-east lies the Old Botanical Garden with interesting glasshouses (see Botanical Gardens), subtropical terraces, an Alpinum and various specialist gardens around the old town moat, as well as two cafés and a refreshment kiosk.

Kleine Wallanlagen

The Kleine Wallanlagen are situated between Jungiusstrasse, Gorch-Fock-Wall, Karl-Muck-Platz and Sievekingplatz with the great law courts in Holstenglacis.
In this part of the Wallringpark can be found a children's playground, outdoor chess, a garden with marsh plants, atrium gardens (around open courtyards) and Wassertreppen (cascades).

Grosse Wallanlagen

Bordered by Holstenwall, Millerntordamm, Glacischaussee (footbridge to the Heiligengeistfeld – see entry) and Feldstrasse, the Grosse Wallanlagen contain a further series of specialist gardens (including a Japanese garden and a Baroque garden), together with leisure facilities such as a model-boat pond, children's theatre, roller-skating rink (artificial ice-rink in winter), a pottery and wall-paintings, as well as an old people's day centre and a café.
At the northern tip of the Grosse Wallanlagen stand the extensive buildings of the Civil Court; in the north-east corner

"Planten un Blomen"; illuminated fountains and television tower

of the park can be seen the equestrian statue of Kaiser Wilhelm I which was transferred here in 1929 from the Rathausmarkt (see entry); in the extreme south of the park is the Museum of Hamburg History (see entry).

Wilhelmsburg

Location
7–10 km (4–6 miles) S from the centre of Hamburg

S-Bahn station
Wilhelmsburg (S 3, S 31)

The large island of Wilhelmsburg between the North and the South Elbe was the property from 1673 of the Dukes of Lüneburg-Celle; in 1927 it was joined to Harburg (see entry) and in 1937 incorporated in Greater Hamburg. Because of its low-lying situation this area suffered particularly severe damage as well as the greatest number of casualties in the catastrophic floods of 1962.

The western part of Wihelmsburg consists of extensive industrial and residential districts, while the eastern part has remained more rural. The oldest part of the region is called Kirchdorf (village church of 1614). In the Amtshaus in Kirchdorfer Strasse 163 is to be found the Museum of the Wilhelmsburg Island in the Elbe. It deals with the development of culture and rural life with particular emphasis on milk production which was once of major importance in the area (1 May–30 October, Sun. 4–6 p.m. or by arrangement; tel. 754 26 09).

Wilhelmsburg Museum (Milk museum)

*Willkommhöft (Ship greeting installation)

Location
in Wedel (Holstein), about 22 km (14 miles) W from the centre of Hamburg

S-Bahn station
Wedel (S 1)

Bus
189

The ship greeting installation Willkommhöft is housed in the Schulauer Fährhaus (ferry house, now a restaurant) in Schulau, part of the Holstein town of Wedel, on the Lower Elbe. Here between 8 a.m. and sunset all vessels of more than 500 gross registered tons are greeted on arrival or wished "Bon Voyage" on departure. An amplified greeting is given in the language of the country of origin and the appropriate National Anthem is played; in addition a flag signal is hoisted. Visitors are given details of the passing ship, where it has come from or its destination.

Buddelschiff Museum

In the basement of the Schulau Fährhaus is the curious B & B Buddelschiff Museum and a souvenir shop. Every day from 10 a.m. to 6 p.m. (closed Mons. in winter). Visitors can admire more than 150 ships from all over the world in bottles which the craftsman Jochen Binikowski (Buddel-Bini; see Practical Information – Souvenirs) has collected. The smallest is in a bicycle lamp, the largest in a bottle of 25 litres capacity. (Buddel = Low German for bottle.)

Harbour Concerts

The Schulau Fährhaus is also the traditional venue for the harbour radio concerts of the Norddeutscher Rundfunk which normally take place on Sundays in winter from 6 a.m.

Footpath to Blankenese

From the Schulau Fährhaus it is possible to walk eastwards along the Rissen bank and the Falkenstein bank of the river to Blankenese (see entry).

Zoological Garden (Carl Hagenbecks Tierpark)

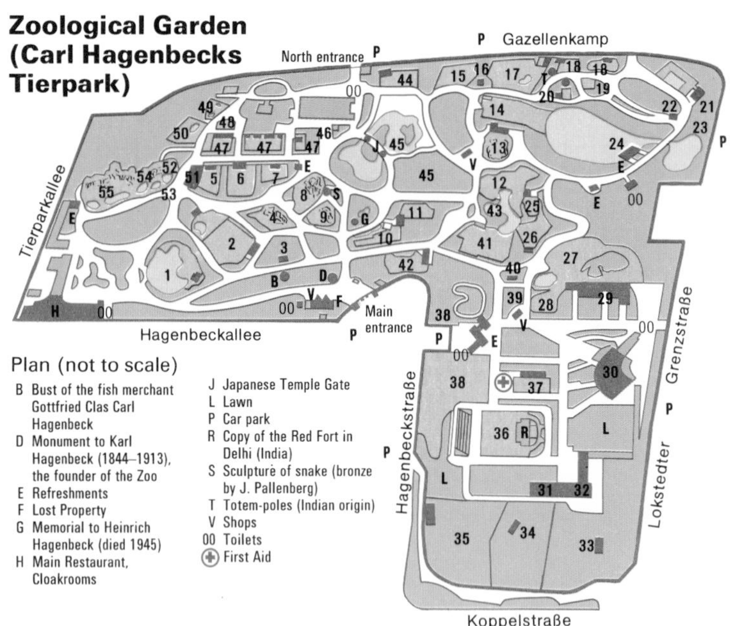

TOUR (2–3 hours): numbers correspond to those on the above plan of the zoo

1 Aquatic birds
2 Animals of the African steppe
3 Pandas
4 Lions
5 Eland antelopes
6 Giraffes
7 Red waterbuck
8 Maned sheep in "the high mountains"
9 Wild Goat Hill (Robinson's goats)
10 Springboks
11 Australian animals
12 Black buck, axis deer
13 Otter house
Monkey Hill (baboon troop)
14 Guanacos (wild llamas)
15 Ostriches of the pampas (nandus)
16 Muntjak (dwarf deer)
17 Bison (Indian buffaloes)
18 Wapiti deer
19 Gluttons
20 Chinese leopards
21 Tiger "Jungle"
22 Porcupines
23 Primeval animals (giant stone sculptures by Pallenberg, 1908/09)
24 Burmese Temple ruin
25 Malay bears
26 Tibetan yaks
27 Indian elephants
28 Rhinoceros (a pair, Pandu and Shita)
29 Elephant and Rhinoceros house
30 Dolphinarium (performances with dolphins, sealions and seals
31 Dromedaries
32 Troparium (fish, snakes, iguanas, turtles, frogs, corals, sea-horses, sea-anemones, humming birds, marmosets, sloths, etc. in 45 terrariums and aquariums); apes (orang-utans and chimpanzees)
33 Shetland ponies, Poitou asses
34 Llamas, Ovambo goats
35 Onagers (Asiatic wild asses)
36 Elephant and camel rides
37 Rhesus monkeys ("monkey saloon")
38 Children's playground, fairytale railway
39 Guinea-pig and rabbit "village"
40 Lynx
41 Zebus (holy cattle of the Hindus); opposite: snowy owls
42 Kodiak bears (open-air enclosure)
43 Asiatic birds (pelicans and other acquatic waterfowl)
44 Asiatic camels (two-humped Bactrian camels)
45 Japanese island garden: flamingo meadow
46 Small monkey house (mandrills)
47 "Parrot alley" (originally bird perches along the lime-fringed walk; at present tapirs, Grevy zebras, Watussi cattle and kudu antelopes)
48 Aviary (for free-flying birds); curlews, ruffs, oyster-catchers, several kinds of ibis
49 Maned wolves
50 Waders (geese, cranes, swans); alpacas
51 Bird house
52 Penguins
53 Walrus (TV star Antje)
54 Reindeer (name from Old Norse hrei'ntier=stag)
55 Polar bears, seals (fur seals, maned seals, sealions)

**Zoological Garden (Hagenbecks Tierpark) H/J8/9

In 1848 the fish merchant Gottfried Clas Carl Hagenbeck put 6 seals on show in a simple washtub in the fish market in St Pauli. They had got into the nets of his fishing smacks from Finkenwerder. The enormous success of this first animal show encouraged G. C. C. Hagenbeck to start a small venture for the sale of animals in addition to his fish business.

Here the people of Hamburg were able to see for the first time exotic animals which Hagenbeck had bought from returning sailors, as well as the first polar bear from Greenland which was brought to him by the captain of a whaler.

Carl Hagenbeck, the fish merchant's eldest son took over the animal business when he was 21. In a very short time he was delivering animals to many zoos at home and abroad and supplying the private collections of emperors, kings, sultans and the Mikado of Japan. He travelled through Africa and America, bought up entire menageries, engaged animal-trappers who explored the farthest corners of the earth for him. For the first time they brought to Hamburg animals which, until then, were unknown even to science, among them the primitive wild horse, the Somali wild ass, Hagenbeck's maral, the sea leopard, the maned wolf and several species of monkey.

Address
Hagenbeckallee
HH 54 (Stellingen)

U-Bahn station
Hagenbecks Tierpark (U 2)

Buses
39, 181, 190, 191, 192

Opening times
Daily 8 a.m.–6 p.m.

Entrance fee

Elephant and Camel rides

Origin

The animal business in the Spielbudenplatz soon became too restricted, and Hagenbeck bought 7060 sq. m (76,000 sq. ft) of land in the Neuer Pferdemarkt 13, where in 1874 he opened Carl Hagenbecks Tierpark. A year later Lapplanders were pitching their tents there. At the instigation of the animal-

Sculptures at the main entrance to Hagenbeck's Zoo

painter, Heinrich Leutermann, Carl Hagenbeck's friend, who conducted his drawing studies every year in the menagerie, the Lapplanders brought their herds of reindeer to Hamburg. They were the forerunners of Hagenbeck's famous ethnological shows of Nubians, Eskimos from Greenland, people from Tierra del Fuego, Patagonia and Ceylon. Subsequently these people exhibited their customs and traditions to enthusiastic spectators and made the name of Hagenbeck known in the countries from whence they came.

Animal Training

Carl Hagenbeck, who detested the cruel methods of animal training of that time, took on the training of beast of prey as well as dealing and exhibiting animals. He recognised that the animals would achieve far more if treated with kindness and understanding. His method of zahme Dressur (quiet training) was at that time a zoological sensation and to some extent anticipated present-day knowledge of animal behaviour and psychology. When in 1887 he opened his circus, Carl Hagenbecks Internationaler Circus und Singhalesen-Karawane, the spectators were delighted with the results of this new quiet training.
In his training school Carl Hagenbeck also carefully studied the distances and heights which beasts of prey could jump. His plan was to create a zoo of the future, a beautiful landscape with lakes, hills and animals in apparent freedom, separated from the public only by invisible ditches. The Imperial Patent Office in Berlin granted him patent No. 91,492 in 1896. Now the only thing lacking was space for this zoo. He found the ideal site in the then Prussian village of Stellingen. After years of hard work potato fields became a landscaped park with artificial rocks, which the Swiss sculptor Urs Eggenschwyler created.

Hagenbeck's Zoo

On 7 May 1907 Carl Hagenbeck opened his new-style zoo in Stellingen. The first ravine without bars for beasts of prey was the greatest sensation for the directors of zoos both in Germany and abroad. Only a ditch separated animals and people. Later emperors, kings, presidents and scientists from all over the world were to pass through the magnificent entrance gate with its two mighty elephant heads, its bronzes of polar bear and lion (modelled by the Düsseldorf sculptor Joseph Pallenberg), with the Indian and Nubian (after models by R. Francke, Berlin), which harked back to the earlier ethnological shows. Carl Hagenbeck was honoured by many scientific societies and presented with decorations by almost every European government. Jean Gilbert composed the song "Gehn'n wir mal zu Hagenbeck" (Let's go to Hagenbeck's) which is still sung and played. Carl Hagenbeck's book "Von Tieren und Menchen" (of beasts and men) became a bestseller in 1909 and was translated into many languages. After his death his sons Heinrich and Lorenz took over the zoo in 1913 and under the most difficult conditions carried it on through the First World War and the subsequent period of inflation. When the Rentenmark was introduced they extended the park as the founder would have wished.

Destruction in Second World War

In 1943 a bombing raid destroyed 80 per cent of the zoo; 9 people and 450 animals lost their lives. Heinrich Hagenbeck died in 1945 and at the end of the war his son, Carl Heinrich, found the zoo in ruins.

Reconstruction

By summoning up all forces Hagebeck's Zoo was rebuilt; to clear the debris, elephants, for example, were employed. When the company celebrated its centenary in 1948 with a great exhibition in the park, the distinguished guests were no longer able to detect any war damage; all the bomb craters had been levelled off. Although the stock was still small, sympathetic zoos sent animals as anniversary gifts. In 1954 Carl Heinrich Hagenbeck went to Persia with the animal-catcher Arnulf Johannes, in order to collect a breeding group of the almost extinct onager in the Persian salt desert. To date 50 foals have been reared from the herd and are maintaining the species in many zoos both in Germany and abroad. The first open-view enclosures for giraffes, antelopes and tigers were built.
Lorenz Hagenbeck, who had made the name known in the whole world by his numerous circus tours, published in 1955 his book "Den Tieren gehört mein Herz" (my heart belongs to the animals). After his death in 1956 his grandson Dietrich joined the company. Like his father Carlo, who had introduced the first rhinoceros from Nepal, Dietrich bought another one from the Khasiranda territory. In August 1963 the first "German" rhinoceros was born in Stellingen and two years later a second one. Today the zoo owns a pair of these rare and valuable animals.

Troparium

With the building of the Troparium in 1960, a successful combination of 45 excellently equipped aquariums and terrariums, reconstruction after the war damage was complete.

In the Dolphinarium dolphins go through their tricks

Dolphinarium

In 1971 Hagenbeck delighted his visitors by opening the new dolphinarium (13 m (43 ft) high; holding 1200 spectators) and putting on a brilliant sealion and dolphin show.
After the death of Carl-Heinrich Hagenbeck, his son, Dr Carl Claus Hagenbeck, who had been a veterinary surgeon in the zoo since 1970, joined the firm in 1977. Since the death of Dietrich Hagenbeck in 1982 Dr Hagenbeck has, together with Dietrich's daughter Caroline, run the zoological garden which has been privately owned since its foundation.
Today the zoo is a magnificent park (25 ha (62 acres)), a happy mixture of landscape-gardening and well-stocked menagerie (about 2500 animals of 365 species) from 5 continents. For children there is a large playground with the most modern apparatus. Several magnificently caprisoned elephants give rides. The visitors' inner needs are catered for by a restaurant and a number of refreshment kiosks.

Practical Information

Access

Hamburg has excellent connections with the USA and Canada by air and with the United Kingdom by air, sea and rail.

Air

Services are operated to the principal airports in the United Kingdom, USA and Canada.

Sea

Hamburg is directly linked to Great Britain by a DFDS car ferry from Harwich every two days, the journey taking about 20 hours. The terminal is Landungsbrücken 9 and 10, situated a few minutes from the city centre.

Rail

There are daily through trains to Hamburg from Ostend and the Hook of Holland.

Road

By road from Ostend it is approximately 690 km (430 miles) and from the Hook of Holland 550 km (340 miles).

For further details see Transport (p. 12).

Airlines

Regional Services

Aeroflot, HH 1, Alstertor 18, tel. 33 59 72
Air France, HH 1, Alstertor 21, tel. 3 28 77
Alitalia, H 36, Gänsemarkt 21–23, tel. 34 15 47
Austrian Airlines, HH 1, Alstertor 18, tel. 32 75 78
British Airways, HH 1, Ballindamm 17, tel. 3 33 91
Deutsche Lufthansa, HH 36, Dammtorstrasse 14, tel. 3 59 55
Finnair, HH 36, Esplanade 41, tel. 34 20 56
K.L.M., HH 36, Neuer Jungfernstieg 6a, tel. 34 15 01
PanAm, HH 63, Flughafen, tel. 5 00 92 81
Sabena, HH 1, Schauenburger Strasse 6, tel. 32 18 19
SAS, HH 1, Spitalerstrasse 16, tel. 3 09 80
Swissair, HH 1, Brandsende 4, tel. 3 28 95

Connections with Heligoland and Sylt

Holiday Express (DLG)
HH 63, Flughafen
tel. 5 08 29 00

Helicopter trips

Helicopter Service Wasserthal
HH 65, Katnerweg 43
tel. 6 40 10 81

Airport
Location

Hamburg International Airport (see A to Z – Airport), is situated in the suburb of Fuhlsbüttel, about 10 km (6 miles) north of the city centre.

Arrival and Departure

Departures of passengers on regular flights are dealt with on the ground floor of the terminal and arrivals on the lower floor. The terminal for charter traffic is entirely separate.

Hamburg Airport
(Fuhlsbüttel)

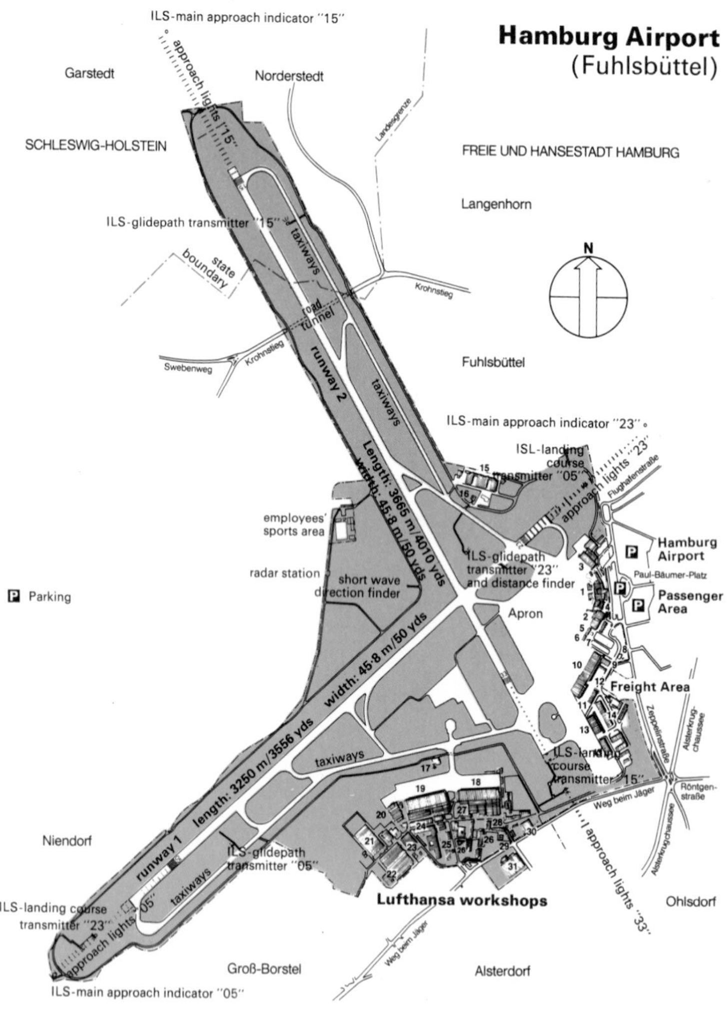

AIRPORT
1 International terminal and Berlin/departure
2 Inland terminal and Berlin/arrival
3 Charter terminal
4 Airport administration
5 Fire brigade
6 Fuel depot
7 Tanker area
8 Radar tower and control building ASR
9 Airmail office
10 Air freight shed
11 Freight forwarding building
12 Freight yard
13 Hangers
14 Workshops
15 Vehicle shed
16 Weather station
17 Air traffic control and tower

LUFTHANSA WORKS
18 Hangers 1 & 2, workshops
19 Hangers 3 & 4, workshops
20 Noise suppression shed
21 Central workshop
22 Engine workshop
23 Electroplating plant
24 Materials buildings
25 ERI workshop (electric/radio instruments)
26 Office building/administration
27 Paint shop
28 Technical school
29 Medical centre
30 Crew building
31 MBB airbus-industry

Shuttle Service

From the city centre the S-Bahn (S 1, S 2) and the U-Bahn (U 1) provide a connection to the airport (as far as Ohlsdorf Station and then by Airport Express bus route 110).

Car Hire

The offices of the large car hire firms (See Car Hire) can be found in a new service centre directly opposite the passenger building (Paul-Bäumer-Platz).

Antique Dealers

Antique Dealers (selection)

Antiquitäten am Dammtor, HH 36, Dammtorstrasse 29
Furniture, Pictures

Beiersdorf HH 36, Poststrasse 22
Jewellery, etc.

Ernst Blass, HH 36, Hohe Bleichen 26
Weapons, Militaria

Birgitt Blume, HH 36, ABC Strasse 51
Porcelain, Glass

Brinkama Kunst & Antiquitäten, HH 36, Hohe Bleichen 23
Art, Furniture, Porcelain, etc.

Bristol Antiques, HH 36, Glosse Bleichen 31
Furniture, Glass, Pictures

Kunsthaus City, HH 36, Gerhofstrasse 2
Furniture, Porcelain, etc.

F. Dörling, HH 36, Neuer Wall 41–42
Books. Drawings

Nicholas Fowler, HH 36, Grosse Bleichen 36
Glass, Porcelain, Silver, Objèts d'Art

Konstantin Greiff, HH 36, Poststrasse 29
Furniture, etc.

Berhard ter Hazeborg, HH 36, Milchstrasse 11
Furniture, Pictures

Jean Hermsen, HH 36, Poststrasse 36
Coins, Medals, etc.

Antiquitäten Hohe Bleichen, HH 36, Hohe Bleichen 25
Silver, Jewellery, Clocks

F. K. A. Huelsmann, HH 36, Hohe Bleichen 15
Silver, Baroque Furniture, etc.

Felix Roman Jagielski, HH 36, Poststrasse 37–39
Africa, Far East, Pacific

Korte Kunst & Antiquitäten, HH 36, Poststrasse 51
Porcelain, Silver, Furniture, Pictures

Kühl & Blume, HH 36, Poststrasse 22
Pictures, Porcelain, etc.

Kunst & Antiquitäten am Ballindamm, HH 1, Ballindamm 25
Furniture, Silver, Clocks

Karl Modschiedler, HH 36, ABC Strasse 7
Silver, Porcelain, Objèts d'Art, Furniture

Urs S. Niederoest, HH 36, Hohe Bleichen 22
Furniture, Porcelain, Silver, Objèts d'Art

Petit Musée, HH 36, Neue ABC Strasse 1
East Asian Art

K. u. M. Reitz, HH 36, ABC Strasse 50
Clocks

Joachim Römer, HH 36, Grosse Bleichen 36
Hanse-Viertel-Galerie
Furniture, Lamps, etc.

Ludwig Rose, HH 36, ABC Strasse 10
Porcelain, Glass, Silver

Rügge im Hansa-Viertel, HH 36, Grosse Bleichen 36
Jewellery, Arts and Crafts

Dr Schmoller, HH 50, Bahrmfelder Chaussee 66
Clocks

Steen, HH 36, Hohe Bleichen 24
Furniture

von der Wense, HH 11, Grosse Johannisstrasse 3
Furniture, Porcelain, Silver

Antique Centre

The Antique Centre in the Markthalle (HH 1, Klosterwall) contains about 25 various antique shops.

Galleries

See entry

Archives

See Libraries and Archives

Banks

Opening Hours

Mon.–Fri. 9 a.m.–1 p.m. and 2.30–4 p.m., Thur. until 6 p.m.

Late and Sunday Service

Bureau de Change at the Main Station, daily 7.30 a.m.–10 p.m.
Bureau de Change at Altona Station, daily 7.30 a.m.–10 p.m.
Bank at the Airport, daily 6.30 a.m.–11 p.m.

Breakdowns

Information

ADAC, HH 1, Amsinckstrasse 39, tel. 2 89 91
ACE, HH 1, Besenbinderhof 57, tel. 2 80 21 64

Breakdown Service

ADAC-Pannendienst, tel. 1 92 11
ACE-Pannendienst, tel. 2 00 29 30
Falcks Rettungsdienst GmbH, tel. 5 40 20 11

Box Offices (Advance Booking Offices

Theaterkasse Alster, HH 76, Hofweg 33, tel. 22 17 97
Theaterkasse Altona, HH 50, Neue Grosse Bergstrasse, Pavillon 5a, tel. 38 62 64
Theaterkasse im HamburgTip, HH 1, Glaspavillon, Gerhart-Hauptmann-Platz, tel. 32 43 12
Theaterkasse Central, HH 1, Lilienstrasse 24, tel. 33 71 24 and 33 52 84
CCH-Theaterkasse, HH 36, Jungiusstrasse 13, tel. 34 20 25
Kurt Collien, HH 20, Eppendorfer Baum 25, tel. 48 33 90
Konzertkasse Gerdes, HH 80, Rothenbaumchaussee 77, tel. 45 33 26 and 44 02 98
E. Schumacher, HH 36, Colonnaden 37, tel. 34 30 44
O. Wichers, HH 1, Adenauerallee 2, tel. 2 80 28 48

Calendar of Events

January/February

North German Art Weeks

March/April

Spring Far (Folk Festival)

May

German International Tennis Championship
Port Birthday (Overseas Day, Folk Festival; about 7 May)
Horse Trials ("Derby") – Jumping, Dressage and Cross-country

June/July

Horse-racing ("Derby Week")
Hamburg Ballet Festival

June/September

Summer in Hamburg (Theatre, Music, Sport, etc.)

July/August

Hummelfest (Folk Festival)

September

Alstervergnügen (Events on the Alster)

November/December

Hamburg Fair (Folk Festival)

Fairs

See entry

Information

Fremdenverkehrszentrale Hamburg (see Information)

Camping

Camping Anders
HH-Eidelstedt, Kieler Strasse 650, tel. 5 70 44 98
Open: all year

City Camp
HH-Eidelstedt, Kieler Strasse 620, tel. 5 70 51 21
Open: all year

Camping Schuldt
HH-Stellingen, Kronsaalweg, tel. 5 40 49 94
Open: all year

Campingplatz Buchholz
HH-Stellingen, Kieler Strasse 374, tel. 5 40 45 32
Open: all year

Car Hire

Avis

HH 36, Drehbahn 15–25, tel. 34 16 51
HH 62, Flughafen Fuhlsbüttel, tel. 50 83 14

Europ Car

HH 1, Spaldingstrasse 77–79, tel. 24 44 55
HH 62, Flughafen Fuhlsbüttel, tel. 5 08 28 09

Hertz

HH 1, Amsinckstrasse 45, tel. 23 00 45
HH 62, Flughafen Fuhlsbüttel, tel. 5 08 23 02

InterRent

HH 1, Amsinckstrasse 58, tel. 23 03 21
HH 11, Rödingsmarkt 14, tel. 36 22 21
HH 50, Holstenstrasse 156, tel. 38 97 07
HH 60, Überseering 3, tel. 6 30 60 06
HH 63, Flughafen Fuhlsbüttel, tel. 5 08 28 12
HH 70, Ahrensburger Strasse 138, tel 66 99 51

Casinos

Spielbank Hamburg (Roulette, Baccarat, Black Jack)
HH 36, Fontenay 10

Automatenspielbank Hamburg (also Roulette)
HH 1, Steindamm 1

Spielbank Hittfeld (Roulette, Baccarat, Black Jack, etc.)
Not far south of the city boundary
D-2105 Seevetal 1, Kirchstrasse 15

Chemists

Emergency Service

In emergency the addresses of chemists open after normal hours can be obtained from any police station or by telephoning the emergency medical service (see Emergency Services).

International Chemists

Internationale Apotheke
HH 1, Ballindamm 39

Roth's Old English Chemist
HH 36, Jungfernstieg 48

Church Services

Information (in English if requested) about the times of church services can be obtained from the following:

Amt fur Öffentlichkeitsdienst der Evangelischen Kirche, HH 13, Feldbrunnenstrasse 29, tel. 45 58 68/69. — Protestant

Katholische Informationsstelle Hamburg, HH 1, Danziger Strasse 52, tel. 24 87 72 24 — Roman Catholic

Judische Gemeinde, HH 6, Schäferkampsallee 29, tel. 44 09 44. — Jewish Faith

St Thomas à Becket, Zeughausmarkt. — Anglican Church

See Music — Church Concerts

Cinemas

Within the city area there are a great number of cinemas; programmes, etc. will be found in the daily papers.

Abaton, HH 13, Allende Platz 3
Alabama, HH 54, Kieler Strasse 622
Arsenal, HH 60, Steilshooper Strasse 317
Blankeneser Kino, HH 55, Blankeneser Bahnhofstrasse 4
Elbe Theatre, HH 52, Osdorfer Landstrasse 198
Kurbel, HH 90 (Harburg), Neue Strasse 13
Magazin, HH 60, Fiefstücken 8a
Metropolis, HH 36, Dammtorstrasse 36
Palette, in Norderstedt, Ohechaussee 11
Thalia, HH 13, Grindelallee 116
Vorführung 6 (Studio Hbg), HH 70, Tonndorfer Hauptstrasse 90

Original Language Films

Amerika-Haus, HH 13, Tesdorpfstrasse 1
Abaton, HH 13, Allende Platz 3
Broadway, HH 36, Gérhofstrasse 1

Autokino

in Billbrook, Moorfleeter Strasse

Communication Centres

Fabrik
HH 50, Barnerstrasse 36
tel. 39 15 63
Music, Literature, Theatre, Films, Youth work

Markthalle am Deichtor
HH 1, Klosterwall 9–21
tel. 33 94 91
Music, Literature, Discussions

Hamburg-Haus Eimsbüttel
HH 19, Doormannsweg 12
tel. 41 12-771
Music, Lectures, Discussions

Lichtwark-Haus
HH 80, Holzhude 1
tel. 72 52-25 10
Exhibitions, Courses, Lectures

Die Brücke
HH 90, Wallgraben 42
tel. 77 42 90
Contact centre and meeting-place

Libresso
HH 13, Binderstrasse 24
tel. 45 16 63
Art, Literature

Consulates

Great Britain: Harvesterhuder Weg 8a, tel. 44 60 71
United States of America: Alsteruferstrasse 27, tel. 44 10 61

Cuisine

Hamburg has always laid great stress on good food; being commericially open to the world, its cuisine was soon influenced by that of other countries. For example, the typical mixed dishes of fish and meat, and of salt, sweet and sour ingredients, which sometimes seem strange, was probably introduced from Nordic countries. In Hamburg the preference is for nourishing, unpretentious and, whenever possible, unprocessed food.

In recent years Hamburg has developed into quite a place of pilgrimage for gourmets. Many internationally renowned chefs serve their culinary creations, and there are very many foreign restaurants. Fish and other seafood feature on every menu, as do oysters, lobster and caviar.

Typical dishes

Hamburg eel soup (originally "sour soup" – the eel was added later): A soup is prepared from a meaty ham bone, smoked meat, carrots (called *roots* in Hamburg dialect), celery, leeks, peas, dried fruit (pears, apple-rings and plums) and other ingredients, the brew being well seasoned with all kinds of herbs and spices, vinegar, white wine, sugar, salt and pepper. Finally pieces of eel are added and lightly cooked.

Fish

Sea fish and freshwater fish: Most Hamburg restaurants serve fish dishes. The visitor should try plaice à la Finkenwerder (especially good in the district after which it is named) – the fish is fried and pieces of bacon added. It is usually accompanied by potato salad.

Pears, Beans and Bacon

Green beans, small whole pears (e.g. bergamots – broken up but not peeled) and pieces of streaky bacon are well cooked together.

Labskaus

The dish labskaus came originally from Norway, the name finding its way into sailors' language via English: It is a seaman's dish, made from pickled meat (preferably pickled breast of beef), fish (herring or cod), mashed potatoes, baked onions and cucumber. The additions are cooked together, sometimes even minced. Usually a fried egg and beetroot are served with the dish, sometimes gherkins as well. Labskaus is now also obtainable in tins.

Matjeshering

(Matjes means young herrings): The dish consists of herring fillets accompanied by a wide assortment of garnishings, from tiny pieces of bacon to semi-sweet cranberries. There are a number of restaurants specialising in this very popular dish.

Rundstück Warm:

Rundstück means a bread roll. This snack consists of two halves of a roll enclosing a slice of roast meat, the whole covered in brown sauce.

Bauernfrühstück

"Farmer's breakfast": Potatoes are fried in lard and a generous helping of cubes of bacon or ham and egg is added.

Rote Grütze

In Low German this is called Rode Grütt. Genuine Rote Grütze (red groats)is prepared from the juice of raspberries and red currants (no other juice and no whole fruit!). The juice is sweetened and stirred into semolina, sago or cornmeal and heated until it thickens. It is then poured into moulds or shallow dishes, cooled and then turned out. Rote Grütze is served with milk or cream, sometimes with custard (although this is less correct).

Fliederbeersuppe

This dish, made from elderberries, is well known and popular with Hamburg people, but is seldom obtainable in restaurants.

Drinks: Beer

Beer is the principal drink; it is bitter and strong. There are several breweries in Hamburg. A popular drink is Lütt un Lütt, a combination of a glass of lager followed by a small glass of Korn (corn brandy) which in Hamburg is known as Köm or Klarer.

Wine

At one time wine was not a very common drink, apart from vintage red wines (especially French but also port and madeira – called Rotspon) laid down in cellars. Nowadays there are many wine bars with a wide selection from very many countries; there are also many wine-dealers. Wine in Hamburg is "in".

Alsterwasser

Alsterwasser (not to be thought of literally as "water from the Alster"!) is a refreshing shandy of equal parts of lager and lemonade (Brause).

Grog

Grog is the classical way of warming oneself up in cold or wet weather. Rum (or arrak) is mixed with hot water and sugar added to taste. According to a local saying: "Rum is essential, sugar may be added, but not water!" A "stiff" grog contains a liberal quantity of rum. A speciality is Eiergrog, made with egg yolks.

Koks

Koks, not to be confused with the slang expression for cocaine, is a rarity today. It consists of a lump of sugar soaked in rum and coated with coarsely ground coffee beans.

Cultural Institutions

Amerika-Haus,
HH 13, Tesdorpfstrasse 1, tel. 44 10 61

British Council,
HH 36, Neuer Wall 86, tel. 36 28 56

Institut Français,
HH 13, Heimhuder Strasse 55, tel. 45 22 79 and 45 56 60

Instituto Italiano di Cultura
HH 13, Hansastrasse 6, tel. 44 04 41

Patriotische Gesellschaft von 1765
HH 11, Trostbrücke 4, tel. 36 66 19
(see A to Z – Patriotic Society)

Disabled Assistance

Information

Club 68, an association for the disabled and their friends (HH 70, Elsässer Strasse 27a), publishes the "Hamburg Führer for Behinderte", which includes information about accessibility for disabled people at places of interest, sports venues, shopping centres, municipal offices, etc., as well as provision for invalid chairs at restaurants, hotels, multi-storey car parks, etc. In addition, addresses of relevant organisations are given, where help may be obtained.

Taxis for the Handicapped

tel. 4 10 54 58

Emergency Services

Police	tel. 1 10
Fire Brigade, Emergency Doctor	tel. 1 12
Emergency Legal Service	tel. 5 11 88 48
Emergency Medical Service	tel. 22 80 22
Emergency Dental Service	tel. 1 15 00
Flood Warning	tel. 1 15 30
ZAB Zentral Ambulanz fur Betrunkene (Ambulance for drunks) HH 6, Karolinenstrasse 46	tel. 44 19 53 74

Fairs

The principal facilities for fairs and congresses in Hamburg are to be found at the Congress Centre (CCH, see entry in A to Z section), not far from Dammtor Station, and at the Messegelände (see entry in A to Z section), which adjoins Planten un Blomen on the south-west.

January, April, December

Hamburg Art and Antiques Fair

January and July/August

Hamburg "Einkaufstage" (Trade fair)

February

Travel and Leisure

March

InternorGa (Special exhibition of gastronomy)

September

"You and Your World" (exhibition for consumers) – shipping, machines, marine technology – (every other year)

EMTEC Trade Days (specialist fair for the boating industry)
German International Boat Show
"Nordbüro" (office equipment, etc.; every other year)

October

NORDPOSTA (philately)
International Caravan Exhibition

November

Information about the current programme of fairs and congresses can be obtained from the Hamburger Messe und Congress GmbH (HMC) HH 36, Jungiusstrasse 13, tel. 3 56 91.

Information

Ferry

See Access

Galleries

Of the approximately 100 galleries and art-dealers of Hamburg which are concerned with traditional, contemporary and avant-garde art, the following should be mentioned.

Selection

art & book Galerie, HH 13, Grindelallee 132
Books, graphic art, etc.

atelier mensch, HH 11, Krayenkamp 10

Louis Bock & Sohn, HH 36, Grosse Bleichen 34
Paintings

Böhrs Kunsthandlung, HH 36, Colonnaden 30
Paintings, etchings, Hamburg art

Elke Dröscher, HH 50, Elbchaussee 140

Galerie Altana, HH 13, Mittelweg 19
Contemporary paintings and sculpture

Galerie Azadi, HH 35, Theaterstrasse 1
Oriental carpets and textiles

Galerie Brockstedt, HH 13, Magdalenestrasse 11
Contemporary graphic art

Galerie Commeter, HH 1, Hermannstrasse 37
Paintings, etchings, Hamburg art

Galerie Crone, HH 13, Isestrasse 121

Galerie für Kunst aus Südostasien, HH 55 (Blankenese), Frenssenstrasse 90

Galerie Hauptmann, HH 36, Colonnaden 96

Galerie Hochhuth, HH 36, Alte Post (Poststrasse 11 to Grosse Bleichen 17)
Art Nouveau, contemporary art

Galerie in der Koppel, HH 1, Koppel 66
Paintings

Galerie in Eppendorf, HH 20, Lehmweg 46

Galerie Kammer, HH 13, Bohmersweg 9
Contemporary graphic art

Galerie 1, HH 50, Elbchaussee 31

Galerie Levy, HH 13, Bohmersweg 24
Paintings, graphic art, sculpture

Galerie Lochte, HH 13, Mittelweg 164
Contemporary paintings and graphic art

Galerie Munro, HH 20, Heilwigstrasse 64
Contemporary art

Galerie Pion, HH 54, Beim Amsinckpark 18

Galerie pro arte, HH 55, Rutsch 2

Galerie Riemenschneider, HH 13, Mittelweg 44
Paintings, graphic art, sculpture, Hamburg art

Galerie Schnecke, HH 13, Turm auf der Moorweide
Contemporary art

Galerie von Loeper, HH 13, Mittelweg 152
Paintings, graphic art

Galerie XX, Uecker & Haase, HH 13, Magdalenestrasse 54

Gemälde Zeiner, HH 36, Neue ABC-Strasse 12c
Paintings, etchings, Hamburg art

Golombek-Kunsthaus, HH 36, Dammtorstrasse 21
Paintings

Hamburger Kunstschule Bouzoubaâ, HH 1, Spitalerstrasse 32
Paintings, drawings, artistic photographs

Hamburg-Galerie, HH 36, Poststrasse 11,
Paintings, Hamburg art

Hans Hoeppner, HH 13, Rothenbaumchaussee 103

Kunsthandlung Klose, HH 1, Steinstrasse 13
Modern and contemporary paintings

Licht-Galerie Fielmann, HH 1, Mönckebergstrasse 19
Holographs

Master's Galerie, HH 36, Grosse Bleichen 21
19th c. paintings

Poster-Galerie, HH 36, Grosse Bleichen 31
Original posters and reproductions

Svanshall, HH 60, Leinpfad 101
Paintings, drawings, books

Photographic Galleries

Fotogalerie der Staatwesen Landesbildstelle Hamburg, HH 54, Kieler Strasse 171

Olympus-Galerie, HH 36, Grosse Bleichen 31

Fotogalerie "The Compagnie", HH 20, Lehmweg 29

PPS-Galerie, F. C. Gundlach, HH 6, Feldstrasse, Hochhaus 1

Antiques

See entry

Hostesses

Guides (Hostesses)

Well-trained young ladies are provided by the Hamburger Hostessen Service (HH 65, Wellingbuttler Weg 88, telephone 5 36 60 16) as guides for groups and interpreters for fairs, congresses, etc. Guides are also provided by the Fremdenverkehrszentrale Hamburg (see Information).

Hotels

Selection

Alster-Hof, HH 36, Esplanade 12, 170 b.
Alsterkrug Hotel, HH 60, Alsterkrugchaussee 277, 160 b.
Alte Wache, HH 1, Adenauerallee 21–27, 76 b.
Ambassador, HH 1, Heidenkampsweg 34, 200 b.
*Atlantic, HH 1, An der Alster 72–79, 449 b.
Baseler Hospiz, HH 36, Esplanade 11, 203 b.
Berlin, HH 26, Borgfelder Strasse 1, 124 b.
Carat, HH 28, Sieldeich 9–11, 160 b.
City Inter Hotel, HH 74, Halskestrasse 72, 300 b.
Crest Hotel Hamburg, HH 60, Mexikoring 1, 231 b.
Eggers, HH 73, Rahlstedter Strasse 78, 136 b.
Elysée, HH 13, Rothenbaumchaussee 10, 602 b.
Europäischer Hof, HH 1, Kirchenallee 45, 620 b.
Falck, HH 54, Kieler Strasse 333, 222 b.
Fürst Bismarck, HH 1, Kirchenallee 49, 91 b.
Garden Hotels Pöseldorf, HH 13, Magdalenenstrasse 60, 120 b.
Graf Moltke, HH 1, Steindamm 1, 180 b.
Hafen Hamburg, HH 11, Seewartenstrasse 9, 250 b.
Hamburg International, HH 26, Hammer Landstrasse 200, 160 b.
*Hamburg Plaza, HH 36, Marseiller Strasse 2, 785 b.
Hanseatic, HH 60, Sierichstrasse, 150, 10 b.
Ibis, HH 70, Wandsbeker Zollstrasse 25–29, 173 b.
*Inter-Continental, HH 36, Fontenay 10, 503 b.
Kronprinz, HH 1, Kirchenallee 46, 111 b.
Norge, HH 6, Schäferkampsallee 49, 169 b.
Novotel Hamburg Nord, HH 61, Oldesloer Strasse 166, 372 b.
Oper, HH 36, Drehbahn 15, 165 b.
Prem, HH 1, An der Alster 9, 74 b.
*Ramada Renaissance, HH 36, Grosse Bleichen, 332 b.
Reichshof, HH 1, Kirchenallee 34–36, 455 b.
St Raphael, HH 1, Adenauerallee 41, 170 b.
Smolka, HH 13, Isestrasse 98, 65 b.
Stadt Altona, HH 50, Louise-Schröder-Strasse 29, 190 b.
Strandhotel Blankenese, HH 55, Strandweg 13, 22 b.
*Vier Jahreszeiten, HH 36, Neuer Jungfernsteig 6–14, 252 b.
Vorbach, HH 13, Johnsallee 63–67, 150 b.

Hotel Reservations — See Information

Information

Tourist Information

Fremdenverkehrszentrale Hamburg e.V.
(with congress and conference bureau)
HH 1, Bieberhaus am Hauptbahnhof
tel. 24 87 00
Mon.–Fri. 7.30 a.m.–6 p.m.

Hamburg Information

Hamburg-Information in der City
(Information about Hamburg)
HH 1, Gerhart-Hauptmann-Platz (Pavilion)
tel. 32 47 58
Mon.–Fri. 9 a.m.–6 p.m., Sat. 9 a.m.–2 p.m.

Hamburg-Information am Flughafen
(Airport Information)
Arrivals Building D
HH 63, Flughafen Hamburg
tel. 5 08 24 57
daily 8 a.m.–11 p.m.

Hamburg-Information am Hafen
(Information about the Port)
HH 4, at St Pauli Landungsbrücken 3
tel. 31 39 77
daily 9 a.m.–6 p.m.

Hamburg-Information GmbH
HH 36, Neuer Jungfernstieg 5
tel. 35 00 10–0
Mon.–Fri. 9 a.m.–5 p.m.

Hotel Reservations

Main Station (concourse)
tel. 2 48 70–230, daily 7 a.m.–10 p.m.
Fuhlsbüttel Airport (Arrivals Building D)
tel. 2 48 70–240, daily 8 a.m.–11 p.m.

Alster Boats

ATG Alster-Touristik GmbH
HH 36, Anleger Jungfernstieg, tel. 34 11 41

Harbour Boats

HADAG Seetouristik GmbH
HH 11, Johannisbollwerk 6–8, tel. 3 19 61

Information about Fairs

See Fairs

Hamburg Transport Authority

See Public Transport

Libraries and Archives

Selection

Bibliothek der Bundesforschungsanstalt für Fischerei
(Federal Research Institution of Fishing)
HH 50, Palmaille 9

Bibliothek der Geographischen Gessellschaft in Hamburg
(Geographical Society)
HH 13, Rothenbaumchaussee 21–23

Bibliothek des Deutschen Hydrographischen Instituts
(German Hydrographical Institute)
HH 4, Bernhard-Nocht-Strasse 78

Bibliothek des Deutschen Instituts für Afrika-Forschung
(German Institute of African Research)
HH 1, Klosterwall 4

Bibliothek des Europa-Kollegs Hamburg
(Hamburg European College)
HH 52, Windmühlenweg 27

Bibliothek des Instituts für Asienkunde
(Institute of Asian Affairs)
HH 13, Rothenbaumchaussee 32

Bibliothek des Instituts für Iberoamerika-Kunde
(Institute of Spanish-American Affairs)
HH 36, Alsterglacis 7

Bibliothek des Unesco-Instituts für Pädagogik
(Unesco Institute of Education)
HH 13, Feldbrunenstrasse 70

Bibliothek und Archiv des Deutschen Orient-Instituts
(German Oriental Institute)
HH 13, Mittelweg 150

Bibliothek und Archiv des Instituts für Wirtschafts-forschung – Hamburg (HWWA) (Institute of Economic Research)
HH 36, Neuer Jungfernstieg 21

Bibliothek für Sozialgeschichte und Arbeiterbewegung
(Research Centre of History of National Socialism at the University of Hamburg)
HH 13, Rentzelstrasse 7

Commerzbibliothek der Handelskammer Hamburg (founded 1735) (Chamber of Trade)
HH 11, Adolphsplatz 1

Deutsches Übersee-Institut (German Overseas Institute)
HH 36, Neuer Jungfernstieg 21

English Library
HH 13, Moorweidenstrasse 40

Hamburger Öffentliche Bücherhallen
HH 36, Grosse Bleichen 13, Kaiser-Galerie
(Central Book and Music Lending Library) over 50 libraries in the city

Norddeutsche Blindenhörbücherei e.V.
(Central Library for the Blind)
HH 76, Adolfstrasse 44–46

Nordelbische Kirchenbibliothek (Church Library of the North Elbe)
HH 13, Grindelallee 7

Staatsarchiv der Freien und Hansestadt Hamburg (State Archives)
HH 36, ABC-Strasse 19

Staats und Universitätsbibliothek Carl von Ossietzky
HH 13, Moorweidenstrasse 40

Theatersammlung der Universitat Hamburg
(University theatrical collection)
HH 13, Rothenbaumchaussee 162

Universitätsbibliothek der TU Hamburg-Harburg
(Technical University Library)
HH 90, Wallgraben 55a

Lost Property Offices

Municipal
HH 36, Bäckerbreitergang 73, tel. 35 18 51

Railway
HH 50, Stresemannstrasse 114, tel. 39 18 1

Post Office
HH 1, Hühnerposten 12 (Post Office), tel. 23 95-1

Markets

Fishmarket

The Fish Market (see A to Z – Fish Market) in St Pauli, is the best-known market in Hamburg and beyond. Every Sunday from 5 a.m. (in winter 7 a.m.) until 9.30 a.m. there is lively and colourful activity on the bank of the Elbe. Even if the sale of fresh fish and fish products still plays a predominant role, the articles on sale now include almost everything under the sun. The area of the market, most of which has recently been newly laid out, is also the venue for the Hamburg Flohdom ("flea-market") and the winter fleamarket.

Weekly Markets

In every district of Hamburg markets are held at least twice a week, altogether more than 40. The undermentioned are a selection:

Markthalle am Deichtor (Tues.–Sat.)
Isemarkt (Isestrasse, Harvestehude; Tues., Fri.)
Grossneumarkt (Wed., Sat.)
Hopfenmarkt (Tues., Thurs.)
Fischmarkt (Sun.)
Offensen (Spritzenplatz/Am Pflug; Tues., Fri.)
Altona (coin market; Wed., Sat.)
Gross-Flotbek (Osdorfer Landstrasse; Wed., Sat.)
Blankenese (Blankeneser Bahnhofstrasse; Tues., Fri., Sat.)
Rotherbaum (Turmweg; Thurs.)
Barmbek-Uhlenhorst (Immenhof; Tues., Fri.)
Bergedorf (Chrysanderstrasse; Tues., Fri.)
Harburg (Sand; Mon., Sat.)

Fleamarkets

Fleamarkets take place in Hamburg several times a year in the following places: at the Fish Market, on Turmweg, in the fair buildings and the wholesale flower market and the Heiligengeistfeld. The times (generally on Sundays) are announced in advance by advertisements and in the daily papers.

Memorials

School am Bullenhuser Damm

In the school on the Bullenhuser Damm (now the Janusz-Korczak-Schule; HH 28, Bullenhuser Damm 92) 20 Jewish children and 28 adult prisoners from the Neuengamme concentration camp were hanged by SS troops in April 1945. The memorial and documents concerning the fate of those murdered can be seen in the cellar of the school.

Former Concentration Camp Fuhlsbüttel

Part of the Fuhlsbüttel prison was used from 1933 as a concentration camp and in 1934 was put under the control of the Gestapo. In 1943 a branch of the Neuengamme concentration camp was set up here.

Former Concentration Camp Neuengamme

See A to Z – Vierlande and Marschlande

Seafarers' Memorial

In 1985 in Hafenstrasse near St Pauli Fish Market a memorial, with a bronze sculpture by Manfred Sihle-Wissel was dedicated to the German merchant seamen who have lost their lives on the oceans of the world.

Museums

Museums described in the A–Z Section

Alster Valley Museum
see Alster Valley

Altona Museum in Hamburg
see entry

Bischofsburg
see entry

Bismarck Museum
see Bismarck Mausoleum and Museum

Buddelschiff Museum
see Wilkommhoft

Ernst-Barlach-Haus
see Jenischpark

Institute of Applied Botany of the University of Hamburg
see Botanical Gardens

Jenisch-Haus
see Jenischpark

Johannes Brahms Commemorative Rooms
see Peterstrasse

Kiekeberg Open Air Museum
see entry

Krameramtswohnungen
see entry

Kunsthalle
see entry

Kunsthaus
see Kunsthalle

Kunstverein
see Kunsthalle

Museum of Art and Industry
see entry

Museum of Bergedorf and the Vierlande
see Bergedorf

Museum of Ethnology
see entry

Museum of Hamburg History
see entry

Museum of Pre- and Early History
see Helms Museum

Neuengamme Concentration Camp Museum
see Vierlande and Marschlande

North German Provincial Museum
see Altona Museum in Hamburg

Oevelgönne Museum Harbour
see Oevelgönne

Oevelgönne Seekiste
see Oevelgönne

Planetarium
see entry

Rade Museum am Schloss Reinbek
see entry

Vierlande Open-air Museum Rieck Haus
see Vierlande and Marschlande

Volksdorf Museum Village
see entry

Wilhelmsburg Museum (Milk Museum)
see Wilhelmsburg

Wine Museum C. C. H. Fischer
see Nikolai Church Tower

Other Museums

Automuseum Hillers
HH 1, Kurt Schumacher-Allee 42
tel. 24 65 77
daily 10 a.m.–5 p.m. (entrance fee)
Cars and motor cycles from 1895 to 1954

electrum (Museum of Electricity)
HH 76, Klinikweg 23
Tues.–Sun. 9 a.m.–5 p.m.
Historic and modern electric apparatus, etc.

Geological-Palaeontological Museum of the University of Hamburg
HH 13, Bundesstrasse 55
Mon.–Fri. 9 a.m.–6 p.m.; Sat. 9 a.m.–midday
Geological and fossil exhibits from the Hamburg region

German Museum of Painters and Lacquer Artists
HH 74, Billwerder Billdeich 72
tel. 7 33 87 06

Heine-Haus
HH 50, Elbchaussee 31
Tues.–Fri. 11 a.m.–7 p.m., Sat. 11 a.m.–4 p.m.
(closed July and August)
Mementoes of the Heine family

Mana Kumaka Museum
(Assids Indio-Museum)
HH 70, Kramerkoppel 24
Sat. and Sun. 11 a.m.–5 p.m.
or by arrangement (tel. 6 56 06 57)
Lifestyle of the South American Indians

Mineralogical Museum of the University of Hamburg
HH 13, Grindelallee 48
Wed. 3–7 p.m., 1st Sun. in month 10 a.m.–1 p.m.
Collection of minerals

Museum of Municipal Drainage Department (Müll Museum)
HH 4, Bei den St-Pauli-Landungsbrücken 49
only by prior appointment (tel. 3 49 13-797)
Curious finds from the sewers

Museum of Work
in the former factory of the New York-Hamburg Rubber Company
HH 60 (Barmbek), Maurienstrasse 19–21
Under construction (information tel. 2 91 81-364)

Panoptikum
HH 4, Spielbudenplatz 3
Mon.–Fri. 11.30 a.m.–9.30 p.m.,
Sat. 11.30 a.m.–midnight, Sun. 10 a.m.–10 p.m.
Waxworks

Postal Museum
HH 36, Stephansplatz 1
Closed until further notice

Reemtsma Collection
HH 52, Parkstrasse 51
only by arrangement (tel. 8 22 05 42)
History of tobacco

Staatliche Landesbildstelle Hamburg
HH 54, Lieler Strasse 171
Mon.–Fri. 8 a.m.–4 p.m., Tues. 8 a.m.–8 p.m.,
Sat. 10 a.m.–3 p.m.
Photographic gallery

Textile Museum (Margot Engel)
HH 11, Krayenkamp 9,
Sun.–Fri. 10 a.m.–6 p.m., Sat. 10 a.m.–1 p.m.
Private textile collections and sales

Toy Museum (Dieter Kurth)
HH 6, Markstrasse 3
Mon.–Fri. midday–6 p.m., Sat. 11 a.m.–2 p.m.

Vehicle Museum "Oldtimer-Gasse"
HH 76, Hamburgerstrasse 197
daily 10 a.m.–6 p.m.
Wheeled vehicles of all kinds

Zoological Museum of the University of Hamburg
HH 13, Martin-Luther-King-Platz 3,
Mon.–Fri. 10 a.m.–7 p.m., 2nd and 4th Sats. 10 a.m.–5 p.m.
Animal specimens

Museum Educational Service

The Department of Culture (HH 76, Hamburgerstrasse 45, tel. 2 91 88 27 52) runs an educational service which arranges special events in conjunction with the museums, especially during school holidays. Teachers and parents can obtain details.

Memorials

See entry

Music

Concert Halls

Musikhalle
HH 36, Dammtorwall 46/Karl-Muck-Platz
tel. 34 69 20

Congress Centre (Great Hall)
HH 36, Dammtor/Marseiller Strasse
tel. 35 92-1

Opera

Hamburg State Opera
HH 36, Dammtorstrasse 28
tel. 35 15 55

Opera stabile (studio theatre; future uncertain)
HH 36, Büschstrasse
tel. 35 15 55

Church Music

Concerts are given in a number of Hamburg churches (e.g. Petrikirche, Jacobikirche and Michaelskirche). Information about current programmes: Amt für Kirchenmusik, HH 76, Uhlandstrasse 49; tel. 2 20 51 31

Radio Orchestra

Norddeutscher Rundfunk
Konzertkasse
HH 13, Rothenbaumchaussee 132–134

Folk Music

Finkwarder Speeldeel e.V.
HH 95, Steendiek 35; tel. 7 42 63 77

Jazz

Blockhütte
HH 50, Grosse Freiheit 66; tel. 31 08 01

Cotton Club
HH 11, Grossneumarkt 50 (temporarily; later Alter Steinweg); tel. 34 38 78

Jazz Forum
HH 80, Weidenbaumsweg 13; tel. 7 24 36 61

Klimperkiste
HH 36, Esplanade 18; tel. 34 30 00

River-Kasematten
HH 11, Ost-West-Strasse 10; tel 36 46 36

Local "Scene"

Logo (jazz, rock, singers)
HH 13, Grindelallee 5; tel. 4 10 56 58

Knust (blues, rock)
HH 11, Brandstwiete 2; tel. 32 49 33

Onkel Pö's Carnegie Hall (folk, rock, blues)
HH 20, Lehmweg 44; tel. 6 41 40 25

Bars with music

Particularly in the vicinity of the Grossneumarkt there have recently come into existence many bars where programmes of a musical and literary nature, including cabaret take place (see Night Life)

Open-air Concerts

Mention should be made of the classical concerts in the inner courtyard of the City Hall, the classical "Frühschoppen" (Sunday from 11 a.m.) at various venues; also concerts of light music by the Hamburger Hafenkonzert (sometimes in the Schulauer Fährhaus), and concerts in the Stadtpark and in Planten un Blomen.

Calendar of Musical Events

Recorded Information: tel. 1 15 15

Night Life

St Pauli and St Georg

As always St Pauli with the Reeperbahn and Grosse Freiheit is Hamburg's premier amusement district. However the area around Steindamm in the St Georg quarter is not far behind. The attractions are outlined under the respective entries in the A to Z section.

Note

Visitors are recommended not to stroll around alone at night in these districts. Useful advice and assistance in cases of fraud are available from the Interessengemeinschaft St Pauli (Spielbudenplatz 27, tel. 3 19 24 15).

Information from the Davidswache (Police Station) for visitors to St Pauli (Speilbudenplatz 31)

In order not to be tempted unnecessarily to exceed one's budget, one should take only as much money (if possible in small notes), as one is prepared to spend.

In any establishment one should do the ordering oneself and make sure to order from the price list which is obligatory everywhere and under no circumstances leave this to a "hostess". After the order has been served one should immediately pay the bill, even if one may intend to order again.

Hamburg by Night

Every evening at 8 p.m. a 4-hour bus tour of St Pauli leaves from the Main Station. There is a stop at the Television Tower, visits to various establishments, including a sex show.

Meeting-places of the "Scene" (Scene-Treffs)

Those who have no inclination to experience the world of the sex-business will of course find other evening entertainments of various kinds in the central area of Hamburg. In this respect certain places have become prominent; around the Grossneumarkt, in the extensive University Quarter, in fashionable but informal Pöseldorf and at many places in the district of Eppendorf. The principal features of the haunts of this "scene" are the musical offerings.

Evening and Night Establishments

Atlantic Bar, HH 1, An der Alster 72–79
Bodega Nagel, HH 1, Kirchenallee 57
Brahmskeller, HH 13, Grindelhof 64–66
Chese, HH 13, Beim Schlump 15
Life Club, HH 13, Rothenbaumchaussee 185
Wintergarten, HH 13, Hartung 1

Discothèques

After Shave, HH 4, Spielbudenplatz 9
Black Market, HH 60, Mühlenkamp 43
Chikago, HH 4, Hans-Albers-Platz 13
Corner 57, HH 76, Wandsbeker Chaussee 57
Leo's, HH 1, Ballindamm 9
Madhouse, HH 36, Valentinskamp 46A
Third World, HH 1, Heidenkampsweg 54
Trinity, HH 19, Eimsbütteler Chaussee 5

Dancing

Boccaccio, HH 1, Kirchenallee 49
Café Keese, HH 4, Reeperbahn 19–21
Kaiserhof, HH 4, Spielbudenplatz 24
Lausen, HH 4, Reeperbahn 58
Lübscher Baum, HH 76, Lübecker Strasse 133

Sex Shows

Club de Sade, HH 4, Erichstrasse 41
Colibri, HH 50, Grosse Freiheit 34
Pulverfass und Crazy Boys, HH 1, Pulverteich 12
Regina, HH 50, Grosse Freiheit 4
Safari, HH 50, Grosse Freiheit 24
Tabu, HH 50, Grosse Freiheit 14

Bars

Cha-Cha, HH 36, Dragonerstall 15
Di Gööle, HH 36, Brüderstrasse 8
Pickenpack, HH 6, Schulterblatt 3
Rick's Harburg, HH 90, Lammertwiete 5–7
Sperl, HH 36, Wexstrasse 30
Zwick am Mittelweg, HH 13, Mittelweg 121 b

Bars with Music

See Music

Opening Times

Departmental Stores

Departmental stores open at 9 a.m. and close on Monday to Friday and on the 1st Saturday in the month at 6.30 p.m. (some at 6 p.m.); on other Saturdays they close at 2 p.m.

Retail Shops

Retail shops open at 8.30 or 9 a.m. and close on Monday to Friday and on the Saturday when shopping in general (mostly in the city centre) at 6 or 6.30 p.m. Many food shops open in the morning as early as 7 o'clock. Boutiques, arts and crafts shops and various specialist shops often have different opening times (e.g. from 10 a.m.).

Banks

See entry

Post

See entry

Parking

City Centre

Glockengiesserwall (260 spaces)
Brandsende (150 spaces)

Gertrudenstrasse (750 and 800 spaces)
Lilienstrasse (600 spaces)
Rosenstrasse (280 spaces; Karstadt, 120 spaces)
Bugenhagenstrasse (Kaufhof, 290 spaces)
Lange Mühren (Horten, 350 spaces)
Johanniswall (400 spaces)
Grosse Reichenstrasse (870 spaces)
Neue Gröninger Strasse (550 spaces)
Rödingsmarkt (850 spaces)
Grosse Bleichen (650 spaces)
Postrasse (443 spaces; Alsterhaus, 120 spaces)
Drehbahn (930 spaces)
Trostbrücke (90 spaces)

Post

Main Post Office

Postamt 1, Münzstrasse
tel. 23 95-1
Mon.–Fri. 8 a.m.–6 p.m., Sat. 8 a.m.–midday

Post Offices with extended opening hours

Post Office at Main Station
tel. 2 39 53 33
24 hours a day (also Post Office Savings Bank)

Post Office at Fuhlsbüttel Airport
tel. 5 91 01-1
Mon.–Sat. 7 a.m.–9 p.m., Sun. 9 a.m.–8 p.m.

Post Office at Harburg Station
tel. 7 71 77-1
Mon.–Fri. 6 a.m.–10 p.m., Sat., Sun. 6 a.m.–9 p.m.

Programme of Events

Current Information in the "Hamburger Abendblatt' and other daily papers

"Hamburger Vorschau" and "Hamburg Führer" appear monthly and give information about events, attractions, theatre programmes, eating places, hotels, shopping and much else. They can be obtained at the official information bureaux (see Information) as well as from many booksellers and newsagents.
Among many other, partly specialised, publications are: "Hamburger Musikleben" (monthly), "Hamburg Tips" (twice a year), "HH Termine" (monthly), "via Hamburg" (quarterly), "Kultur für alle" (monthly) as well as the publications tending to favour the alternative and pop "scenes" – "Was'n los in Hamburg" (monthly), "Szene Hamburg" (monthly) and "Ox-Mox – Hamburgs Stadtmagazin" (monthly).

Public Transport

Hamburg Transport Authority (HVV)

The Hamburger Verkehrsverbund (HVV) is a combine of 8 transport undertakings (railways, buses and boats on the Elbe and Alster) the timetables of which are co-ordinated and which have developed a common tariff system.

Tariff System

The network of routes served by the HVV (with the exception of a few lines serving the outer suburbs) is divided into tariff zones 1 and 2. Subdivisions in the tariff zones are of interest only to holders of weekly and monthly tickets.

Leisure Weekend and "after 6" Ticket

The Freizeit- and Feierabend-Karte (FF-Karte) is a monthly ticket valid in tariff zone 2 on Mondays to Fridays between 6 p.m. and 4.30 a.m. and on Saturdays, Sundays and Public Holidays at any time. By paying a supplement express buses and first class on the S-Bahn can also be used. The ticket is obtainable from HVV ticket and information offices.

Tourist ticket

For individuals or small groups for one or several days as required. Obtainable in advance at HVV passenger offices.

Family ticket

The Familienkarte is valid on Saturdays, Sundays and Public Holidays in tariff zone 2. With this ticket up to 4 adults and 3 children can make as many journeys as they like; express buses and first-class on the S-Bahn are subject to supplement. The ticket is obtainable from bus drivers or from automatic ticket machines.

Day tickets

The daily network ticket for the whole area is valid for any number of journeys in the entire network of the HVV, also on routes which serve places beyond the boundary of tariff zone 2, between the start of services until 4.30 a.m. on the following day.
The daily city ticket is valid for any number of journeys within tariff zone 2 between 9 a.m. (Saturdays, Sundays and Public Holidays from the beginning of services) and 4.30 a.m. on the following day.
Both kinds of daily ticket are obtainable from bus drivers or automatic ticket machines. Express buses and first class on the S-Bahn are subject to supplement.

Children's tickets

Valid for children between the ages of 5 and 13.

Passengers' bicycles

These are carried on the S- and U-Bahn from Monday to Friday between 9 a.m. and 4 p.m. and 6 p.m. and 4.30 a.m.; tickets valid all day on Saturdays, Sundays and Public Holidays.

Night Buses

Between midnight and 5 a.m. bus services operate from Rathausmarkt on various routes; the fares are subject to a supplement.

Information

Further details, including information about tourist tickets tailored to individual needs, senior citizens' tickets, "two-city" tickets, etc. can be obtained from the HVV Information Office (tel. 32 29 11; open daily 8 a.m.–7 p.m.

Radio and Television

North German Radio

The Norddeutscher Rundfunk (NDR; see A–Z – North German Radio) has developed from the previous North-West German Radio Service which was founded in 1948 and which existed until 1955. Today the NDR, which transmits over the area embracing Hamburg, Schleswig-Holstein and Lower Saxony, is the second largest regional broadcasting company in the

Federal Republic of Germany. It broadcasts three radio programmes and produces about one-fifth of the television programmes of the ARD (including the news and magazine programmes "Tagesschau" and "Tagesthemen"); in addition it supports a third TV programme in association with neighbouring broadcasting companies.

Norddeich-Radio, Elbe-Weser Radio

The stations Norddeich-Radio, Elbe-Weser Radio and Kiel Radio serve the worldwide marine radio traffic (telephone, telegraph, telex) of the German Federal Post Office (Deutsche Bundespost). Co-ordination and operation is controlled by the Fernmeldeamt Hamburg 6.

Hans-Bredow Institut

Hans Bredow (1879–1959) was one of the leading pioneers of radio. He initiated the marine radio service and played a leading part in the early days of radio broadcasting in Germany. The institute of the University of Hamburg which is named after him has as its principal function research and documentation of the history of broadcasting.

Restaurants

German and International Cuisine

Alsterpavillon (Café-Restaurant), HH 36, Jungfernstig 54
Alsterufer 35, HH 36, Alsterufer 35
Alter Elbtunnel, HH 4, St-Pauli-Landungsbrücken (Br. 7)
Althamburger Aalspeicher, HH 11, Deichstrasse 43
Alt-Hamburger Bürgerhaus, HH 11, Deichstrasse 37
Alt-Helgoländer Fischerstube, HH 4, Fischmarkt 4
Am Michel, HH 11, Englische Planke 8
Arkaden-Kajüte, HH 36, Alsterarkaden 11
Bavaria-Blick, HH 4, Bernhard-Nocht-Strasse 99
Block-House, HH 36, Gänsemarkt-Passage and HH 80, Sachsentor 2, also HH 90, Sand 8
Caspian (speciality caviare), HH 60, Maria-Louisen-Strasse 25
*Deichgraf, HH 11, Deichstrasse 23
Dimanche, H 36, Karl-Muck-Platz 11
*Ehmke, HH 11, Grimm 14
Finkenwärder Hof, HH 95, Auedeich 61
Finkenwerder Elbblick, HH 95, Focksweg 42
Finnlandhaus, HH 36, Esplanade 41
Fischerbörse Elbterrassen, HH 50, Elbchaussee 139
*Fischereihafen-Restaurant, HH 50, Grosse Elbstrasse 143
Fischerhaus, HH 4, Fischmarkt 14
Fischerstube, HH 4, St-Pauli-Landungsbrücken (Br. 3)
Fischkajüte, HH 4, St-Pauli-Landungsbrücken (Br. 5)
Fischrestaurant Möwen-Blick, HH 52, Oevelgönne 6
Flic-Flac, HH 55, Blankenese Landstrasse 29
Friesenhof, HH 76, Hamburger Strasse 1
Friesenkeller, HH 36, Jungfernstieg 7
Fürst-Bismarck-Mühle, in Aumühle, Am Mühlendeich
Galerie-Stuben, HH 11, Krayenkamp 10
Globetrotter (Café-Restaurant), HH 36, at the Alster landing-stage
Gustav Adolf von Schweden, HH 36, Grosse Bleichen 32
Hafenterrasse, HH 4, St-Pauli-Landungsbrücken
Hamborgher Kücherie, HH 76, Hamburger Strasse 1
Hamburger Fischerstube, HH 36, Esplanade 31
Harmonie, HH 1, Pumpen 17

Hofrestaurant, HH 60, Alsterdorfer Strasse 2a
*Jacob, HH 52, Elbchaussee 401
*Johann Cölln (speciality oysters), HH 11, Brodschrangen 1–5
Kleines Fähraus, HH 13, Fährdamm 13
Kranzler-Grill, HH 36, Marseiller Strasse 36
*La Fayette, HH 76, Zimmerstrasse 30
*Landhaus Dill, HH 52, Elbchaussee 404
*Landhaus Scherrer, HH 50, Elbchaussee 130
Landhaus Walter, HH 60, Hindenburgstrasse 2
Landungsbrücken-Restaurant, HH 4
*l'Auberge Française, HH 13, Rutschbahn 34
*Le Canard, HH 20, Martinstrasse 11
Le Délice, HH 1, Klosterwall 9 (market hall)
Le Relais de France, HH 65, Poppenbütteler Chaussee 3
Mellingburger Schleuse, HH 65, Mellingburgredder 1
Michelangelo, HH 20, Eppendorfer Landstrasse 74
Michelsen (delicatessen), HH 36, Grosse Bleichen 10–14
Mövenpick (with bakery, wine bar, artistes' café and expresso bar), HH 36, Grosse Bleichen 36
Mühlenkamper Fährhaus, HH 76, Hans-Henry-Jahnn-Weg 1
Nikolaikeller (speciality Matjeshering = fillets of young herring), HH 11, Cremon 36
Oevelgönner Fährhaus, HH 50, Neumühlen 53
Old Commercial Room, HH 11, Englische Planke 10
Op'n Bulln, HH 50, Blankenese landing-stage
*Peter Lembcke, HH 1, Holzdamm 49
Provençal, HH 60, Lattankamp 8
*Ratsweinkeller, HH 11, Grosse Johannisstrasse 2
Riper (ale-house), HH 11, Reichenstrasse 56
Saseler Dorfkrug, HH 65, Saseler Chaussee 101
*Schümanns Austernkeller (Art Nouveau décor), HH 36, Jungfernstieg 34
Sellmer, HH 20, Ludolfstrasse 50
Skyline Turm Restaurant (revolving restaurant in Television Tower), HH 6, Langerstrasse 2–8
St-Pauli-Theater-Restaurant, HH 4, Speilbudenplatz 29
Strandhof, HH 55, Strandweg 27
Süllberg, HH 55, Süllbergterrasse 2
Tante Anna, HH 95, Landscheideweg 100
Thalia-Restaurant, HH 1, Gerhart-Hauptmann-Platz 1
To'n Peerstall, HH 52, Hochrad 69
Trześniewski (tasty snacks), HH 11, Börsenbrücke
Überseebrücke, HH 11, Vorsetzen
Valentin's Restaurant, HH 36, Neuer Wall 30
*Vegetarische Gaststätte, HH 36, Alsterarkaden 11a
Vierländer Kate, HH 50, Museumstrasse 23
Vitell, HH 36, Wexstrasse 38
Witthus Teestuben, HH 55, Elbchaussee 499a
Wuppermans Kochstube, in Halstenbek, Bahnhofstrasse 22
Zum Alten Lotsenhaus, HH 52, Oevelgonne 13
Zum Alten Rathaus, HH 11, Börsenbrücke 10
Zum Brandanfang, HH 11, Deichstrasse 25

Hotel Restaurants

Atlantic Grill (in Hotel Atlantic), HH 1, An der Alster 72–79
Brasserie (in Hotel Inter-Conti), HH 36, Fontenay 10
Danmark (in Hotel Falck), HH 54 Kieler Strasse 333
Drehbahn Restaurant (in Hotel Oper), HH 36, Drehbahn 15
English Grill (in Hotel Hamburg Plaza), HH 36, Marseiller Strasse 2

Fontenay Grill (in Hotel Inter-Conti), HH 36, Fontenay 10
*Haerlin (in Hotel Vier Jahreszeiten), HH 36, Neuer Jungfernstieg 9–14
Hafen Hamburg (in Hotel Hafen Hamburg), HH 11, Seewartenstrasse 9
Hamburg Restaurant (in Hotel Europäischer Hof), HH 1, Kirchenallee 45
Jahreszeiten Grill (in Hotel Vier Jahreszeiten), HH 36, Neuer Jungfernstieg 9–14
Kon-Tiki-Grill (In Hotel Norge), HH 6, Schäferkampsallee 49
La mer (in Hotel Prem), HH 1, An der Alster 9
Noblesse (in Hotel Ramada Renaissance), HH 36, Grosse Bleichen
Reichshof (in Hotel Reichshof), HH 1, Kirchenallee 34–36

Afghan

Saidal, HH 20, Schrammsweg 10

Argentinian

El Argentino, HH 60, Dorotheenstrasse 105
La Estancia, HH 1, Hermannstrasse 30

Bulgarian

Rila, HH 76, Finkenau 1

Chinese

Asia, HH 1, Steindamm 35/1
Chop-Sue, HH 11 Grosse Burstah 3 (in Allianz-Haus)
Hsi Lin Men, HH 50, Nobistor 14
Mandarin, HH 4, Zirkusweg 20, Millerntorplatz
Man Wah, HH 4, Speilbudenplatz 18
Pak Sun Lam, HH 11, Ferdinandstrasse 55–57
Peking-Enten-Haus, HH 13, Rentzelstrasse 48
Sommerpalast, HH 11, Brandstwiete 32
Sun Kwong, HH 36, Gänsemarkt-Passage
Suzy Wong, HH 13, Mittelweg 141

Italian

Al Pincio, HH 1, Schauenburger Strasse 59
Angelo, HH 70, Wandsbeker Markstrasse 170
Bologna, HH 60, Hudtwalckerstrasse 37
Casa della Pasta, HH 36, Gänsemarkt 50
Cuneo, HH 4, Davidstrasse 11
Da Paolino, HH 36, Alsterufer 2
Ennio's Ristorante, HH 1, An der Alster 23
Il Ristorante, HH 36, Jungfernstieg-Passage
La Barca (Alster boat), HH 1, Ballindamm 28
La Vite, HH 13, Heimhuder Strasse 5
Martini-Osteria, Hh 13, Badestrasse 4
Massimo, HH 36, Colonnaden 15
The old spaghetti factory, HH 36, Neuer Gänsemarkt

Hungarian

Zigeunerkeller, HH 4, Reeperbahn 48

Japanese

*Daitokai, HH 13, Milchstrasse 1
Daruma, HH 1, Stadtdeich 1
Fuji, HH 76, Richardstrasse 18
Kogetsu, HH 1, Gurlittstrasse 11
Matsumi, HH 36, Colonnaden 96

Korean

Arang, HH 11, Kleine Reichenstrasse 16

Malayan

Rasa Sayang, HH 76, Deseniss Strasse 62

Portugese

Portugal, HH 20, Loogestieg 3
Sangria, HH 1, Lange Reihe 83

Swiss	Klösterli, HH 20, Eppendorfer Landstrasse 61 Luzerner Fondu Stübli, HH 76, Wandsbeker Chaussee 130
Thai	Baan Thai, HH 11, Hopfenmarkt 28
Turkish	Anadolu, HH 13, Grindelberg 3 At Nali, HH 13, Rutschbahn 11
Vietnamese	Dong Nai, HH 19, Stellinger Weg 47 Vietnam, HH 60, Ohlsdorfer Strasse 45
Yugoslavian	Bei Marija, HH 1, Klosterwall 4a
Wine Bars	Brahms-Stuben, HH 20, Ludolfstrasse 43 Butzirus, HH 36, Colonnaden 72 Sperl, HH 36, Wexstrasse 30 Weinkrüger, HH 13, Milchstrasse 3–4 and HH 90, Lämmertwiete 6–10 Weinstuben am Grossneumarkt, HH 11, Grossneumarkt 10 Wiener Marie, HH 13, Rentzelstrasse 36 Zur Traube, HH 50 (Altona), Karl-Theodor-Strasse 4
Cafés	Alsterpavillon – see Restaurants Bobby Reich, HH 60, landing-stage at the Fernsicht Café des Artistes (in Mövenpick) – see Restaurants Café l'Etage, HH 36, Neuer Wall 18 Café Schöne Aussichten, Hh 36, Old Botanical Garden Café Wirth, HH 1, Spitalerstrasse 28 Condi (in Hotel Vier Jahreszeiten), HH 36, Neuer Jungfernstieg 9–14 Danny's Caf'Conc', HH 76, Lübecker Strasse 25 Elbterrassen, HH 50, Elbchaussee 139 Funk-Eck-Café, HH 13, Rothenbaumchausee 137 Lessing, HH 36, Gänsemarkt-Passage (Gallery) Lindtner, HH 20, Eppendorfer Landstrasse 88 Mövenpick Espresso – see Restaurants Mövenpick in Café Vernimb, HH 1, Spitalstrasse 9 Vienna, HH 6, Fettstrasse 2 Wiener Café Bohème, HH 13, Milchstrasse 1
Ale-Houses	Alt-Pöseldorfer Bierstuben, HH 13, Milchstrasse 7 Bierpalast, HH 36, Dammtordamm 1 Klein Kleckersdorf, HH 11, Grosser Burstah 46–48 Posemuckel, HH 36, Bleichenbrücke 10 Tiroler Engel, HH 20, Eppendorfer Landstrasse 61 Uhlenspieker, HH 11, Grossneumarkt 6–8 Zum Franziskaner, HH 36, Colonnaden/Grosse Theatrestrasse 9
"Trendy" Bars	Das Herz von St Pauli, HH 4, Spielbudenplatz 9 Fleetenkieker, HH 11, Börsenbrücke 10 Zillertal, HH 4, Spielbudenplatz 27
Recommended Establishments South of the Elbe	Estehof, pleasant inn in the Altes Land, D-2155 Jork, Estebrügge 87 Zille's Weissbierstube, artists' rendezvous in Sottorf, D-2107 Rosengarten, Paul-Roth-Steinweg 2 Zum Hundertjährigen, ethnic inn in Hittfeld (speciality good plain cooking and "Hittfelder Korn" schnaps). D-2105 Seevetal 1, Harburger Strasse 2

Shopping

Addresses in local telephone directory; yellow pages

To the south-west of the Main Station (Mönckebergstrasse, Spitalerstrasse) mainly department stores and shops of the popular kind are to be found; the area around the Jungfernstieg, Neuer Wall and Grosse Bleichen (see A to Z – Passages) is predominantly the home of specialist high-class emporia. Outside the immediate city centre, north of the Dammtor, lie the shopping districts of Rothenbaumchaussee, the district of Eppendorf and in Pöseldorf the area around Milchstrasse (for high-class and accordingly expensive merchandise).

Antique Shops

See Antiques

Art-Dealers

See Galleries

Sightseeing

Boat trips

From April to October the Alster Touristik GmbH (ATG, tel. 34 11 4) operates sightseeing trips on the Alster and the Elbe, as well as on the associated fleets and canals. All trips of this company start from and return to the Jungfernstieg landing-stage.

Circular Trip on the Alster

Duration about 50 minutes; the route covers the Inner and Outer Alster. Departures every half-hour from 10 a.m. to 6 p.m.

Alster Cruise

Duration about 2 hours; the route runs to Winterhude. There is a stop at every landing-stage.

Trip on the Fleets

Duration about 2½ hours. The route passes through the fleets (canals and locks) of the Inner City, through the Speicherstadt and parts of the Free Port.
Departures 10.45 a.m., 1.45 and 4.15 p.m.

Canal Trip

Duration about 2 hours; the route is on the Alster and its side canals to the north of the city centre.
Departures 9.45 a.m., 12.15 and 5.15 p.m.

Vierlande Trip (to Bergedorf except Tuesday)

Duration about 3 hours (one way) or 7 hours return trip; the route is along the Elbe and the Bille. Departure from Jungfernstieg at 10.15 a.m., Bergedorf Harbour 2 p.m.

Bridges Trip

Duration about 3 hours; the route takes in the most important bridges over the Fleets and the Port. Departure Tuesday 10.15 a.m.

Evening Trip ("Dämmertörn")

Duration about 2 hours; the route is on the Alster and its canals. Departure 8 p.m. (only mid May to mid September).

Tours of the Port

The HADAG Line and various smaller shipping concerns organise round trips in the port of about 1 hour's duration throughout the year. Departures 10 a.m.–6 p.m., every half-hour from St-Pauli-Landungsbrücken, landing-stage 2/3.

Evening party trip in the port (April to December); duration about 3 hours; trip through the illuminated port with music, substantial buffet on board. Departures Saturday 8 p.m. from St-Pauli-Landungsbrücken.

City Tour (Information tel. 24 87 00)

Departure point is the Kirchenallee bus station on the north-east side of the main railway station. Duration, depending on bus route, $1\frac{1}{4}$–$2\frac{1}{2}$ hours; combined bus and harbour trip is possible.
Hamburg by Night: duration about 4 hours; short boat trip from the Outer to the Inner Alster, then bus to the Reeperbahn with visit to a show, etc. Departures daily 8 p.m. from the Main Station/Kirchenallee.

"Happy Hamburg" inclusive booking

For a short visit the Hamburg tourist board offers bargain package arrangements (Friday to Monday from 1 November to 28 February and for an unlimited period from 1 July to 31 August). Included is the so-called "Happy Hamburg" ticket with coupons for city and harbour tours, visits to museums and the casino, tickets for public transport (see entry), etc. The holder is also entitled to reduced fares on the Alster services, boat excursions, etc. Booking through the Fremdenverkehrs-zentrale Hamburg (see Information), or direct with the hotels.

Informative Tours (Municipal Building Department)

From May to October the Municipal Building Department organises sightseeing tours on 4 routes which offer a general view of the building work going on in the city called Sieh dir an, wie Hamburg baut (have a look at what Hamburg is building). Duration about 3 hours; departure from Moorweide/Mittelweg every Saturday at 2 p.m. Prior booking: Baubehörde, HH 36, Stadthausbrücke 8, tel. 3 49 13-26 62.

"Hummelbahn" (trip by train)

Leaving from the Main Station the "Hummelbahn" (also called "Inner-City") with its nostalgic third-class carriages makes a circular tour via the Lombardsbrücke, Jungfernstieg, City Hall, Port (facility for a round trip of the port at the Landungsbrücken (see above) and Speicherstadt (visit)) and back to the Main Station. Departures daily at 10 a.m., midday, 2 and 4 p.m.

HVV Day Ticket

For sightseeing using the Hamburger Verkehrsverbund (HVV; see Public Transport) the HVV day ticket is especially convenient and good value.

Souvenirs

Nautical

There is an especially rich variety of nautical articles, which are attractive to "landlubbers" because of their decorative qualities. Excellent old examples can be found, including ship's instruments and furniture and various articles of equipment, but prices tend to be quite high. Many kinds of articles are made from linen and rope (e.g. hammocks).

Souvenirs of Old Hamburg

Apart from Hamburgensien (old views of the city, etc; Die Hamburgensie, HH 36, Poststrasse 11), mention should be made of model ships, figureheads, Buddelschiffe – ships in bottles – (Buddel Binikowski, HH 20, Lokstedter Weg 68; Captain Billy's Nautic Shop, HH 13, Alsterchaussee 3), sailor's clothing and boat equipment in the broadest sense (Hechelmann, HH 11, Vorsetzen 42); sailor's kitbags of all sizes and shapes can be obtained from Daddeldu's Segelkoje (HH 4, St-Pauli Landungsbrücken 1). Captain's Cabin (HH 4, St-Pauli Landungsbrücken 3) offers nautical souvenirs of high quality; a wide selection of nautical charts can be found at the specialist book and chart dealer Eckardt & Messtorf (HH 11, Rödingsmarkt 16) and at Bade & Hornig (HH 11, Stubbenhuk 10).

Exotic Articles

In St Pauli there are a number of shops specialising in exotic articles brought home by seafarers. Among these suppliers is Harry's Hamburger Hafenbazar (HH 4, Bernard-Nocht-Strasse 63).

Food

Among culinary products which visitors may like to take home are Labskaus (in tins), smoked eel and Hamburger Rumtopf (soft fruit in rum).

Hummel

The figure of the water-carrier Hummel, the symbolic figure of the city, can be obtained in many versions.

Sport

Bowling

Brunswick-Bowling-Anlagen; HH 4, Am Millerntor (36 rinks); HH 50, Max Brauer Allee 206; HH 60, Fuhlsbüttlerstrasse 334. Also Elbe-Bowling HH 53, Osdorfer Landstrasse 119; Bowling-Anlange Hamburger Strasse, HH 76, Wagnerstrasse 2.

Cycling

Information: Radsport-Verband Hamburg, HH 26, Griesstrasse 38; tel. 2 00 93 42.

Equestrian Sport

Racecourse in Horn, Derbyplatz (jumping, dressage and cross-country riding) in Klein Flottbek, trotting course in Bahrenfeld; some 40 riding-schools.
Information: Landesverband der Reit- und Fahrvereine, HH 36, Neuer Wall 26; tel. 36 66 06.

Football

Hamburg has two well-known football clubs; the HSV (Hamburger Sport-Verein, many times German champions, last in 1983) and the FC St Pauli. The principal ground is the Volkspark Stadium.

Golf

18-hole golf courses:
Golfclub Hamburg-Ahrensburg, D 2070 Ahrensburg, Am Haidschlag 39–45 (Bredenbeker Teich)
Golfclub Falkenstein, HH 55, In de Bargen 59
Golf Club Gut Waldhof, D-2359 Kisdorf
Golf Club Hamburg Walddörfer, D-2071, Ammersbek 1 (Schevelbarg)
Golf Club auf der Wendlohe, HH 61, Oldesloher Strasse 251
Golf-Club Hoisdorf, D-2050, HH 80, Wentorfer Strasse 11
Hamburger Land- und Golf-Club in der Lüneburger Heide, D-2105 Seevetal 1 (Emmelndorf) Am Golfplatz 24

Ice-skating

Artificial ice-rinks (in winter) in the Grosse Wallanlagen (Wallringpark), in Stellingen (HH 54, Hagenbekstrasse 124) and in the Eissporthalle Farmsen (HH 72, Berner Heerweg 151).

Polo

The Hamburg Polo-Club (HH 52, Jenischerstrasse 26; tel. 82 06 81) has its own polo field.

Roller-skating

Roller-skating rinks (in summer) are situated in the Grosse Wallanlagen (Wallringpark), in Stellingen (HH 54, Hagenbekstrasse 124, in the Eissporthalle Farmsen (May–July; HH 72, Berner Heerweg 151) and in Bergedorf (HH 80, Osterrode 53). Roller-discos can be found in Eppendorf (HH 54, Osterfeldstrasse 34) and in Bergedorf (HH 80, Billstedter Haupstrasse 7–15).
Skateboard Centre in Lohbrügge (Bergedorf).

Skittles (Kegeln)

Like football, the game of skittles stands high in public favour. It is played in many purpose-built Kegelsporthallen as well as in innumerable pub skittle-alleys.

Tennis

Every year Hamburg is the venue for the German International Tennis Championships (Rotherbaum, ground of the Club der Alster). A great many tennis-courts (some belonging to clubs) are available.
Information: Hamburger Tennisverband, HH 34, Derbyweg 20; tel. 6 51 29 73.

Water-sports

Prime place goes to rowing and sailing. The Outer Alster, however, although popular for sailing, is not without problems for novices, on account of frequent squally winds; private motor-boats are not allowed on the Alster. There are a number of clubs, rowing, sailing and windsurfing schools, as well as boats for hire.
Information: Allgemeiner Alsterclub/Norddeutscher Ruderbund, HH 76, Schöne Aussicht 39, tel. 2 20 97 48; Hamburger Kanuverband e.V., HH 6, Schäferkampsallee 1; tel. 4121-204; Hamburger Segler-Verband e.V., HH 76, Uhlenhorster Weg 22, tel. 2 20 16 78.

Sports Hall

The Sportshalle Hamburg in Alsterdorf (HH 60, Krochmannstrasse 55) is exceptionally well equipped to cater for a wide variety of sporting events.

Information

Information about sporting facilities in and around Hamburg can be obtained from the Haus des Sports, HH 6, Schäferkampsallee 1, tel. 41 21 0, and from the Sportamt HH 1, Johanniswall 4, tel. 24 82 51.

Stations

Main Station

Main Station, situated to the east of the Inner Alster (see entry in A to Z), is primarily of importance for suburban traffic (see Public Transport). It is a "through" station and lack of space makes it only moderately suitable for long-distance traffic.
The Inter-City trains (see Access) stop at Main Station and at Hamburg-Altona, some of them also at Hamburg-Harburg.
For information at and in the vicinity of Main Station see Information.

Altona Station

The extensive terminus of Altona Station makes it an important hub of national and international railway traffic. The S-Bahn provides a link with the city centre.

Dammtor Station

Dammtor Station (Kongressbahnhof) to the west of the Outer Alster, is the second most important connection in the inner area between the main-line services and the S-Bahn.

Harburg Station

Harburg Station, to the south of the Elbe in the district of Harburg, is primarily of importance for services to Bremen, Bremerhaven and Cuxhaven. It is linked to the city centre by the S-Bahn.

Train Information

tel. 33 99 11

Swimming-pools

Heated open-air swimming-pools are generally open from the middle of May to the middle of September; unheated pools from the beginning of July until the end of August.
Indoor swimming pools are open all the year.

Open-air Swimming-pools

Aschberg, HH 26, Rückersweg
Aussenmühle, HH 90, Gotthelfweg 2
Bille-Bad, HH 80, Reetwerder, 25
Billstedt, HH 74, Archenotzstrasse 50a
Bondenwald, HH 61, Bondenwald
Dulsberg, HH 70, Am Dulsbergbad 1
Eimsbüttel "Kaifu", HH 19, Kaiser-Friedrich-Ufer
Eppendorf, HH 20, Goernestrasse 21
Farmsen, HH 72, Neusurenland 63–67
Finkenwerder, HH 95, Finksweg 82
Langenhorn, HH 62, Hohe Liedt 9
Lattenkamp, HH 20, Meenkwiese 39
Marienhöhe, HH 55, Luzerneweg 3–5
Neugraben, HH 92, Neuwiedenthaler Strasse
Ohlsdorf, HH 63, Im Grünen Grunde 1
Osdorfer Born, HH 53, Am Osdorfer Born
Rahlstedt, HH 73, Wiesenredder 85
Schwimmstadion Altona, HH 50, Schnackenburgsallee 85
Stadtparksee, HH 60, Südring 5b
Volksdorf (naturist), HH 67, Moorbekweg 100
Wilhelmsburg, HH 93, Zeidlerstrasse 52

Indoor Swimming-pools

Alster-Schwimmhalle, HH 76, Ifflandstrasse 21
Barmbek-Uhlenhorst, HH 76, Bartholomäusstrasse 95
Bille-Bad, HH 80, Reetwerder 25
Billstedt, HH 74, Archenholzstrasse 50a
Bismarckbad, HH 50, Ottenser Hauptstrasse 2
Blankenese, HH 55, Simrockstrasse
Bramfeld, HH 71, Fabriciusstrasse 223
Dulsberg, HH 70, Am Dulsbergbad 1
Eimsbüttel, HH 19, Hohe Weide 15
Elbgaustrasse, HH 53, Elbgaustrasse 110
Finkenwerder, HH 95, Finksweg 82
Harburg, HH 90, Rathausstrasse 40
Holthusenbad, HH 20, Goernestrasse 21
Niendorf, HH 61, Bondenwald
Ohlsdorf, HH 63, Im Grünen Grunde 1
Rahstedt, HH 73, Rahlstedter Bahnhofstrasse 52
Süderelbe, HH 92, Neugrabener Markt 9
St Pauli, HH 4, Budapester Strasse 29

Volksdorf, HH 67, Rockenhof
Wandsbek, HH 70, Wendemuthstrasse 14
Wilhelmsburg, HH 93, Dratelnstrasse 30

Tattooing

The art of tattooing, which originated in the Pacific area, was brought to Europe by seafarers. Specialised establishments for this somewhat painful form of personal adornment can be found mainly in St Pauli.

Tattoo Studios

Tatoo-Artist Herbert Hoffmann
HH 4, Hamburger Berg 8

Tatoo-Studio
HH 4, Seilerstrasse 56

Taxis

Central Taxi Office

tel. 44 10 11, 6 56 20 11, 61 10 61

Taxis for the Handicapped

tel. 4 10 54 58

Theatres

State Theatres

Deutsches Schauspielhaus und Malersaal
HH 1, Kirchenallee 39–41
Associated theatre: Malersaal in the Kampnagel factory (future uncertain)
HH 60, Jarrestrasse 20–26

Thalia-Theater,
HH 1, Raboisen 67
Associated theatre: tik (Thalia in der Kunsthalle; future uncertain)
HH 1, Glockengiesserwall 1

Hamburg State Opera
HH 36, Dammtorstrasse 28
Studio theatre; Opera stabile (future uncertain)
HH 36, Büschstrasse

Private Theatres

Hamburger Kammerspiele, HH 13, Hartungstrasse 9
Operettenhaus, HH 44, Spielbudenplatz 1
Ernst-Deutsch-Theater, HH 76, Mundsburger Damm 60
Atelier-Theater, HH 50, Stresemannstrasse 375
Theater in Zimmer, HH 13, Alsterchaussee 30
Altonaer Theatre, HH 50, Museumstrasse 17
Harburger Theater (in Helms Museum), HH 90, Museumplatz 2
Theater an der Marschnerstrasse, HH 76, Marschnerstrasse 42
Theater am Holstenwall, HH 36, Holstenwall 19
CCH-Boulevard-Theater, HH 36, Jungiusstrasse 18

Haus im Park, HH 80 (Bergedorf), Gräpelweg 8
die kleine komödie, HH 36, Neuer Wall 54
Piccolo-Theater ("smallest theatre in the world"; in the Fürsthof), HH 50, Juliusstrasse 13–15

Theatre Ship

Das Schiff, HH 11, Nikolaifleet, Holzbrücke landing-stage

Folk Theatres

Ohnsorg-Theater, Hh 36, Grosse Bleichen 23
St-Pauli-Theater, HH 4, Spielbudenplatz 39–40

Children's and Youth Theatres

Klecks Theater der Jugend, HH 11, Alter Steinweg 43
Theater für Kinder, HH 50, Max-Brauer-Allee 76

Puppet Theatre

Hamburger Puppentheater, HH 6, Moorkamp 5
Farmsener Marionettentheater, HH 72, Tegelweg 28
Figurentheater Fundus, HH 65, Huuskoppel 68
Puppenbühne Rhabarber, HH 50, Bahrenfelder Strasse 73d
Puppenbühne Bergner, in Marxen, Moorburg 26

English Theatre

The English Theatre, HH 76, Lerchenfeld 14

Variety

Hansa-Theater, HH 1, Steindamm 17

Cabarets, Experimental Theatre

Fools Garden, HH 13, Bornstrasse 18
Kellerbühne Hamburg in the MC-Club Pauline Courage, HH 4, Kastanienallee 22
Kellertheater Hamburg, HH 36, Colonnaden 9
Macadam-Theater, HH 11, Niedernstrasse 117
Theater Monsun, HH 50, Friedensallee 26

Literary Cabarets

Ahrweiler's Rendezvous, HH 36, Neuer Wall 54
Klein-Neumarkt, HH 11, Grossneumarkt 10
Schwender's, HH 11, Grossneumarkt 1
Villon, HH 1, St Georgskirchhof 7

Opera

See Music

Youth Hostels

Auf dem Stintfang, HH 11, Alfred-Wegener-Weg 5, 330 b. (only for members of the Youth Hostels Association).

Horner Rennbahn, HH 74, Rennbahnstrasse 110, 286 b. (only for members of the Youth Hostels Association).

Hamburger Jugendpark Langenhorn, HH 62, Jugendparkweg 60, 250 b. (only for groups).

Useful Telephone Numbers at a Glance

Emergency calls	
ACE breakdown and recovery service	2 00 29 30
ADAC breakdown assistance	1 92 11
ADAC emergency service	23 99 0
Ambulance	24 82 82 82
Bites, stings and rabies	31 10 21
(Bernhard-Nocht Institute)	31 28 51
Central ambulance for drunks (ZAB)	44 19 53 74
Central contact number for car insurers	33 66 44
Emergency dental service	1 15 00
Emergency doctor	1 12
Emergency legal service	5 11 88 48
Emergency medical service	22 80 22
Emergency pharmaceutical service	22 80 22
Emergency veterinary service	43 43 79
Eppendorf dental clinic (emergency service)	4 68 32 60
Falcks Rescue Service (breakdown assistance)	5 40 20 11
Fire Brigade	1 12
First Aid	1 12
Flood Warning	1 15 30
Poison Information Centre	6 38 53 45/46
Police	1 10
Rescue Helicoptor	1 12
Rescue Vehicle	1 12
Information	
Accommodation service	2 48 70-230
Airport	5 08-0
Alster-Touristik	34 11 41
Central tourist office	24 87 00
Central theatre box office	32 43 12
Church information	11 57
Fairs information	3 56 91
German Railways	33 99 11
HADAG (port shipping services)	31 96-1
Hamburg Information at the Airport	5 08 24 57
Hamburg Information in the City	32 47 58
Hamburg Information Neuer Jungfernstieg	35 00 10-0
Hamburg Information in the Port	31 39 77
North German Radio traffic studio (road conditions)	4 13 21 03
Traffic information HVV (8 a.m.–7 p.m.)	32 29 11
Taxis	
Autoruf	44 10 11
Hansa Radio Taxi	21 12 11
Radio Taxi Agency	6 56 20 11
Taxiruf	61 10 61
Taxis for the handicapped	4 10 54 58
Telephone	
Samaritans	11 10 1
Speaking clock	11 91
Telephone information	11 88
Weather forecast	11 64
Telegrams	
in foreign languages	11 33
in German	11 31

Notes

Notes

Notes

Notes

Notes